Where Cool Waters Flow

Four Seasons with a Master Maine Guide

by Randy Spencer

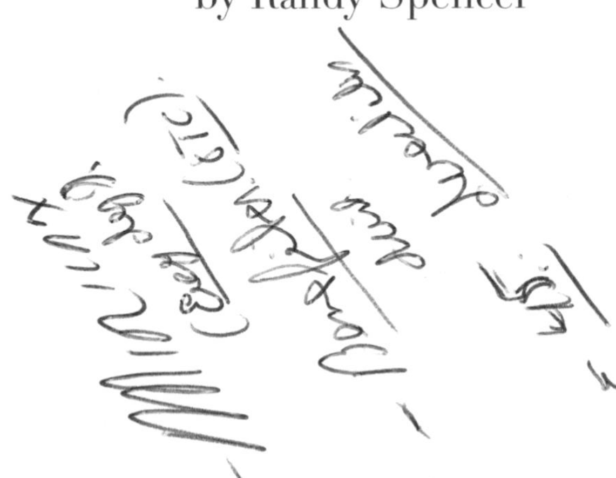

Other books from Islandport Press

Contentment Cove
by Miriam Colwell

Stealing History
by William D. Andrews

Shoutin' into the Fog
by Thomas Hanna

down the road a piece: A Storyteller's Guide to Maine, and
A Moose and a Lobster Walk into a Bar
by John McDonald

Windswept, *Mary Peters*, and *Silas Crockett*
by Mary Ellen Chase

Nine Mile Bridge
by Helen Hamlin

In Maine
by John N. Cole

The Story of Mount Desert Island
by Samuel Eliot Morison

The Cows Are Out! Two Decades on a Maine Dairy Farm
by Trudy Chambers Price

Hauling by Hand: The Life and Times of a Maine Island
by Dean Lawrence Lunt

These and other Maine books are available at:
www.islandportpress.com.

Where Cool Waters Flow

Four Seasons with a Master Maine Guide

by Randy Spencer

Islandport Press

Frenchboro • Yarmouth • Maine

Islandport Press
P.O. Box 10
Yarmouth, Maine 04096
www.islandportpress.com
207.846.3344

ISBN: 978-1-934031-28-5
Library of Congress Control Number: 2009933222

First Islandport Press edition published September 2009
Second Islandport Press edition published May 2010

Book design by Michelle A. Lunt / Islandport Press
Cover design by Karen F. Hoots / Hoots Design
Cover image courtesy of Dean Lunt

To David Kotok, the gentleman fisherman who has brought recognition from the outside world to the unique guiding culture of Grand Lake Stream

Acknowledgments

While mentors and certain legendary guides were acknowledged in context, my indebtedness to them is not slaked. In some cases, their widows helped me with information that became part of this manuscript. My thanks to Edith Sprague, Barbara Wheaton, and Annie Fitch for the contributions they knew they made, and for all that they bestowed unknowingly. Jack Perkins, now one of our oldest guides, is a reservoir of lore and fact. I drink there often. The brothers Sockabasin, Ray and David, have always been generous with information on the tribe, guiding, and their father Lola. I am grateful to them both. Donald Soctomah, history and preservation officer for the Passamaquoddy Tribe, provided me with history when I needed it and was always there to answer a question throughout the production of this work. I am also grateful to members of the Elsemore family, descendants of Eben Elsemore, who provided important information for the history section. Thanks to Paul Laney for both bear and bobcat guiding help, to Gerry Flanzbaum for the "words" section, and to "K" Bolduc and Arline Ritz for the finer points of their stories. Thanks to Brad Allen of Maine's Migratory Bird Project. Most of the texts that served bibliographically are, unfortunately, out of print. The *Professional Guide's Manual* by George Leonard Herter and Jacques P. Herter is still, wherever it can be found, a strong source for any guide or would-be guide. Eric Wight's *Maine Game Wardens* is a wealth of outdoor information. Anna

Chambers Cataldo and Ada Chambers's *Pod Run* and *Guides for Hire* are essential Grand Lake Stream reading, as are *Upriver and Down* by Edmund Ware Smith, and *Grand Lake Stream Plantation* by Minnie Atkinson. All are difficult to find, as those, like me, who own copies are covetous of them. Thanks, too, to the clients and others who helped me get facts straight and were kind when they weren't. The OBASS group, the David Kotok party, and many others were supportive for the long haul until completion. When it came to friendly encouragement and support, Kurt and Kathy Cressey, owners of the Pine Tree Store, John and Mary Arcaro, owners of Canalside Cabins, and Al and Sue LaPlante, owners of Chet's Camps, are all headliners with me. My late father, Kerwin A. Spencer Sr., either put the love of the woods and waters of Maine into me, or let it out, I'm not sure which—either way, I owe him. The same goes for Warren Whiting and Sonny Sprague, Kenny Wheaton, and Val Moore, all models to me in some way, and all must receive these thanks posthumously. Finally, if not for the patience, listening, love, and caring of Shelley Marie Spencer—the postcard girl—this book would never have happened.

Table of Contents

Foreword

New England is becoming homogenized. Its once unique sense of place is falling victim to corporate conglomerates that have made one town look much like another. Strip malls and chain stores have driven out mom-and-pop pharmacies. General stores that once offered everything from dill pickles in a barrel to penny candy, and hardware stores, with wooden floors where nails were measured out by the pound and owners would dispense advice on how to fix a leaky faucet or shingle a barn, are mostly gone—but not everywhere.

You must travel a bit to find places that would look familiar to New Englanders of yore. Washington County, Maine, is such a place. On the pages of this book Randy Spencer brings it to life, a sprawling land of sky-blue lakes rimmed by pointed firs; icy rivers and streams that cascade to the sea along the eastern border of the United States and Canada; and hardscrabble townships where people struggle to make a living as did their forebears—harvesting timber, raking blueberries, weaving Christmas wreaths, and guiding men and women from the cities who seek out moose, deer, landlocked salmon, and smallmouth bass.

Yes, even in Spencer's territory, times have changed, but really, not that much. There are 4-stroke outboards now on the transoms of the Grand Lakers, sleek, square-stern canoes just shy of twenty feet. The Grand Lakers offer comfort for guides and fishermen and can be paddled home should those fancy new motors develop a glitch. The canoes are symbols of the town where most were built, Grand Lake Stream, a settlement wedged between two lakes on the banks of a legendary salmon river.

Spencer knows the turf as well as anyone. He's a versatile fellow, at home equally guiding from the stern of a Grand Laker, on stage singing folk songs of his own creation—tunes that draw on the blue-green landscape and the struggles, joys, and wisdom of the people—or in front of a microphone narrating radio and television presentations. The man can do it all, and cook up a mean fish chowder for his "sports" as well. (Salt pork in the chowder must never be forgotten, says Spencer. It's all part of the guide's mantra, and its omission is said to be cause for flunking the Maine guide's licensing exam in the old days.) He captures the spirit of this special region as only one who has lived there can. It is an area peopled by descendants of the original white settlers and members of the Passamaquoddy Indian nation, and all are struggling to hold on to a traditional way of life far from the big city centers of commerce. Spencer cites the irony of the impressive efforts to preserve the area's lakes and forestland, efforts that offer little to feed a family in the bitter months when the tourists are far away. Visitors may hold their noses at the stench from pulp mills, but the natives call it the smell of money.

With all their differences, the people of far eastern Maine have forged strong bonds over the years with those from away who've been coming to the area for generations, to hunt, fish, or, increasingly, to merely savor the calm of a West Grand Lake sunrise or a canoe trip down the wild Machias River. Spencer counts many of these visitors as friends. You forge special bonds in the intimate space of a twenty-foot canoe, which Spencer rightly compares to the aura of the confessional.

If you can't get to eastern Maine in the near future, go there in these pages. They offer a whiff of Grand Lake Stream's pines, echoes of the loon as the sun dips low over the grand lakes, the splash of the salmon coming to net, and the homespun wisdom of the native people dispensed from the Liar's Bench at the Pine Tree Store. It's time you made the trip.

—Peter Mehegan

Award-winning journalist Peter Mehegan has been a fixture on Boston television since 1967 when he made his on-air debut covering Kevin White's election as mayor of Boston. In 1982, he became co-host of WCVB's Chronicle *and traveled the world, including assignments in Ethiopia, Israel, Italy, and France. Perhaps his best-known stories, however, were his travels through Maine in the "Old Chevy." Inherited from his wife's aunt, the 1969 Impala found new life on Maine's back roads, from remote fishing villages to inland lakes and mountains. In 2005, Mehegan semi-retired from WCVB.*

Author's Note

Before undertaking this project, I consulted a friend whom you'll meet in these pages. He is no man of letters, but I value his uncomplicated observations just the same. His counsel to me in this case: "Go about it the same way you'd brush out a trail. In the beginning, it'll all be chain-saw work. Lop off the big stuff. When you're done with that part, you should be able to stand back and at least see there's a trail there. Then, take the cruisin' ax and trim anything that hits you in the face. From then on, every time you go back, take a handsaw."

At publication time, I thought of including a handsaw with each copy. I hope you can find your way down this trail, a trail originally blazed by people who are now almost mythic in Grand Lake Stream. They carved out a life that is barely possible today, but that somehow, extraordinarily, endures.

Randy Spencer
Grand Lake Stream, Maine
July 2009

Prologue

The Path to Grand Lake Stream

". . . and everything is green and blue
and everybody smiles at you,
and Daddy, can we stay a few more days?
I never want to leave this place."

—from "One Road In" by Randy Spencer

I don't know how long I sat on my guitar case on the Grand Lake Stream town dock that June afternoon thirty-six years ago. I wondered how I was going to make the final twelve miles of a journey that began eighteen hours earlier in Maryland, but it didn't seem like an emergency. The view stretched forever and I was lulled.

There wasn't a soul in sight until an orange Duratech emerged from a cove across the way and moved toward me. As the boat approached the dock it turned broadside to reveal a bedraggled, sixtyish man with an even more bedraggled Pug pooch in his lap.

"Can you play that thing?" he hollered over the outboard.

I nodded and gave him a thumbs-up.

"Where ya goin'?"

"I'm supposed to be at Darrow Camp today, but I don't know how I'm going to get there."

The man—Warren Arthur Whiting—got up and weighed the boat's fuel tank in his hand.

"Tell ya what. You play, the dog and me'll listen, and if you're any good, we'll get you to Darrow's."

This looked like the only game in town, so I threw my lot into the hands of a complete stranger, never bothering to ask what might happen if I didn't pass the audition.

Stepping into that orange boat was one of the most fateful decisions of my life.

Grand Lake Stream, Maine, is a tiny, six-street village surrounded by eleven interconnecting lakes in northern Washington County, 35 miles from the Canadian border. "GLS," as it is colloquially known, has a population of 125 people.

The road to Grand Lake Stream began for me in Annapolis, Maryland, where I had moved not long after graduating from Elon College in North Carolina. I shared a rented house with a college pal and was trying to be a club musician. There I met a special girl named Shelley and her beautiful three-year-old daughter, Erin. On the Maryland music scene, I met David Mack, who in the summer worked as a camp counselor at Darrow's. He told me about a job opening that sounded idyllic. George Darrow owned a wilderness canoe camp on The Birches, a completely self-contained island with generated power, located

Photo courtesy of Randy Spencer

My brother Al Spencer (left) and me on Peabody Pond in 1953. Our visits served as a pressure valve for my father.

twelve miles by water from Grand Lake Stream. George needed someone to meet up with canoe groups at different checkpoints and resupply them. I'd have a van and all the gear they'd need to complete their trips down Maine's storied waterways. Escaping the Maryland summer heat was a big draw—I didn't ponder long.

Maine, after all, was already forged into my fiber. My father, Kerwin Alton Spencer Sr., had taken his three sons to his brother's camp on Peabody Pond in Sebago since their births. Dad was working his way through the white-collar labyrinth of the Connecticut banking hierarchy. One by-product was stress, and the Sebago camp was his pressure valve. There, at all hours of the day and night, he fished and taught his sons to fish. Landlocked salmon were the most prized quarry, and nothing put a perk in his gait like a chilly morning with a good "salmon chop" on the lake. Rowing, paddling, swimming, hiking, frogging, trapping bait, and fishing were the stripes we earned thanks to Dad and Mom. Although for Mom, to call those trips

Photo courtesy of Randy Spencer

My parents Kerwin and Harriett Spencer at Peabody Pond in 1981. My father imparted his love of fishing to me.

vacations might be a stretch. She worked as much as ever, only without plumbing and electricity.

And so it was that in June of 1973 I loaded a VW bug and headed for the state where my happiest memories were born. I would turn twenty-five in Grand Lake Stream and that sounded fine to me. It was a withering 700 miles for the poor, battered VW bug that had taken me through college and beyond. Like all elderly travelers, it now needed more stops—stops to cool down those four overworked cylinders and give the crankcase a drink of oil. Once in Maine, I made the mandatory stop at L.L. Bean in Freeport to make sure I was equipped to catch a salmon, and to feed the VW one more quart of oil that surely would get it the rest of the way. It did, and when I reached the town dock five hours later, I felt that my faith had been requited by the steaming, crackling Beetle parked there humbly under the tall pines on its too-smooth treads.

And it was there that I first met Warren Arthur Whiting, he of the orange Duratech, and who from that day on treated me like his long-lost son. And how could I avoid being intrigued by a man who could whittle a model ship, hook a wool rug, build a solid camp with hand tools, and write a good poem, all on a steady drip of Narragansett Lager Beer? And, as if that weren't enough, he had once met Hank Williams. From our many conversations that summer, I ascertained that in the distant past there had been a family. Pain, loss, estrangement—whatever the details were, they only made themselves known in the lines of his face at certain times. I never pressed the point. Warren gave me a history lesson on his native Grand Lake Stream replete with recitations of local poems and songs. He taught me a host of wilderness shortcuts and tricks that would behoove any traveler in those woods to know. He bought me a new guitar and an amp and bade me write a song about Maine's infamous black flies, those "devils in disguise." In return, Warren asked for something valuable to him in his solitary life—a visit whenever I was passing through.

Every now and then, I come across the birch-bark postcard I fashioned and mailed to Shelley back in Annapolis that summer, thinking it might impress her. She later agreed to take a chance on me for life, so it couldn't have hurt. We both still marvel that the postcard actually made it through the U.S. Postal Service maze intact. On it I had written, "for as far as the eye can see, the world here is green and blue."

That entire summer's labors yielded only $350. But the outdoor skills I learned, the 1957 Old Town river canoe I restored, the salmon I caught trolling a fly as I paddled "downlake" on leaving day, the messages the vast wilderness whispered—they all made their indelible imprint. I'd leave Grand Lake Stream, but I sensed that it would not leave me.

During that summer of 1973, absence played its fond role for Shelley and me. By fall, after three months apart, we knew we were destined to be a team. So back in Maryland, we immediately laid plans to relocate together to New England. Shelley continued to waitress as Erin started preschool. On a lead from David Mack, I traveled to Woodstock, Connecticut, to investigate work, rents, and schools. I shared a lake house that winter in beautiful northeastern Connecticut, supporting myself by playing club dates in Massachusetts, Connecticut, and Rhode Island. Woodstock seemed like an excellent place to raise children, with its rural character, farms, lakes, and streams. Shelley visited a few times and agreed.

Our plan was interrupted that spring by two deaths. The owners of the Sebago camp, my father's brother Henry and his wife Ethel, had succumbed to asphyxiation from a propane refrigerator gas leak while staying at the camp. They were found dead on the floor by a family friend. The camp would go to my parents, but my father was not emotionally ready to take on the project and all the work needed. Shelley and I volunteered.

That June we made the journey that would begin our life together as a family. Great sadness had given way to great happiness as we settled into the lake house and became attuned to the beauty of that place. Shelley quickly found work at a local inn open to summer tourists and I started playing in area pubs. That scheme afforded Erin a good babysitting schedule—one of us was always available and on duty to take her swimming or fishing or hiking.

The end of summer brought school considerations. The work we were doing, lucrative while the summer lasted, would shortly dry up. Erin needed a school and a home base. We returned to Woodstock and found a fixer-upper farmhouse with insufficient heat, little to no insulation, and years of neglect. We traded the owner elbow grease and improvements for rent. We both knew we would find work, and did—Shelley at the Publick House in Sturbridge, and me in any gin joint of my choosing, playing the guitar and singing. Every spare penny went into paint, fuel, and home improvement tools. I also landed a job at a golf course as a greenskeeper.

Our Connecticut years were punctuated by several life-changing events. Shelley had emergency surgery for an ectopic pregancy and while recovering decided to enroll in nursing school. This led all the way to graduation from Worcester State College with a bachelor's degree and an RN. While still performing nights and weekends, I became a certified greenskeeper at the golf course, and we built a home in Woodstock.

Meanwhile, I had taken Warren's suggestion to write a song about black flies, and it was scheduled for release in the spring of 1981. I couldn't wait to send the acetate master recording of "Black Flies" to Warren just before it came across his local radio station. The single came out the same week Shelley and I were married—the first week of May. It had caused such a ruckus by the day of the ceremony that the band and I hit the road the very next day, putting a honeymoon on hold. By June, a monster had been created and the phone went crazy.

In July, singer Harry Chapin was killed on the Long Island Expressway in a tragic tractor-trailer collision. We were asked to perform at a benefit concert for Harry's impassioned cause—world hunger—and it was there, on a stage in Hartford, Connecticut, that "Black Flies" reached a wider audience. From there, we rode the storm out for all it was worth.

The song, released as a mere novelty, topped radio charts in two countries, and no one was more surprised than me.

By Labor Day weekend I was ready for a break, and Shelley was eight months pregnant with our son, Ian. We decided on Grand Lake Stream for some R&R, and called ahead to let Warren know we were coming. On Shelley's and Erin's first visit to the place I'd been raving and writing about for years, we were met with a line of children at the Pine Tree Store, all wanting their copy of "Black Flies" signed. These were the final days of the vinyl, 45 rpm single, and there was a stack of them on the counter.

The store owners, Robert and Bonnie Gagner, let us use their camp uplake for our stay. With Warren's orange Duratech and some coordinates from Robert on how to find the place, we set out with a guitar, a fly rod, and enough food for three days. I owed Shelley a honeymoon and this one would've been difficult to top. The weather smiled. The salmon cooperated. Robert and Bonnie's camp was fully appointed and comfortable. Even Ian, preparing for his final descent, seemed mellowed.

One day, the three (almost four) of us hiked the jagged shoreline until we were surprised by a ramshackle camp almost hidden from view by overgrowth. Hemlocks and jack pines

Photo courtesy of Randy Spencer

This is the cabin that I stumbled upon while hiking with the family. I was able to buy it, and it helped change my life.

enshrouded the place, and it was clear no one had ventured there for a long time. When I pressed on the door it creaked open. On the table in the middle of the very dark, main room was a note. It read, "Please leave as found. Kindling in the woodbox, few staples in screen cupboard. Thank you—the owner."

Shelley and I had recently been to Concord, Massachusetts, to see Walden Pond and Henry David Thoreau's cabin. This place was its first cousin. There was a main camp and a smaller camp, both built with cedar logs. In the larger was a wood cookstove, a wood heating stove, a sink and pitcher pump, a rough-hewn table and benches, and two double-sized bunks accommodating eight. I stayed there far longer than Shelley's lower back would've liked, but I was caught up in a daydream. I was looking not at the holes in the floor and in the roof, not at the log sills sunk low in the mud, not at the mouse batting in those old camp mattresses, but at what it all might look like with some intense TLC. We finally left, but once again I had the distinct feeling that this place wasn't going to leave me.

One day that fall after Ian was born, Shelley said out of the blue, "Why don't you find out who owns it and write to them?" How did she come by these strange powers? Apparently, I'd been staring into space more than usual. Her words ignited a blitz of research that yielded a name and a New Hampshire address. I wrote a spare note, trying not to reveal that I'd be crushed if the response was negative—it was, and I was.

Seven months later I was still staring into space.

"Write again," Shelley said. "Water under the bridge, changes, who knows?"

This time, I penned a more honest representation of what was in my heart. I praised the place despite its disrepair. I wrote about the feeling I had when I saw it, about my family, and about our ideas for giving the place a new future. I also made a modest offer with consideration that Shelley was in nursing school and I was playing Mr. Mom to Ian and Erin.

I remember trembling holding the return mail that came so quickly. The envelope was thicker than the previous response. As I read the smooth hand of the widow who owned my dream, my eyes welled up. She confessed that she had never seen the place. Her husband, a banker just like my father, had used it as a sporting hideaway until he became too ill to keep it up. They had a handicapped son whom she had hoped would be able to use the place one day, but over the winter, following my first letter, she had done some soul-searching and realized that those ruminations outreached reality. Yes, she would accept my offer, and she was happy to think it could bring so much joy to someone.

Beginning that first summer and for the next sixteen years, Shelley and I shepherded our children to the woods and waters of Grand Lake Stream where they too earned their outdoor stripes. For the first ten years it was almost all work, trying to reclaim the two buildings and give them a second wind. From our primary residence in Connecticut, we made the trip at least once each season of the year. Once in Grand Lake Stream, our first stop was always Warren's. We nicknamed him "Cowboy" because of his tireless hobby of recording and chronicling classic country and western songs. Shelley and the kids grew close to Warren who seemed to love having a family around him.

By the mid-1990s, we were visiting Grand Lake Stream up to ten to twelve times a year. Bags would remain unpacked between trips. I began to see that we were viewing Grand Lake Stream the same way my father had viewed Sebago—as a pressure valve. Shelley had been promoted to the top positions of her career as a registered nurse. The work now had less to do with patient care and more to do with clerical duties and endless forms. I was creating music-based marketing campaigns and making regular trips to Manhattan to produce George Plimpton as a voiceover artist and company spokesperson.

A new conversation topic made its debut: a major life change. Talking about it was like painting on a blank canvas. It was both therapeutic and heartening. Sometimes, the very prospect of such a change seemed like a riddle we had to solve before we could act.

The dialogue continued for months until July 1994, when there was news from the north, and it wasn't good. Warren, my friend of twenty years, was dying. He had held his own against emphysema for nearly ten years, but the toll had caught up with him. I had kept up my promise to visit him each time I went to

Photo courtesy of Randy Spencer

Warren Whiting and his dog, Pepe.

GLS, and now, with a huge lump in my throat, I prepared for my final visit.

I flew out of Hartford to Bangor, rented a car, and drove straight to the hospital in Calais, where Washington County borders Saint Stephen, New Brunswick, Canada. When I saw Warren in his room, the gleam in his eye was there as usual. A nurse with a dour expression on her face came into the room talking baby talk to him. He looked at me impishly for a reaction and I rolled my eyes. That made him smile, and I knew he was not in any great distress.

After the nurse left, Warren said, "Stop the world, I want to get off."

I didn't respond right away. "Are you sure?" I finally asked.

"I'm sure," he said.

I'd learned years before that when Warren's mind was made up, it was like a block of granite. He had smoked too much in his life until he decided not to, and that was the end of tobacco. He had drunk way too much Narragansett in his day until he decided not to, and that was the end of alcohol. This time, he had decided to stop eating, and no doctor or nurse was able to dissuade him. I tried, too, until I saw that my admonishments were upsetting him.

Warren had made other decisions, too, some of them a long time previous. The cemetery in Grand Lake Stream slopes gently eastward, and on its easternmost border is a modest grave with a veteran's stone commemorating Warren's service as an aviation cadet in the U.S. Army Air Corps. He requested the stone, and he requested that a flag be placed there each Memorial Day. He wished to be cremated, and he wanted his ashes scattered at the mouth of Oxbrook Stream where his most joyful, youthful memories lived. He wanted no funeral or memorial service. And, in the simple will he had drawn up eight years earlier, he had specified that he wanted his house and property to go to Shelley and me. All that time, he had been carrying a key to our future. I believe today that this knowledge brought him consolation in his final days. Warren had been painting on a canvas of his own, and he had an uncanny talent for solving riddles.

Perhaps the biggest riddle that could face anyone was the one I was facing then. Warren had seen to it that a door would open for me and that I would be confronted by my own dream. Was it real or had it simply been a useful fiction? Had I really meant it, or was it merely a concoction that served some purpose as an imagined escape from reality? Shelley's and my nightly conversations now turned to mapping out a plan.

If Shelley was going to be a nurse, she made it clear, she wanted to do nursing, not paperwork in a cubicle far from any patient. Surely nurses were needed in the far reaches of eastern Maine. For my part, the Internet had taken hold by 1998 in even the most rural Maine haunts. I could continue my commercial music recording and transmit music files to clients by e-mail. Erin was living in Washington, D.C., and soon to be wed. Ian was a sophomore in high school and enthusiastic about a move to Maine. Supporting ourselves and Ian seemed plausible. And, once we hit the ground in GLS, I would work quickly to become a Registered Maine Guide, a goal that was crystallized for me because of one George Lee "Sonny" Sprague.

The man with the same initials as Grand Lake Stream was known far beyond its borders. The fact that film documentaries and feature stories had been done on Sonny Sprague served mostly to amuse him. He had been in the Philippines during World War II. He had worked the woods camps in his home environs. He had owned sporting camps. He had followed in the footsteps of his father to become one of a handful of renowned craftsmen who built "Grand Lakers," the twenty-foot, square-sterned, cedar and ash canoes invented in Grand Lake Stream. While the image and persona of this rugged individualist and freethinker was known far from his native Grand Lake Stream, Sonny himself rarely left home. He embodied the very essence of the place he loved above all others, and so, who better to sport a personalized license plate that read "GLS"?

Photo courtesy of Randy Spencer

The one and only, Sonny Sprague.

It was not long after acquiring our camp that I first met Sonny, whose daughter, Bonnie Gagner, co-owned the Pine Tree Store with her husband, Robert. Sonny was then in his late fifties. He invited me to accompany him on a number of unspecified adventures, and it was a privilege. I watched him start fires in gales and in gully-washing rains. I watched him build quiet winter sanctums in the middle of windswept lakes using spruce poles and tarps. I saw him produce ice-fishing rigs out of pucker brush and playing cards. I followed him as he blazed new trails home after I had given us up for lost. His sense of direction was fabled in those territories where hunters sometimes left the camp door never to be seen again. Sonny navigated in the deep woods as though an inner azimuth guided him wherever he wanted to go, and home again. I never once saw him use a compass.

Sonny, a working guide since his late teens, became my mentor and friend. When it came time for me to take the state of Maine's fourteen written exam sections and three oral boards in order to become a licensed guide, Sonny laughed, saying, "I'd flunk that test with flying colors." In his day, the process was different. Then, you had to get a Maine game warden to vouch for you and you could then become licensed to guide for hire. Sonny believed that the brains to pass the test and the brains to do the job were two entirely different things.

I learned from Sonny that the relationship between a guide and clients, or "sports" as clients are known, is unique because it takes place in a vacuum—in this case, a twenty-foot Grand Laker. Things that are said between sport and guide are held sacred in an unspoken rule of confidentiality, much the same as with a psychiatrist or lawyer. I learned that beyond hiring Sonny to put them over fish, these people were placing their lives in his hands. Dramatic, sometimes violent weather could befall them at any time, and they needed to be confident that in his care, they would return safely. It took brains, indeed.

When our Connecticut home sold in May of 1998, renovations on Warren's place, including a recording studio, weren't

Photo courtesy of Randy Spencer

The house on the right is the one left to me by Warren. By the time of this picture in 1998, we had begun making renovations.

finished yet. We went anyway. We planned to stay at our camp for the summer and work on the house in the village. We hoped to be moved in by the start of school. Not quite. Taking baths in the lake in mid-October is a story you may want to tell your grandchildren, but at the time it was something other than exhilarating. Ian will always remember doing his first homework assignments in a remote camp under a gas light, and that'll be a story for his grandchildren, too. Relief came just as temperatures were dipping into the twenties at night—we finally moved into a working home.

We had executed the major life change that had headlined our conversations for the previous two years, and our new life had begun. Shelley applied for work at the same Calais hospital where Warren had been a patient. The studio was set up and ready for me to resume commercial recording from my new, northern outpost. And, I mustered the brains to pass the state's exam to be a Registered Maine Guide. Now it remained to be seen whether I could muster the brains to do the job.

Getting Ready

Grand Lake Stream, Maine

Just fifty-five miles west of the easternmost promontory in the United States is the tiny town of Grand Lake Stream, Maine.

With a U.S. Post Office, a general store, a salmon hatchery, and a year-round population of 125, give or take, it is surrounded in every direction except one by unorganized, wilderness townships—each thirty-six square miles, and each with only a numeral for a name. They are designated on DeLorme's *Maine Atlas and Gazeteer* as T 42 and T 43, etc. To the east, across Big Musquash Stream, is the Peter Dana Point / Indian Township Reservation, home to about 700 Passamaquoddy.

There is a lone memorial in the center of town. It is not a Revolutionary War or Civil War general on a steed, nor is it a bronze cannon. On a marbled, granite stone a simple scene is etched—a twenty-foot, square-sterned "Grand Laker" canoe with a guide paddling and two "sports" fishing. In this town, "Grand Laker" is the name applied both to townspeople and to this special canoe. In the etching, the forward sport is playing a fish while a nearby bald eagle, wings arched, picks something off the lake's surface. It depicts a day-in-the-life snapshot of a Grand Lake Stream guide, an image essentially unchanged for more than a century. The monument commemorates two centennials: the incorporation of Grand Lake Stream, and the inception of the

Photo courtesy of Randy Spencer

Map of the Grand Lake Stream area.

Registered Maine Guide. More than one hundred years ago, both of these milestones inspired hope when the town's young life seemed imperiled.

Just prior to the incorporation of Grand Lake Stream in 1897, there were rumblings of great changes in the destiny of

Photo courtesy of Randy Spencer

Here you can see the stack at the old tannery and logs on the stream. The tannery is now the site of the salmon hatchery.

what was then Hinckley Township. The township had grown up around the Shaw Brothers Tannery, located on the site now occupied by the state salmon hatchery. At the time, it was the largest tannery in the world, consuming colossal quantities of hemlock bark, which was needed to make tanning liquor, harvested from woods camps dotting the broad wilderness around the tiny village. But as the Industrial Revolution gathered steam and chemical tanning began to come into its own, the fortunes of Shaw Brothers faltered along with those of Hinckley Township—soon to become Grand Lake Stream Plantation.

Not far from where Grand Lake Stream flows into Big Lake after its three-mile run from West Grand Lake, an enterprising man named William Gould around 1870 hacked out a clearing that came to be known as Gould's Landing. His industriousness proved far more promising than he could have foreseen. Access to

Photo courtesy of Randy Spencer

A turn-of-the-century "sport" at Grand Lake Sream.

Grand Lake Stream and its incredible salmon fishing, then known to few, became viable. Before this time, trudging with dunnage was the only means of accessing the desirable fishing grounds of Grand Lake Stream. As the tannery-based economy of the village wound down, an attraction like this offered a possible lifeline to the future.

The rough "road" from Gould's Landing to the village of Grand Lake Stream was called "Indian Carry," and to it the town owed its earliest sporting business. Until 1870, all camping, cooking, fishing gear, and canoes came over the trail on the backs of tribal guides. Once more, William Gould saw opportunity. He crafted a special wagon with "floating" wheels that slid back and forth on their axles to help the wagon negotiate the rocky road. Grand Lake Stream was now positioned to do business as a sporting destination, a business that was sorely needed by the close of the nineteenth century. The tannery went into bankruptcy on March 19, 1898, its contents sold to junk dealers and later shipped to Boston.

Photo courtesy of Randy Spencer

One of the paddleboats that brought early sports from Princeton to Grand Lake Stream.

Guided fishing as a lucrative resource required two things: good marketing and better access to the remote northern Washington County location. These were already in the works. In the 1890s Cornelia Thurza "Flyrod" Crosby was busy marketing outdoor sporting in Maine at shows in Boston, New York, and Philadelphia. An expert fly fisher, a dead aim, and good outdoor writer, she wowed audiences at fairs and expositions in a too-short deerskin skirt, showing photos of fish and game exploits beyond the wildest dreams of Dapper Dan sportsmen to the south. Her chief area of operations was the Rangeley region, but her promotions brought attention to all of Maine. Crosby received the state's first Registered Maine Guide's license in 1897.

The timing couldn't have been better when the railroad opened to Princeton, just ten miles from Grand Lake Stream, in 1898. From Princeton, located at the headwaters of the West Branch of the St. Croix River, there was unblocked access to

Photo courtesy of Randy Spencer

Early-twentieth-century sports at Rosie's Camps in Grand Lake Stream.

Gould's Landing. Sports and other visitors leaving the train depot boarded a steamer, *Captain Lewy* or *The Wood Duck*, which passed through Lewy Lake, Long Lake, and Big Lake before docking at Gould's Landing. A steamer made the trip back and forth daily. Eventually, Gould's floating wagon gave way to a Ford. The guided sporting business began to pour into Grand Lake Stream like warm maple sap.

Indeed, Minnie Atkinson in her book, *Hinckley Township or Grand Lake Stream Plantation,* wrote that when the clock tolled a new millennium, "the village turned from the humble task of providing the world's sole leather to the pleasanter task of catering to its pleasures and its health."

David Cass

David Cass, the first white man to permanently settle his family in these environs in about 1820, set the tone for many to follow. He cared for neither the comforts nor the limitations of society, seeking instead to invent his own life despite inhospitable surroundings. He was known as "The General" by everyone from nearby Indians to the lumbermen who occasionally stopped through his outpost for a night's debauchery.

Cass weighed 380 pounds, almost four times the weight of his wife, who was known to the settlers who soon followed the Cass family as "Aunt Nellie." Cass either had some slight medical training or was self-taught, and his services were often called for among neighbors. It was this and the many other skills he brought to the backcountry that leveraged him against failure. Living on a bluff overlooking Big Lake, Cass carved from scratch a life of relative prosperity with over a hundred acres cleared, livestock, and a viable fur and lumber trade.

From Cass's time to the present day, other individualists have sought similar lives amid the thousands of acres of timberlands and almost innumerable lakes and streams that surround Grand Lake Stream.

Grand Lakers and the Streamer Fly

Among the other factors critical to the development of Grand Lake Stream as a first-class fishing destination were the highly effective "streamer fly" and "Beaver Canoes"—later to be called "Grand Lakers"—built to accommodate outboards. Both came courtesy of the Bacon brothers, Alonzo and Herbert.

The following passage was first published in the April 1910 issue of *National Sportsman* describing a version of how the streamer fly was created:

"There was a time when the chanticleers of Grand Lake Stream [Maine] used to rule the yards with uplifted white tails; but their pride was crushed when a guide named Alonzo Stickney Bacon demonstrated that the hen's long feathers made attractive lures for landlocked salmon. This is how it came about . . .

"Alonzo was in his canoe, fishing with artificial flies. He could not get a rise. He was seated on a cushion filled with hen's feathers. There was a hole in the cushion and a long white feather protruded. Alonzo plucked the feather from the cushion, tied it to a hook, and used it as a lure. The salmon took it with avidity. Other fishermen copied the lure. Soon in all the barnyards of the plantations all of the hens were rifled of their caudal appendages and the stream was flecked with anglers using a long straggly fly, misnamed by Boston flymakers the Morning Glory."

The story is reprinted in Joseph Bates's authoritative text, *Streamer Fly Tying and Fishing*, in a chapter that examines the origins of the streamer fly. In Maine, Bates concedes, the streamer fly was most likely born in Grand Lake Stream. To claim that there were no streamer flies before they were introduced by Alonzo "Lon" Bacon would doubtless be met with challengers

Photo courtesy of Dean L. Lunt

Here I am in a modern version of the famed Grand Laker. This one was made by the late Sonny Sprague.

from around the fly-fishing world. Nevertheless, from these ignoble beginnings as a canoe cushion "lure," the streamer fly blossomed in Grand Lake Stream into other Leghorn variations with names like Rooster's Regret. Regardless of its true origins, the streamer fly soundly hooked the fly-fishing world.

Around the same time, another need knocked on the hopeful fishing town's door. Gas-powered propulsion had arrived in the form of outboard motors, and one man saw how to incorporate that convenience without sacrificing the grace and efficiency of canoe travel. He was none other than Alonzo's brother, Herbert "Beaver" Bacon. His original square-sterned canoes were called "Beaver Canoes," later to be named "Grand Lakers."

Sadly, the life of Alonzo Bacon ended tragically when, mistaken for a bear in a hunt at the north end of West Grand Lake, he was shot in the thigh and bled to death during the transport downlake. Meanwhile, Herb continued to polish and perfect the square-sterned creation in a modest shop that still stands on Shaw Street in Grand Lake Stream.

Grand Lake Stream Guides

In a relatively short span of time, several factors and developments worked together to transform remote Grand Lake Stream from a small mill town to a nationally known sporting destination. And the people who came into this sometimes treacherous wilderness needed help to not only find fish, but to survive. This need gave opportunity to the locals who knew the woods so well. In her history, Atkinson describes the mystique that surrounded the early guides:

"They possess the sturdy traits of the first pioneers in America. The conditions of their lives make them self-reliant and unaffected in manner. Shut away from the rest of the world all winter, save for the slender ties of more or less regular mail, they are ready with a hospitable welcome for returning friends or strangers when the fishing, vacation, and hunting season comes again . . . With two or three exceptions every family in the village is represented [in the list of local guides]."

That list, in Atkinson's day, exceeded fifty-four guides. Today, the region still boasts the highest concentration of Registered Maine Guides in the state, with upwards of eighty, although less than half that number are working guides. An informal system of journeymanship preserves the original, 1897-style of a guided fishing trip in Grand Lake Stream. Newcomers learn the trade from veteran guides who not only pass along the skills of the business,

Photo courtesy of Randy Spencer

Maine Guides, David Sockabasin (left) and Ray Sockabasin.

but also those aspects unique to Grand Lake Stream guiding, including the Grand Laker, which can be maneuvered into places barred to other boats; distinctive methods for preparing a three- to four-course shore lunch cooked over an open fire; and exposure to some of the most productive salmon, togue (Passamaquoddy word for lake trout), and smallmouth bass waters in Maine.

Most of the earliest guides were woodsmen working out of remote camps. Some years they didn't return home for months at a time. All entertainment between long hours of hard labor had to be invented. Storytelling, one of the most prized talents, was the product of mentoring and practice. Together with their woodsmen skills, storytelling proved a handy tool for guiding. The day in the canoe is long if the fish aren't biting. These earliest guides who wintered in timber-cutting camps were experts at passing the time pleasantly. Games, limericks, and stories—especially stories—were employed to make the long days shorter.

The traditional shore lunch likely was born during these seminal days of guiding. The midday break is no place to skimp. It's a chance to stretch limbs, but it can also be an escape from the elements. Cold rain and relentless wind eventually penetrate the hardiest sport. The shore lunch revives and warms, rejuvenates, and informs the afternoon with a fresh outlook. Lunch baskets are packed to overflowing with the fixings for fish chowder, "bannock"—a kind of biscuit easily made outdoors—potatoes, onions, homemade pies, cookies, and other treats. Guides brewed tea in the old days, and later, coffee with an egg.

The guides' reclusiveness in winter and interaction in summer with ladies and gentlemen from the big cities produced one-of-a-kind, colorful characters. The first Grand Lake Stream guides charmed their well-to-do clients not just with their woods savvy but with their wits. Day after day, they delivered unaffected eloquence in Down East dialect from the stern seat of a canoe. They set the standard for a new profession while saving a town from extinction.

Photo courtesy of Dean L. Lunt

A monument to Maine Guides that sits in the middle of Grand Lake Stream.

Joe Mell

Passamaquoddy guide Joe Mell's canoe-making skills and fishing and hunting talents were well established locally, but it was noted photographer and Massachusetts Institute of Technology bacteriologist William Lyman Underwood who carried Joe's name and fame outside of Maine. Underwood kept detailed notes about their trips together and later published two books drawing heavily from his experiences with Joe. They were *Wilderness Adventures,* published in 1927, and *Wild Brother,* published in 1921. By the close of the nineteenth century, Underwood had been spending an average of a month each summer with Joe, camping, canoeing, fishing, hunting, and exploring.

"Joe Mell, the Passamaquoddy guide, stalked the woods and canoed the lakes and rivers of Maine and New Brunswick," Underwood wrote. "Joe was an astute reader of natural signs, an interpreter of animal movements and habit, a namer of birds, a survivor who knew how to build canoes and shelters from natural materials and how to supply fish and game for meals."

Underwood saw in Joe "an example of what men could be if they remained close to nature."

The Underwood family had a seasonal residence at the headwaters of the St. Croix River, fifteen miles north of Joe's home. Over the many hours they spent together, Joe's life story slowly came to light for Underwood. When Joe was four years old, his father was mysteriously shot by an unknown assailant while tending his traps. Joe went out on his own at a very early age, but later returned home to care for his ailing mother until her death at the age of ninety. He was by then raising his own family on the proceeds of his own outdoor ingenuity, and on his growing reputation as a guide.

"Nothing escapes Joe's keen eyes," Underwood wrote. "His power of sight, especially the knack of finding things, is nothing short of marvelous. Often with the naked eye he has seen a canoe hugging the farthest shores of a cove in the lake, while I with powerful binoculars have difficulty in locating it."

When the two men traveled together on the St. Croix, Underwood was bowman, while Joe guided from the stern. When they camped overnight, Joe built lean-tos. They were made, said Underwood's journal, with "three sides of logs and a roof of sapling trees shingled with boughs of spruce and fir. Fir boughs also carpeted the floor and furnished us with beds. The open side of our bower faced the water and just in front a big fireplace was constructed and piled with logs ready to be lighted when the chill of evening should descend after sunset."

Underwood's writings about his wilderness adventures with Joe Mell reveal that he wasn't just hiring a guide in the usual sense. He was studying, admiring, and celebrating the unique ways of an extraordinary individual and of native life.

Once, when the two were hunting for black duck, three flew over and Underwood discharged both barrels of his shotgun. "Missed," he muttered in self-disgust. Joe disagreed. "You got one," he said. Joe added that he heard it fall and break off a cedar limb on its way down in a nearby swamp. As the day darkened, Underwood shook his head while Joe assured him they would find the duck the next day.

They hunted ducks again the next morning, and on the way back to camp for lunch, Joe steered off to one side and parked the canoe next to a stand of dead cedars. He disembarked, all the while listening to Underwood beseeching him to abandon the idea and go have breakfast. Joe refused and waded waist-deep into the swamp. Underwood pulled out a book to pass the time. When Joe sloshed his way back to the canoe, he got in and pushed off without saying a word. Underwood couldn't resist. "I told you it was no use. How could you find a duck that you only heard drop in the dark? Even if you had seen him fall in the swamp in the daylight you would have a hard time finding him." At that, Joe pulled something out of his coat, turned around, and said, "Look, I got him." Underwood, beholding the black duck that he had missed the night before, remained silent.

Many times after Joe had made a campsite for the two to inhabit for a night, he pronounced it "too comfortable" for himself, and retired to sleep under his canoe on the shoreline. One time, Underwood crept down to the shoreline after they had both retired to witness Joe's humble "abode." He brought his camera with him.

There slept Joe Mell, swathed in a blanket, canoe overhead as a roof against the elements. Underwood snapped a picture and *BOOOSH!* went the flash. Joe came off the ground from a sound sleep and banged his head on the underside of the canoe. "By golly! What you do? I think I struck by lightning!" screamed Joe.

Underwood's photograph, "Joe Mell, Asleep in his Canoe," ca. 1895, resides at the Smithsonian American Art Museum.

A century later, Joe Mell's legacy is still known to some people of the region, and local canoe makers are aware of the influence of his canoe-making style.

Lola Sockabasin

I've worked for several years in the off-season as audio archivist for the Passamaquoddy people. My job is to take old tapes, digitize them, clean them up so that they're more listenable, then return them to the tribe for archiving. Some of them are destined for the Museum of Indian History in Washington, D.C. Ever since recording devices were invented by Thomas Edison, tribal elders have been interviewed on "tape," sometimes in sessions lasting for days. Without scripting, these informal, often mundane conversations yield an extraordinary result: They sum up an oral history of the Passamaquoddy tribe.

The act of speaking freely about one's life, especially in the twilight years, is perceived in the tribe as an unselfish enterprise; a gift to those who follow. Reviewing hundreds of hours of these oral tracts, some of them in English, some in Passamaquoddy, one can hear wit, sadness, humor, and, most of all, honesty, perhaps illustrating that the truth of a life is best crystallized near its end. No interviews exemplify this candor so well as those with one of the region's most famous guides, Lola Sockabasin.

Lola passed away in July of 2001 at the age of ninety-one. In the early 1990's, he indulged me by meeting with me at his home for informal discussions about his knowledge, experiences, and memories.

His recollections reached back to the last days of the "longhouses," when it was still not uncommon to see teepees, or wigwams, as they were sometimes called. These birch-bark dwellings were used as the people moved back and forth seasonally between the salt water and the inland lakes.

Birch bark, a staple of Indian life, was used in various thicknesses for different purposes. For fishing spears, quarter-inch-thick bark was used to form a kind of spring-loaded trap around the sharp point to hold the fish firmly once speared. The bark was best suited for canoes (*aguidon*) when stripped in the winter. A controlled fire was started around the trunk, allowing the heat to follow the tree up until the bark could be easily removed.

Lola said that one of the best sewing materials for canoe seams was the sinewy strips on the inside of cedar bark. I later tested this by using it to string together a log railing and it held for three years. If it was stripped when green, it was strong and durable. Pine pitch was boiled down to the consistency of a thick, black tar and applied liberally to the sewn seams. Lola remembered how fascinated he was as a young boy to see that the canoe did not leak at all after this process. It would be repeated as a maintenance regimen over the life of the canoe. If tribal members suffered from infections, some of the boiled pitch would be used to fashion a poultice to be applied to the wound.

For drying and preserving game meats and fish, salt water was gathered at Pleasant Point (*Sepayik*), Lola said. Large bowls of it were left in the sun to evaporate and the remaining salt was collected to use on cod, salmon, deer, and moose meat. Cod was the chief food source for the tribe while residing on the coast, and they also carried salt cod inland. The tribe moved up the St. Croix River to Skoodic Falls, portaged, canoed past Woodland Lake (*Wapskonikonok*, or "white rock carry"), portaged again at Grand Falls, and then had direct access to the hunting and fishing grounds of today's reservation.

Most native names tended to be toponyms, at once descriptive and mellifluous to the ear. Sysladobsis Lake, for example, just twelve miles northwest of Grand Lake Stream, means, "lake with shark-fin-shaped rocks." Anyone who has guided or fished "Dobsy," as it is nicknamed, will readily avow that this is an accurate toponym.

Lola was still trapping beaver in the winter and muskrats in the spring when we first met. Later, he helped his sons by "fleshing" the animals. He used a sharp gouge to scrape fat off the hides. I saw Lola fleshing out three and four beavers a day in his late eighties—no small feat for much younger men.

The skill for which Lola became known far beyond the borders of Maine, however, was basket weaving. Later in life, he added birch furniture to his repertoire. Ash, the wood prized in basket making, is of seminal significance to Maine's aboriginal peoples. Glooskap, the beloved figure of oral Passamaquoddy legend and song, fired an arrow into an ash tree, from which fell the first female and the first male. Ash is "pounded" for basket making, helping to make it supple for weaving. Lola's mastery extended to large, utilitarian pack baskets, smaller, artful baskets, picnic baskets, and decorative baskets for mantel or shelf.

What leaked out between the lines of Lola's stories were handy tricks and shortcuts that are indispensable in the outdoors. With a scarcity of doctors or conventional medical resources, home remedies were lifesavers in the tribe. Lola described "Black Stem," which grows three to four feet tall, developing a large, roundish, white flower. When the flower fell off in September, the entire plant was dug up and the root system was hung in a bag. These roots were then minced or shaved into cheesecloth so that they could be boiled and steeped as a tea. This elixir treated common colds, flu, and other respiratory ailments. "Yellow Root" (*wisaweyik*), Lola said, grows in bogs, shallows, and swamps. Its long, yellowish vines grow up from the bottom, and it, too, was used as a tea to combat common illnesses.

Lola's adeptness at hunting was renowned. He knew, both as a guide and provider for his family, to wait for a side view of a bull moose (*mus*) to be able to tell how big it was. If the antlers reached to the back of his ribs, it was trophy size. If you cannot maneuver for a side view, the next best way to judge size is by the ears—extra long ears are the sign of a very large moose. In guiding moose hunters, it is important to know how to preserve the "cape" for later mounting. If the skinning process is begun immediately after the kill, the hair will come out in clumps, spoiling the mount for the taxidermist and the client. After the animal has been dead for ten minutes or so, the hair will "set," and it is then safe to skin the moose. One of the hardest times to find a bull moose is right before the fall rut begins. At this time they are hiding in thick cover or swamps, laying low prior to the mating ritual. It can be next to impossible to find one or to move one from its cover during this period. Making a megaphone-shaped moose call out of birch bark served to beckon many a mus to Lola's muzzle, as did other tricks known to few. For example, out of sight of a bull, slowly pouring water from a bucket into a stream or lake mimicked the sound of a cow moose urinating. This, in combination with a few well-placed grunts, could ensure meat for the table in lean times.

By the 1990s, few living people other than Lola still had firsthand experience with the tribal tradition of spearing salmon (*ouananiche*) during the spring and fall salmon runs. Fluvial narrows or "oxbows" were sought where heavy salmon migrations bottlenecked, forcing a large biomass of fish into a small area. Key sites included an oxbow section of Junior Stream, connecting Junior Lake with Junior Bay and West Grand Lake. Many of the Indian artifacts housed in the state museum were found at this site. Another is "The Thoroughfare" between Junior Bay and Pocumcus Lake. Here, the flow of thousands of years, before any dams created an alluvion, approaches the middle of the narrows from opposite shores. The largest salmon runs occurred at night, so the ingenious "birch light" was devised long before the days of Coleman lanterns. Lola described a six- or seven-foot pole, cut and then split at the top with a hatchet. Into the crevice, birch bark was stuffed. Once lit, it would burn brightly for a long time, and many of these could illuminate the killing grounds enough to ensure a bountiful harvest.

Surely a wealth of knowledge passed on with Lola Sockabasin, for these and all other interviews could not be exhaustive. I also suspect that like other exceptionally learned guides and woodsmen I've met, Lola practiced a personal sacrament of saying a little less than he knew.

Harley Fitch

Harley Fitch and his wife, Helena, up to the early 1970s, ran the Trading Post located close to today's town dock in Grand Lake Stream. The building is no longer standing. They also rented cottages. Helena's first husband was Dr. Nye Whiting, father of my old friend Warren. I had the pleasure of once meeting Harley, but his legend grew for me thanks to a man I guided, Rodney Maddison, Warren's childhood friend.

Rodney, seventy-six at the time I guided him, had lived in Grand Lake Stream until he was sixteen, learning proficiencies that would last him all his life. As a boy, he learned about cold, and how to keep warm when there was too much of it; about sustenance and how to survive when there was too little of it. By the time he was sixteen, he knew both more and less than sixteen-year-olds from the population centers. They could've taught him how to panhandle for a soda pop. He could've taught them how to set a snare and catch a bear, or use the right amount of dynamite to free up a logjam in the river.

Rodney credits Harley with a lot of this learning. His favorite recollections go straight to Harley's storytelling mastery. One of his favorites came when as a teenager, he and a friend spent time at Harley's Oxbrook Camp one fall. By evening firelight, Harley held them spellbound with tall tales of whitetails. He knew how to build his story from the ground up, adjusting his cadences to the enthusiasm of his youthful audience. Harley had been on the trail of a massive buck for days, camping out at night and picking up the track again the next morning. The buck, of course, knew he was being stalked. Periodically, he would stop and wait. He waited only long enough to either smell or see Harley, then bolted. As the days passed, Harley just wore down the animal with perseverance. These near-miss encounters started coming closer together. Finally, early one morning when the wind had shifted and the buck miscalculated Harley's position, Harley was ready with his rifle shouldered and the safety thrown. He took a bead on the buck's brisket.

Right then, Harley stopped the story, filled his pipe, took extra long to do it, and asked the boys if they wanted some popcorn. Rodney said he and his friend were giddy with the suspense. Harley then produced, for his wide-eyed young audience, an old Polaroid of the fourteen-pointer hanging from a game pole outside the Oxbrook Camp.

Drummond Humchuck

Earl Bonness, whose family originally hailed from New Brunswick, Canada, spent most of his adult life in Grand Lake Stream, and finally worked his last guiding job in the mid-1990s at the age of eighty-six. That day, he guided Vinnie Lobosco, a New Jersey native and thirty-year GLS visitor. When I guided him ten years after his trip with Earl, Lobosco told me that Earl had taken him salmon fishing that day at the head of West Grand Lake around Junior Bay. He marveled at the way Earl navigated and prepared a shore lunch as though he could do it blindfolded. At eighty-six, the "Old Trapper," as he was called by his sports, regaled Lobosco with stories so vividly detailed, so expertly told, the client didn't know and didn't care whether he was hearing fact or fiction.

Drummond Humchuck embodies that long tradition of real-or-not-real mythical men. For seven years, I wrote a weekly column in the Calais-based *Down East Times* called, "A View from Grand Lake Stream." At least once each season of the year, I reported on my visits to Drummond, far off the beaten track in a place he calls Township Unknown. According to the terms of our special covenant, I could only write about him on the condition that I did not reveal his whereabouts. I have never violated that pact. When the columns appeared, people approached me, wishing to make contact with him. Guelie Roberts, manager of the landfill in Grand Lake Stream, seemed best to understand who Drummond is and what he is all about. When he was once asked on dump day whether he thought Drummond was fact or fiction, he said, "Neither."

Storytelling is an important tool for a Maine guide. My goal in writing about Drummond was only to show a portrait of an uncommon life lived deliberately, and despite all modern odds. Many would say that a feasible explanation for "Township Unknown" is required, and I agree. Maine's unorganized territories are without governments, schools, post offices, and effectively, law enforcement, since, by and large, they are often without people. At surveying time when townships were being portioned up, certain small, odd-shaped "junks" of land, which for one reason or another couldn't be shoe-horned into a 36-square-mile township, were termed "gores." There was yet another surveying oddity—a small piece of land that was just plain unaccounted for, or otherwise overlooked. Afterward, if the mishap was acknowledged at all (and not all were), it was referred to on maps as a "surplus," or, alternately, a "mistake." That's if it was discovered. These points are raised not to offer a

The Pine Tree Store

As the first trains delivered sports to nearby Princeton in 1898, a native son was delivered in Grand Lake Stream. Paul Hoar was one of eight children, not an unusually large family at the time, but one that was sadly bereft of its father when the boy was only seven. As a young man, Paul became a guide, and as the Great Depression wound down in the early 1930s, he was already laying plans to start a business. His bride, Edith, convinced him it should not be a sporting lodge. Her disinclination toward cooking and kitchen work, she said, would not be an asset to a family-run business.

Paul had been guiding an executive in the Woolworth's department store chain with whom he finally felt comfortable enough to share his dream: Instead of a lodge; he would open a store. It would stay open year-round, and offer not only groceries, but also hardware and building supplies, and would cater to fishermen by stocking tackle and flies tied by Paul and Edith. Since Paul was postmaster, the store would house the Grand Lake Stream post office. The businessman, apparently impressed by Paul's enthusiasm, wrote Paul a check for $800 and handed it over as seed money. To give context to that gift, guides' fees in 1934 were $3.00 per day (they are over $200 today).

Paul enlisted the services of Fred Lacey, who owned camps on Munson Island on West Grand Lake, to help design the store. After a full day of guiding, Paul worked evenings digging the full basement with pick and shovel. The Pine Tree Store opened in 1934. To supplement income from the budding business, Paul continued to guide in the summer while his wife ran the store and the post office. By the mid-1940s, Paul also offered life insurance, as well as insurance for homes and camps.

A future store owner was already peering over the counter at the parade of summer customers and helping to stock shelves when she was only seven. Barbara Hoar Wheaton took over the business with her husband Kenneth in 1964. The daughter of the store's founder also did double duty in the post office as Kenneth guided during the season and built canoes in the off-season. This became the norm as the Pine Tree Store's third owner/operaters, Robert and Bonnie Gagner, took over in 1978 after it was leased and operated for a year by Sam and Joanne Thompson of Calais. With comfortable living quarters above the store, they raised two sons who, like Barbara Wheaton, were helping out from an early age.

True to store tradition, by the time she was an eighth grader, Kara Cressey was tending to customers in 2007. Her parents, Kurt and Kathy Cressey, had then been running the store for thirteen years. In 1994, they had left jobs at DeLorme, the mapping company in Yarmouth, Maine, to begin a new life as store owners.

While fly-fishing one of Grand Lake Stream's classic salmon pools in the spring of 1989, I looked up to see a distinguished-looking gentleman observing me from the ledges above Little Falls. I fished down and then walked over to say hello. He spoke softly and knowingly about the stream and its pools, then reached into his pocket and produced a fly he had long since tied himself. I was taken by the obviously practiced craftsmanship. He handed it over, saying, "How do you do. I'm Paul Hoar." He passed away in 1993 at the age of ninety-five.

crash course on surveying terminology, but to illustrate at least the possibility of Drummond's unique situation.

I don't know everything about Drummond Humchuck, since he was already in his mid-seventies when we met. He's now well into his eighties. We met because I dropped my compass in a heath one deer season, got turned around, and walked unwittingly right into his dooryard. I was a long, long way from home and overwhelmed to see someone living in such a remote place. The fit, agile, bearded man graciously took me into his very modest cabin, telling me that lost hunters comprised his entire society—one every five years or so. The time spent in his presence flew by fast. I became concerned that I couldn't make it out before dark to the twitch trail that led to the woods road that led to the old logging yard where I had parked my truck. Just before I departed, Drummond reminded me that without my compass, I could always find north on a clear night. Just line up the bottom two stars on the Big Dipper (even if they're on top) and they will point to that ancient navigational celestial body, the North Star. The horizon directly beneath this star will be north. I used that reliable tool for the long trek out of there, marking my way as I went with hash marks on trees. I knew I'd be back.

Drummond is simple, but not simple-minded. He is matter-of-fact, but never rudely so, and he is of this earth in a way that makes his company a veritable therapy. I also love to watch him. Despite his age, Drummond's movements are a masterwork of economy. Not an ounce of energy is ever wasted. He portions it out judiciously to fuel all his waking hours. He cuts a little wood every day to stay ahead of his needs in case he's ever laid up for a bit. Depending on the season, rainwater or snowmelt collects in a barrel inside the cabin thanks to clever piping channels he's arranged. Dried, salted meats and smoked fish such as eels are put by in cool storage. Cranberries, blueberries, raspberries, and blackberries all grow within easy reach of his cabin.

Drummond procures his entire sustenance from the land—land he doesn't actually own, but has use of through a kind of squatter agreement, either with the tribes, the timber companies, the state, or someone else—that topic is always avoided. It has occurred to me that whoever the landowner is might not even know he's there, though I doubt that. The more puzzling part is his exemption from Fish and Game laws as we know them. He is allowed to set a gill net for himself, trap in the old ways, and hunt out of season. We should emphasize that he does not do these things for sport, but for survival. He chums, baits, snares, and spears with the adeptness of Passamaquoddies I've only read about. He may, in fact, have some native blood. In short, by our standards, Drummond Humchuck is a poacher, a game bandit, and an outlaw. But in that one little junk, or gore, or mistake in unorganized territory, Drummond lives as he pleases and as he needs to, and it's somehow okay.

Drummond made his decision long ago to live in this place far away from hustling, bustling humanity. To talk to him, you get the impression he knew his destiny from the day he was born. He is where he should be, doing what he should be doing. He seems to me, by any ruler I apply, to be happy. He has never talked specifically about his early life, although I know he hasn't been in this place forever. Sometimes it's what goes unspoken that spills the most beans. I have had a peculiar feeling that this world had shown a young Drummond Humchuck, perhaps through its wars, things that forged the man I know now. It's only speculation.

The outside walls of Drummond's shack are lined with snares and traps of every variety, most of them homemade. Also bucksaws, drawknives, axes, and other tools hang there under the eaves. The inside walls are caulked and chinked in the style of the early woods camps, with mud and hewn sticks. Half the year he cooks outside, half the year in. A broiler, a teapot, and a #8 cast-iron "spider" frying pan make up his kitchen wares. He boils water in a #10 coffee can to which he has added a bail by punching out two holes and attaching wire. He weaves his own snowshoes out of hide strips from game he has trapped, reloads his own shells by melting lead, ties his own flies from duck feathers and bucktails, and whittles for business and pleasure. He once told me that whittling gave his mind wings to go anywhere it pleased, and that way, he didn't need to leave Township Unknown. He often whittles all the way through my visits.

Drummond has taught me many things that are of absolutely no value in most of today's world. They are important to me because they are lessons in tenaciousness, resourcefulness, and in many instances, genius. Drummond Humchuck is a man who carries credentials from another era, credentials unrecognizable in our time. For example, who needs to know these days that sprinkling soap flakes on the surface of a lake or stream will drive fish away from that area and into another (a more favorable one) for catching or spearing? Who needs to know that an aspirin in a bait bucket will revive dying minnows? And, who cares if you can make a washing machine as good as any from Sears when you have no running water or electricity? Drummond does. His galvanized tub and plumber's plunger clean clothes amazingly well, even if it takes a little elbow grease. Drummond is a repository of knowledge from yesteryear, and not all of these nuggets are anachronisms. He never kills a ladybug because ladybugs control the populations of many kinds of indoor, unwanted insects. In fact, I have to date not seen, even in likely seasons, any houseflies or sweet-loving ants in Drummond's home.

What most people today know about obtaining lamp oil from fish comes from Melville's *Moby-Dick*. Well, Drummond, for all I know, may not have read that briny tome, but he actually makes his own lamp oil from freshwater fish. By extracting the liver and boiling it along with the fatty portions that surround the other vital organs in the body cavity, he is able to skim off small quantities of fish oil. Multiplied by the many fish Drummond takes in a year, this sums up to all the lamp oil he needs to light his cabin, plus some fish oil for his diet. He says it keeps him regular. He makes wicks for the lamps by pounding raspberry vines into fibrous, sinewy wads that burn beautifully.

We're not supposed to have cougars or timberwolves in Maine, but for some reason, they still exist in Township Unknown. That's not simply hearsay—he's shown me tracks and two hides! He looks at me incredulously when I tell him they're supposed to be extinct.

"Who told ya that?" he asked one day.

"Game biologists," I replied, and at that, Drummond broke into a fit of laughter that left his cheeks stained with tears and his beard covered with spit.

"Ohhhh, that's a good one," he spattered when he finally reraveled himself. "Game biologists!"

Spring

The Long Wait

Surrounded by 17,000 acres of lakes, Grand Lake Stream might be Maine's most island community possible without actually being at sea. Residents are attuned to the water's moods and to the corresponding changes in themselves. "Ice-out" is not a meaningful term in about two-thirds of the lower forty-eight states. It doesn't mean spring is about to burst wide open anytime soon. Rather, its significance is symbolic. Ice-out marks the beginning of a long process that eventually leads to spring. Although, hindered by more cold and snow and, finally, mud, spring is indeed on its way, and that means that Grand Lake Stream will soon reconnect with the outside world.

The glacial, stratified lakes of the region go through several preliminary stages before giving up their ice. Some years, ice-out may not happen for two full months after the vernal equinox, March 20. The lakes may be perfectly safe to ice-fish until the season closes March 31, but anglers become more watchful and wary. When the augers begin to drill through too easily, it's a sure sign that the ice is getting "punky." The snow on top takes on a granular consistency. Snow fleas show up as tiny, black, moving specks. The days, by now, have been lengthening for three months, and this solar benefit brings up the lake's temperature, which in turn wears away, or "rots," ice from the underside. Fishermen turn to wearing two layers of clothing instead of four or five.

One day the snow and ice will appear to become one as the lake's covering steadily darkens. Fissures open between large floes of ice, and these floes move about, bumping into each other. The ice in the coves hangs on the longest, but even there it pulls away from the shoreline. Fishing shacks not off the lakes by this time are doomed because there will be no safe way to get them. On shore, southerly-facing hillsides are bare, and so are the shelves in the Pine Tree Store, at least compared to what they'll look like shortly—the regular fishing season opens April 1. The snow is dirty, receding from the roads and from around tree trunks. A winter's worth of sand covers the road, which gives up its dust with each passing vehicle or gust of wind. Woods roads lose their snow and soften. Runoffs flood all the trails. Rocks and roots rear up to bash errant snowmobile skis into scrap metal.

No matter what the weather is doing on April 1, the faithful flock to the stream to join casting rotations on its five classic pools. The spectacle of fly fishermen lashing Grand Lake Stream's Dam Pool with nymphs and streamers on April 1 can be difficult to conjure. After suiting up in polypro long underwear, pulling on neoprene waders, down vests, and even ski masks, hardened anglers sometimes have to scale high snowbanks pushed up along the edge of the Dam Pool parking lot. Often there are huge snowdrifts right to the water's edge. The drop-off from the drifts into the stream is steep, but that doesn't stop these anglers. Any obstacles to the fishing season opener are overcome.

To find open water on the lakes, some years fishermen must wait as long as five or six weeks after the season opens. Other than diehards fly-casting the stream, it's a tough time for outdoorsmen. Nothing to fish for, nothing to hunt, and too long to wait. Potholes are murder on a pickup's ball joints, and frost heaves jostle the truck enough to scramble eggs inside the cab. Patience wears thin.

White, green, and blue, the colors of winter that have predominated for at least four months, cede the stage to brown. Much has been written about the therapeutic properties of green and blue, but plugs for brown are scant. The snow's disappearance amounts to the emotional equivalent of a plastic surgery gone bad. When the gauze is unwrapped, the patient sees the result and is horror-stricken.

No one is in a rush to see what they know lurks beneath the melting snow. All winter long, each storm spiffed and polished everyone's home and grounds with an all-forgiving luster. Now, the rude guest arrives with a vengeance, splattering advertisements everywhere—it's Mud Season! When it comes, all sins are uncovered. An embargo on trodding anywhere off the beaten path takes effect. Every garden hose, dog bone, child's toy—all of fall's flotsam that was lost to sight and memory is exposed. No one and nothing looks its best. It doesn't help that the calendar says it's spring.

The mood of mortals is frayed at the edges. What a time for Mother Nature to demonstrate that she has more foul weather than people have patience. She's too stingy with her gifts at a time when most would gladly trade another gray, grim, raw day for a good black-fly bite. People start looking for the subtlest signs of spring as if their lives depended on it. It's not uncommon to receive a phone call from someone who has just seen a robin. If the ice goes out of a five-acre pond, it's worthy of notice on the Pine Tree Store's Liar's Bench. A moth, sweet-loving ants, woodcock sightings—all earn a headline.

Some try to force some forsythia in front of a well-lit window. Some check and recheck the seeds they've started under a grow light. A lot of the guides make several trips to the boat launch each day to see how much the waterline has widened. It's not really winter. It's not really spring. How long things will remain suspended this way is anyone's guess.

Time for Work

After living in Grand Lake Stream for several years, I noticed that canoe makers share one thing in common: They start work in March. This is when Sonny Sprague would steam ribs and saw out the planking for three or four canoes. The same was true for Kenny Wheaton. This is when Val Moore would fit the slats to the frames of his beautiful ash canoe seats. Jack Perkins might repair or restore a canoe relic from a sporting camp, or weld a boat trailer back into serviceable order.

"Why March?" I wondered. I finally realized it wasn't that there was anything special about the month of March—it just wasn't good for much else. Wheaton, interviewed by an outdoor magazine, was asked why he chose March for this work. His answer was revealing: "My time's not worth much then." It was simple deduction: Work in March beats sharing house space with impatience and cabin fever, and by early May, guiding fills the hours leaving little time to spend in the shop.

It was also during the spring in days long past that Grand Lake Stream's housewives worked at the local hatchery clipping salmon fins. Today, volunteers make the annual clipping chore manageable. About 40,000 fish pass through their hands in just

Photo courtesy of Dean L. Lunt

The town dock at Grand Lake Stream.

two days, readying the spring yearling salmon for stocking, mostly in the waters of Washington and Hancock counties. Their average length is seven and one-quarter inches and their general health and appearance are excellent.

Hatchery staff corral the fish using a screened gate and then net them, perhaps a couple hundred at a time, and drop them into holding buckets. In the buckets a potion of clove oil and ethanol stuns the fish for a few minutes. Workers stand on cinder blocks in the pools so that released salmon, still doped from the sedative, won't get underfoot. Because of such precautions, mortalities from the operation are quite rare.

Various fin clips in alternating years help fisheries managers age fish later in their life cycle, and also gauge weight, length, and general health indexes when some of these same fish show up in future fall samplings. A four-year clipping cycle eliminates confusion and keeps each age class separate. No pectoral fins are ever clipped from landlocked salmon. These are the "feathering" fins that keep the fish stable in their "lies."

Of the 40,000 landlocked salmon clipped in recent springs, a little over 10,000 were destined for West Grand Lake. About 20 percent were "air-stocked" with a floatplane. The balance of the stocking occurred south of Farm Cove on the west shore, and south of Kitchen Cove on the east shore of West Grand Lake.

At a spring clipping a few years back, one young salmon did not look as healthy as the rest. He had a large chunk taken out of his back near his dorsal fin. A fisheries staffer said that the injury came compliments of a mink. In January of that year, the furbearer with the expensive coat found its way under the eaves of one of the hatchery buildings. Once in, he thought he'd died and gone to Haynesville. His euphoria was brief, however, for he soon found himself in a live trap being transported to Grand Falls Flowage.

Evidently, however, his replacements were notified. Within a couple of weeks, another mink scaled the fence and feasted on fat yearlings until he too met his Waterloo. Off to the Flowage he went to join his partner in crime.

The punishments were apparently not effective deterrents. You guessed it—the third-string mink was off the bench and on the job in a jiffy. He also got his free ticket to the Flowage.

Trapping Bait

Spring is a great time to trap bait. P. T. Barnum may have said, "There's a sucker born every minute," but did he ever try to trap one in a wire basket? It's not all that easy unless you've been

Lovely Lillian

Lillian Fawcett, seventy-one, was born and raised in Grand Lake Stream. She is married to a guide, Joel Fawcett, eighty-five, who has enjoyed a long, distinguished career as an outdoor sporting writer for national and international periodicals. Lillian serves as an exemplary model for fighting the spring doldrums.

The woman for whom I wrote a song of admiration simply titled, "Lillian," gets around by bicycle in warm weather and by pickup truck in cold. Her missions, though many and varied, usually amount to the same thing—she brings care. She might bring lunch for a shut-in, visit a widow, or deliver the mail. Lillian is kind to even the most unsuspecting souls, and it is next to impossible to remain stone-faced in her presence. Whether those she visits expect her or not, she's coming, and she leaves you a little more light-hearted than she found you. If the treachery of the season affects Lillian Fawcett at all, it has made no significant claims on her disposition.

exposed to tricks of this trade. Suckers are one of the preferred live baits for experienced togue fishermen, summer or winter. There must be something about a bottom feeder that attracts a bottom feeder, but even while a nice shiner (minnow) can certainly catch a fine togue, the catch rate, some say, seems to increase when you switch to suckers. As a fringe benefit, they have firmer flesh and sew onto hooks more easily, therefore remaining intact longer than some shiners. They also last longer in the bait bucket.

During the spring and summer, a large shiner or sucker is typically "sewn" onto a leadered hook in such a way that while trolling, it will track in a spiraling, erratic pattern. The trolling depth will increase as the heat of the season proceeds and gamefish are driven downward.

It's always fun to find an out-of-the-way brook or deadwater to try your luck at bait trapping with a little dry dog food or bread inside a two-piece wire trap attached to a line. Traps are made with plastic, too, nowadays, but give me wire for sink-ability and a more bountiful catch. This method is for the amateur bait trapper who only wants to stay ahead of himself with bait for the season, or maybe even stock up for winter. Although, for that, he'll eventually need some kind of tub and pump. For the more serious, licensed trapper, these small wire baskets won't catch the numbers or the size needed to sustain a bait business.

Professional trappers often design and build their own baskets that dwarf store-bought varieties. The holes at the ends are much larger and sometimes there is just one. The mesh may be quarter-inch, and the business end of the trap is always a wire cone turned inward. Bread may be used only as an attractant, for it is known from observation that suckers will earn their name by remaining outside the trap, actually sucking the bread through the wire mesh. The professionals use a more durable bait inside the trap and out of reach of that downturned suction cup of a mouth. They sometimes run a wire through the center with a hot dog, piece of salt pork, or other meat skewered on it like a shish kebab. Eventually, that sucker's coming in after that meat picnic!

Those of us who only need to keep a modest supply of bait on hand will be checking one or two small traps every couple of days. Those traps bear the name and address of the trapper; even the holding boxes must have a name and address on them. To do this kind of "amateur" trapping, all you need is a valid fishing license.

"Fly bait" is the most common bait used as spring fishing gets under way. This may be a smelt or a small shiner, which is attached to the hook of a streamer fly and trolled near the surface. Tandem-hooked streamers are also used, and in this case, the fly bait is attached to the aft hook. Both salmon and togue cruise the cold surface waters at this time of year.

Much of this bait will have been trapped previously, possibly even during winter by licensed trappers. Smelts are trapped or jigged through the ice from shacks set out just like ice-fishing shacks. Nighttime is the right time, and if the run is good, 100 to 150 dozen or more may be harvested through the use of an attracting light and fine-mesh nets. Competitive pricing that may run $8.50 and up per dozen smelts compensates for the labor.

Fish biologists always conduct spring surveys, but a question not asked is whether an angler's catch was taken with bait or with artificial lures, including flies. No data I know of sheds light on which is more effective. With fishermen, it tends to be a matter of comfort and preference, often traceable to the method learned from Dad or Grandpa.

The heyday of the bait dealers is now past. Bill White was the best-known bait name in Grand Lake Stream up to the early 1970s. Eddie Brown kept worms in his basement, and before selling to a customer, he'd spread them out on a newspaper on his kitchen table. He would not sell a dead worm. Baitmen of that day worked hard nearly year-round to keep their customers supplied. These days, most convenience stores sell some kind of bait, some of it imported from places like Arkansas, some of it grown commercially in Maine. Bait fishing is not as popular as it was in former times, but, after June 21 when live bait is allowed for catching bass, many anglers fish for their bait first, then they go fishing.

Name that Baitfish

In the state of Maine you can only sell, possess, or use one of the following baitfish legally: smelt, lake chub, Eastern silvery minnow, golden shiner, emerald shiner, bridle shiner, common shiner, blacknose shiner, spottail shiner, Northern redbelly dace, finescale dace, fathead minnow, blacknose dace, longnose dace, creek chub, fallfish, pearl dace, banded killifish, mummichog, longnose sucker, white sucker, creek sucker, American eel, and blackchin shiner.

I have yet to meet the person who could identify all of the above, although he or she is probably out there. In guides' school, some deliberation is given to smelts, golden shiners, emerald shiners, common shiners, blacknose dace, creek chub, banded killifish, longnose suckers, and mummichogs. On the oral exam, more than a few initiates are unable to identify an impromptu, freehand drawing of one particular baitfish. If it has an adipose fin, it's a smelt. It's the only baitfish that has one.

First Visitors

Soon, fresh faces from away begin to arrive in Grand Lake Stream—folks who left places where spring had a perfectly firm foothold. Their arrival offers us a look, through their eyes, at ourselves, and we are perennially flattered by their exuberance. These visitors perform an invaluable service: They show us a picture of our town that, while it may look murky to us, is a masterpiece if only you step back a little. These first visitors

Photo courtesy of Randy Spencer

Opening day on the stream, the woods still filled with snow.

don't know it, but they give us a lifesaving transfusion in addition to room, board, and guides' fees.

Spring days are chilly ones for the guides and their sports. No thought of mothballing the long johns has suggested itself so far. Staying warm and keeping sports warm is a top priority during this, the year's best salmon weather. What to wear for warmth, what to feed fishermen for warmth, what bodies of water to choose in certain winds—these are the first thoughts on the guide's mind upon awakening each day.

Maiden Outing

A guide's inner clock wakes him up two hours before he's supposed to meet his sports for the maiden outing of the season. The amount of preparation and the number of things to remember are dizzying. To pronounce the Grand Laker "ready" means to have gone over it again and again, probably right up until it's time to go.

Maintenance on the Grand Laker was done in March or April. Now, it's what goes into this sleek cargo barge that counts. Few first-comers to Grand Lake Stream fail to observe how much stuff a Grand Laker can hold without compromising it in any way. The guide's personal wangan is as important as the canoe itself. The guide knows that for any number of reasons, the canoe has to be outfitted to stay out much longer than the standard day of guided fishing.

Most Grand Lake canoes are still powered by outboards of no greater horsepower than 9.9. In recent years, though, stronger sterns have been built to accommodate heavier 15 hp motors. They move the canoe faster, but they can be more unwieldy when you need to take the motor off and put it back on at least once a day, sometimes more. One sure gain is that newer motors, especially the 4-strokes, are quieter. The old guide who answers "Eh?" to his sports may be answering to too many years beside a loud outboard. Now it's possible to hear the sport in the bow seat at full throttle, and for that person to hear you. No small mention should be given to the environmental friendliness of the 4-strokes, which effectively ended the days of the multicolored gas slick behind the boat.

The stern seat is usually built to the express specifications of the guide. If he or she is heavy, it may have greater supports. If they're tall, or just prefer a lower center of gravity, the stern seat can be lowered from the gunwale level with carriage bolts and spacers. It can be caned or webbed, or it may be solid. Its width and virtually everything about it can be designed to accommodate the seat of the person who'll be spending six or seven hundred hours on it per season.

Photo courtesy of Randy Spencer

A fully stocked Grand Laker.

Since all space is utilized in a Grand Laker, the space under the stern seat doesn't go to waste. Some guides install one or more storage drawers under it in which to keep licenses, boat registration, a light tool kit, first-aid kit, hook extractor, tackle, snacks—you're apt to find almost anything there. Other guides keep the outboard gas supply under the seat. Behind or beside the gas can is room for anchor and rope, an extra personal flotation device, a personal dry bag for items like a camera and matches, and the guide's rain gear.

Ahead of the stern seat, and midway between the guide's knees and midships, is usually a canoe thwart. Some designs have widened them almost to the extent of being a serviceable seat. The midships sport can about-face, sit on this thwart, and cast. It can also serve as a surface on which to clean fish when the canoe hits the beach at the lunch ground. Some guides attach a fish finder to the thwart. Under it, more gear such as tackle boxes or the sport's "carry-on" bag can be stored.

The midships sport faces the guide. For the sport who needs more assistance or instruction, it's the perfect position, up close and personal. Most parents put their kids in this seat and many husbands ask that their wives be seated here. (Later, when she has outfished him all morning, he'll be rethinking this magnanimity.)

The back of the midships sport's seat rests against the center thwart. Between this member and the next one is the most spacious cargo area in the canoe. The lunch basket, firewood, canoe ax, Thermoses, cooler, and more all easily fit here. The forward structural member that borders it may, once again, be a simple thwart or a casting seat. It too may be caned, webbed, or solid. Its advantage is that it gets a sport up "off the water" where there is better casting leverage and a superior view. The downside is that this raises the center of gravity, putting the craft at risk in the event of overzealous rocking. There is storage room under the casting seat as well.

The forward sport, when seated, also faces the guide, a design surely derived from the earliest days of guided fishing in the Grand Lakes region after outboard motors arrived. At last an angler could put down the paddle or oars and take their feet off the butt section of the rod on the floor. Outboards were to trolling what the streamer fly was to salmon fishing. With two hands at the ready, a greater percentage of strikes can be answered with a stiff report that hooks the fish. Did catch rates go up with the introduction of the outboard motor? Yes. More water could be covered with full attention paid to the rod.

The back of the forward sport's seat rests against the forward, and usually final thwart. The guide's bow bag is often stored between the forward-most thwart and the bow for easy access when the canoe lands at the lunch site. There may be additional room for the clients' rain gear, a spare collapsible paddle, rope, tarp, etc. Dozens of items are carried in a completely outfitted Grand Laker, and one thought bothering the guide's mind as he steps back before embarking is, what has he forgotten? Fire extinguisher? Bait? PFDs for everyone? Leatherman tool? Net? A checklist has saved many a guide's bacon.

The contents of the bow bag is critical. The success of a three- or four-course traditional shore lunch depends on it. Some guides take out their long-handled large and small fry pans—most use the smaller pan for cooking fish and the larger for potatoes and onions—and season them before the season opener. Seasoning involves a hot, hardwood fire and an eighth of an inch of cooking oil in the pan. At close range, the fire will heat that amount of oil to roughly 350 degrees in about two minutes. Allow the oil to completely coat the pan by moving it in circular motions, and then wipe it out with paper towels or a clean cloth. The seasoned pans must be kept out of kitchens where nothing is considered clean unless scoured with soap and water—the death knell of all good fry pans. Seasoning a pan leaves it with a good, polymer-coated surface that is full of advantages. It tends to be nonstick, cooks uniformly, and will sustain very high temperatures without burning, with the added benefit of keeping bacteria unwelcome.

A chowder pot is essential spring cookware in this part of Maine. A chowder pot is typically smaller than a lobster pot, and it can double as a potato and onion pot. It has a bail for hooking with a hookaroon, which allows the shore chef to move cookware around on the fire without having to keep track of pesky potholders. The coffeepot, too, always has a bail, and guides search far and wide for the particular pot of their preference. Many want the old-style spout that comes all the way up so that its top is even with the top of the coffeepot. When the guide's coffee and egg mixture is added to boiling water and the pot is placed directly in front of the fire, a rolling boil, front to back, thoroughly cooks the floating "raft" of grinds to perfection.

The bow bag also holds one or more broilers of various sizes. These are rarely placed above the fire but go in front where they can be turned one way and then another with the hookaroon. This affords more space on top of the grill for the fry pan and the chowder pot, and for bringing the coffee water to a boil. Long-handled spatulas, forks, and tongs are the other tools of the trade, saving the guide's hands from being singed every day.

The most personal tool on the lunch ground is the guide's knife. Always sharp enough to split hairs, it is constantly honed to make clean, injury-free work of cleaning fish, peeling potatoes, dicing onions, and whatever else is required. Losing this knife can toss the guide into a blue funk for days or weeks.

The bow bag itself is usually sturdy canvas. Mine are replaced often as a result of their second use—a wind block next to the fire. With a shoulder strap, it is easily lugged to the fireplace area, freeing up both hands to carry other dunnage.

As for the guide's paddle, in the course of a season, the "beaver tail" section gets scuffed, dented, and abused. In rivers and in lake shallows in wind and waves, it takes the damage and saves the canoe. A paddle is easily "tuned" with sandpaper and any one of many oils available to protect the wood, which is usually ash. It tends to be roughly as tall as the guide, has good flex when pressure is put on it, and is not thick in the blade. It becomes another appendage to the guide who quietly maneuvers it all day with a range of powerful, effective strokes. The guide will likely have his or her paddle tuned and ready for day one.

On this first day, the Grand Laker looks the best it will all season. Later on, off-road travels to outlying lakes will coat it with gravel dust. Scales, blood, pickerel grasses, and slime will set it apart as a legitimate, working Grand Laker. Today, though, is a time for gawking and picture-taking. It's the time to admire and delight in this one-of-a-kind, eastern Maine guided fishing vessel that has looked pretty much exactly like this on the season opener for well over a hundred years.

Stalwarts

Soon after ice-out, four fishermen in their mid-seventies show up at seven o'clock one morning for the start of a three-day adventure. Bob Siebert, Rich Carle, and Mike Fastoso, friends since college—the University of Bridgeport in Connecticut—and their friend Fred Baran are always my first guiding clients of the season. It's so predictable that it's going to be freezing, blowing, and raining during their stay, it has become our annual joke. Thanks to the age of instant communications, all details of their trip are coordinated beforehand via e-mail. I hear from some of them as the time draws near with questions about conditions. Can we come in on the logging roads or are there washouts? Are the fish up "on top" yet? What colors seem to be working? They know that even though they're my first clients, I will have fished on my own before they arrive.

They come from Florida, Massachusetts, and Connecticut, and have their own system of travel. The southernmost group member drives north to the next guy's house, spends the night, leaves his car, and then the two of them travel to the third guy's place. They stay there a night, then those three pick up the fourth guy and travel all night, arriving in Grand Lake Stream just in time for breakfast in the sporting camp dining room. You'd think they'd be spent and bleary-eyed from an itinerary that would wilt younger men, but instead, they answer the fishing bell with big smiles and straight spines. All are retired and have no time constraints, but, as fifty-year veterans of this routine, this is how they always did it and continue to do so.

There are occassional glitches. A few years ago, it was bypass surgery for Rich. Of all times of the year, it happened during the annual spring fishing trip. He went into surgery just as the other three were pulling away from the dock with their guides. When they returned at day's end, they gathered around the pay phone at the Pine Tree Store to call the intensive care unit and check up on their friend, who had insisted that they all take the trip as usual. The following year on the trip, Rich was twenty pounds lighter, talked in softer tones, smiled more, and cherished the time with his friends more than ever—his new outlook giving everybody a booster-shot of enthusiasm. They all came to acknowledge the value of having their whole group intact after all these years. They go out, two to a guide, varying the combinations, and, no matter who winds up together, they share fond, funny memories.

I can't help but laugh, too, thinking of these older men as the young pranksters who nearly got thrown out of college. One time they met behind the student union at 2:00 a.m., each carrying bags of women's apparel. They had plans for the college patriarch and founder whose bronze sculpture stood smack dab in the middle of the quadrangle between the four main buildings of the campus. They also had a stepladder.

They dressed the poor old patriarch up to look like Jayne Mansfield, a contemporary Hollywood screen goddess, generously endowed in the thoracic area. One of the guys had raided the makeup closet of the college's drama department and found a perfect blonde wig. Another collected hay from a local dairy farm, which they used to pack the rear end of Jayne's tight skirt. When Jayne's derriere was complete, to the extreme, they set a beer can on top of it. Their crowning achievement, they thought, was the overstated, oversized chest. For this work, they chose Easter basket grass. They took turns on the stepladder getting the protuberances to everyone's satisfaction. "The right one's sagging, it's got to come up a little," etc.

The next day, they barely got to savor their great campus caper. No sooner had they joined the crowd in the quad in raucous laughter, than the dean of students walked up behind them. He asked them to accompany him to his office. Noticing a few stray strands of the green Easter grass peeking out from Jayne's bustline, the dean had also noticed that Bob, Rich, Fred, and Mike had similar strands clinging to their clothing, which they had neglected to change since the wee hours of the morning. They would never make career criminals.

Fortunately, the dean had a sense of humor, and meted out a punishment to fit the crime. The drama department had a production of *The Hothouse* by Harold Pinter coming up, and the director

Photo courtesy of Randy Spencer

The setup for a typical guide's shore lunch.

needed three walk-on female extras. The dean had just the thing—overdressed, overendowed, highly made-up female impersonators. The department had all the props, like the padding for hips and buttocks, but the dean insisted that they use hay instead.

On our first day out this trip—a cold rainy day, of course—Mike and Rich, in my canoe, had netted seven salmon and a togue by 11:45 a.m. The sports decided to keep one of the salmon and the togue for lunch. Three inches of water sloshed back and forth at our boot bottoms. We all had the hoods pulled up on our rain suits, gloves on, but still the biting wind and cold rain found its way to our cores. We needed shelter, warmth, and sustenance.

Luckily, we had a welcome refuge close at hand, a camp, on the east shore of West Grand Lake, that sat out of that day's prevailing winds. As we slowly made our way from the fishing ground to the lunch ground, one of those not-so-subtle weather events caught my attention—the skies opened up. The intense velocity of the rain actually quelled the waves or "salmon chop" on the lake. Each raindrop hit the lake so hard, bubbles remained on the surface afterward like so many mothballs. The lake gave the confusing impression of being calm despite the strong wind. We motored on as the men huddled low in their seats, buried beneath their slickers.

On a day like this, there's one meal that will restore, warm, and revive frozen fishermen, and I knew we had it in the bag. Even though the lodge had sent along a lunch, I was carrying the fixings for a fish chowder, counting on my sports to come through with the main ingredient.

Birch bark and cedar kindling were already laid up in the woodstove when we got to the camp. I touched it off, showed the guys the woodbox, and they soon had the stove dancing a jig while, hovering close, they warmed themselves, rotisserie-style. By that time, my cut-up potatoes were almost at a boil, and I was adding the diced onions. In another skillet, chopped salt pork sizzled. The smells and the warmth now permeating the camp were working their magic. This brew would be ready, start to finish, in fifteen minutes. Meanwhile, they had pickles and cheese to tide them over.

As the rain gear dried on nails on the log walls, a slurping feast saved the stalwarts from second-stage hypothermia. They then pulled up platform rockers, encircling the stove. In seconds, all rocking ceased. A whimper, a sigh, and all, save the guide, were sawing wood for warm dreams. Soon they'd be rested and fortified for an afternoon of great salmon weather, and even more memories.

Guide's Fish Chowder

Fish chowder has been integral to the guiding profession of Grand Lake Stream for well over a century. As a welcome part of a shore lunch on chilly days, it warms the inner furnace fast. Smallmouth bass, landlocked salmon, togue (lake trout), and white perch have all been used by guides to make the hearty concoction, but no chowder is considered complete without the keystone ingredient: salt pork. It is said that in days gone by, in order to pass the Registered Maine Guide's exam, it was necessary to mention salt pork when asked how to make a fish chowder.

Ingredients:

4 medium-sized potatoes
2 medium-sized onions
¼ lb salt pork
4–6 filets from 10"–12" smallmouth bass,
  or 6–8 filets from 10"–14" white perch
4 filets from an 18"–22" salmon or togue
2 cans evaporated milk
⅛ lb butter
black pepper

Instructions:

Chop potatoes, peeled or unpeeled, into quarter-sized pieces, cover with water in chowder pot, and start fire. Dice salt pork and fry in a skillet to a golden brown. Drain off fat, chop onions to preferred size, and add both to the potatoes. When the potatoes soften, it is time to add the fish. Chop fish into chunks and add to chowder. When the fish turns white (2–3 minutes), add evaporated milk, and remove to milder heat. Don't scald the milk. Add butter. When the butter melts, stir chowder, cover the surface with pepper, and serve. Guests may salt to taste. Will serve 4–6 people.

A Fly is Born

Fish for salmon long enough—either landlocked or Atlantic—and you'll eventually figure out that getting up at the crack of dawn has zero impact on catch rates. That doesn't matter to one particular group of spring fishermen—Dave, Stewart, Steve, Don, and Dennis. They typically begin the clanging and cursing in their "housekeeping" cabin before daylight. The first object of ire is the coffee machine. Same thing happens every morning; it boils over and makes a huge mess on the countertop. There's a small eruption of tempers that jolts the rest of the fishing camp awake and aflutter.

These five men always opt for the housekeeping cabin because it's cheaper than the American plan, which, by the way, includes the shore lunches. They don't need to be served and pampered, have their cabin cleaned daily, or find a warm fire waiting for them at the end of the day. They do it all themselves and save a bundle. (This is what they say openly, anyway, but privately, they probably wonder just how fine the other way might be.) So, they take turns cooking, a new cook each day for five days, and it has worked for them for almost twenty-five years—except on occassional mornings like this one. Dave, the one they affectionately call "the fly guy," stayed up late tying flies at the kitchen table and, as usual, left hackle all over the place. A vise is still clamped on the table's edge and there are hooks, thread, glue, and flashaboo cluttering up the whole eating surface. Of course, the culprit is the last one up.

Today, it's hash and eggs, coffee (with grounds in it), orange juice, and English muffins with blackberry jam. This is special jam because the guys picked the berries themselves the previous September during their fall fishing trip. Lots of the salmon anglers come spring and fall. One of the five's wives took all the berries, made a big batch of jam, and then gifted all the members of the fishing group over the holidays. Each of them saved his jar all winter to bring it on this trip, thinking they'd be the only one. Now, they have a refrigerator full of the stuff. So, it's toast and jam, muffins and jam, French toast with jam, and for lunch, peanut butter and blackberry jam sandwiches. By day three, they had two days and two jars to go, and no one had figured out how to incorporate blackberry jam into dinner.

They go out each day in two boats, three in one, two in the other. Each boat is fully equipped with depth- and fish-finders, GPS, trolling motor, downriggers, bimini tops, and swivel captain's chairs. A few years ago, Don added planer boards to his boat after he went to a fishing seminar hosted by his local rod and gun club featuring two fishing guides from the Lake Ontario region. A video demonstrated how, through the use of planer boards, several people could troll from one boat at the same time and not get their lines crossed. Wow! This had been his group's problem for years. In the past, they'd tried all kinds of different combinations—two trolling deep and one up top, two up top and one deep, but they always managed to get into trouble at least once a day, especially when someone got a fish on. Now their lines could be separated by a safe distance with this wonderful invention.

It's a good thing they have these well-outfitted boats for their early spring trip with all the protection they afford. Dennis, an accountant, has calculated that over the twenty-five years they've been doing this, the wind blows during their spring trip 85 percent of the time and it rains 65 percent of the time. With these numbers, the group plans accordingly. It's right there in their journal that they always catch more fish on long-john days with the bimini top up than on bluebird days of high barometric pressure, cloudless skies, and the first blooms of black flies. Many things might be said about salmon anglers as a group, but they are not fair-weather fishermen. If they're serious, they are out there in the most miserable conditions Mother Nature can dish up. This group's goal: Have one good fish dinner the last night of their stay. They've always achieved it. One year, Stewart brought a smoker and smoked a five-pound togue. They've tried every conceivable recipe for preparing salmon, but no matter what, they never tire of it. The fact that they release most of what they catch makes that "last supper" all the more memorable.

This year had been rough—too much fierce wind. By day four, prospects for their last supper looked bleak. They've bounced around all week, and one day they stopped early because one of their group actually got seasick. On the fifth and final day, they are about to throw in the towel, thinking an early toddy in a warm cabin preferable to more tossing and heaving. Dave, the kitchen fly-tying mess-maker, is trolling a homemade, as-yet-unnamed fly between two planer boards when the decision is made. He starts to reel up, disconsolate, but with visions of toddies dancing in his head. Suddenly, the rod is yanked out of his hand. Don grabs the butt section just before the whole rod goes over the boat's transom.

"Fish on!" Things had been so slow, everyone is caught off guard. The torque being applied from the other end of the fly line is incredible. Dave can think of little else than his eight-pound Maxima leader, praying it will hold, praying his knots are good, and just plain praying. Down, down, down the fish pulled. Everyone decides it must be a togue. Salmon tend not to go deep and stay deep. It seems to take forever to get this fish turned and coming in the general direction of the boat.

It makes two more big runs before Dave stands up on a seat, shouting commands. "Net him on the next pass!" He raises his rod and gingerly brings the tired togue amidships. Don summarily swoops it into the boat, which is now side-to the waves and rocking violently. Twenty-nine inches, and eight pounds on the Deliar scale! The group's other boat has pulled up within eyeshot, and when Dave holds up the fish, their loud cheers can barely be heard above the crashing waves.

While having his second toddy in the cabin and preparing to broil his prize togue for the Last Supper, Dave gets to thinking about the only other time he'd caught a togue this big—in Labrador with a native fishing guide. At lunch, that guide broiled the togue next to an open fire, then drizzled heated maple syrup over the filets. It was a meal Dave has never forgotten. And that's when the idea came to him: If maple syrup works, why not blackberry jam? He heated some in a saucepan, added a touch of brandy to it, and when the time came, glazed the beautiful lake trout with a rich, dark swath of brandy jam. This was it, he thought! The prototype fly he'd created—the one that had caught the eye of the togue that saved the group's Last Supper tradition—would henceforth be known as, The Brandy Jam. The Brandy Jam continues to prove itself as the group continues making this trip together.

Fifth Lake Stream

After one long winter and during another reluctant spring, Kurt Cressey, owner of the Pine Tree Store, and I decided to superimpose some adventure onto our too-routine lives. Assessing the spring high-water conditions throughout the region, we planned to float-trip down Fifth Lake Stream. This beautiful, very remote waterway connects Fifth Machias Lake to Fourth Machias Lake after five miles of deep woods perambulations over granite ledges, veins of gneiss, through thick alders and into miles of marshes, comprising a good day's journey in fast water.

On a Sunday in early May, the appointed time for departure greeted us with rain, wind, and temperatures in the forties. Beholding this from eye slits at six in the morning, doubts rose up threatening to sack the day. Sturdy wills prevailed, however, and we proceeded as if nothing was going to ruin our planned escape. At just past seven-thirty, we were in two vehicles bouncing up the dirt, wash-boarded Wabassus Road, known to locals as the Wabash Road, which in May resembles a moonscape of craters, ruts, and washouts. Winter had not been kind to the road. We dropped Kurt's Subaru wagon at Fourth Machias Lake and stood on the shore only long enough to make a wish: "Let's hope this south wind holds so we'll have a tailwind paddling across it tonight."

We piled into my Ford Explorer carrying a seventeen-foot Old Town Discovery canoe and made for the headwaters of Fifth Machias Stream. A quick perusal of the Gassabias Lake Region topographic map reveals that almost the entire trip—beginning where Fifth Machias Stream flows out of Fifth Lake, ending where it empties into Fourth—is in Hancock County. To get to the starting gate (not an actual gate), there's a good side route off the Stud Mill Road that passes the Machias River outlet at Third Machias Lake and continues for almost twelve miles to the "put-in" at the Fifth Lake Stream. To call this a put-in is like calling Grand Lake Stream's baseball diamond Wrigley Field. It's a game path on the downstream side of a culvert.

The good side route wasn't good. Two-thirds of the way out, we were greeted by a gully, eight feet across, the result of night crews of beavers working overtime to prevent human passage. As we studied the situation, spring arrived with a bloom of black flies coming at us like heat-seeking missiles. It must have clouded our thinking, because in short order, we decided to back up, rev the engine, and the devil take the hindmost. This was one of those classic instances where once committed, there can be no reversal. After two bog-downs with wheels spinning up mud, the Ford made a final, desperate lurch in four-wheel low and fought its way up the other side. We thought we could hear the Army Corps of Beavers letting out a sigh as the dam let go. "There'll be no coming back this way," Kurt observed as the trip continued in high spirits.

Our forge-ahead attitude was rewarded at launch time when the skies cleared. Bright sun peeked through fast-moving, puffy clouds, and the wind stayed south to southwesterly, boding well for the last leg of the trip.

In short order, we loaded our dunnage into the canoe, including my bow bag containing all the cookware for a shore lunch. As we put the last of the gear into the canoe, I noticed that I'd failed to bring along a spare paddle. I looked at the ash paddle that had served me since my summer at Darrow's Wilderness Canoe Camp thirty years earlier and found enough faith to drive away all doubt. I jumped into the stern and hollered, "Let's go!"

After a few "J" strokes, the spring current caught us and we were off, rounding the first few hairpin turns at a moderate clip. Beyond the second bend, a bald eagle bestirred and launched himself, then circled behind taking careful note of us with his telescopic vision. Kurt fumbled for his camera and squeezed off a late shot.

Up ahead was another beaver dam, a work in progress. Fording it looked possible from our upstream vantage. Kurt yelled, "Give it hell!" And that's just what I did. I planted my paddle firmly into beaver slag, applied torque, and, *Snap!*

"Uh-oh," I heard from the bow. We got past the dam, but once in calmer water, Kurt turned around, and I held up two paddle halves. Now, the real humiliation of what "no spare" meant came home to me. I knew better, but didn't do better. As the Old Town Discovery limped into a deadwater pit stop, I slumped in my seat, passing public sentence on myself for having a strong back and a weak mind.

If getting the last gasp out of equipment was an academic discipline, Sonny Sprague was a Rhodes Scholar. Here, in this predicament, if redemption for me was possible, it lay in somehow "Sonnying" this paddle. I pulled two types of line out of my pack–one a waxed ice-fishing line, the other a fly-line backing. I fitted the two halves together carefully, exactly as they had broken. Just above the break I began a tight wind with the waxed line and continued past the break. Then I came back in the opposite direction with the fly-line backing, wetting it as I wound. Wet lines wrapped tightly in opposite directions provide strength, Sonny said of last-ditch efforts. On misadventures with him, I'd seen it work. When I'd finished, I held up the mended halves for Kurt and gave it the flex test. It held! Relieved that he wouldn't be chauffeuring me for the balance of the day, Kurt happily snapped a shot of me and my "Sonnied" paddle.

Under way again, we found quickening current. Green paint shone on passing subsurface boulders, and we knew that someone had tried this before us. We crossed more beaver dams with the help of a stout pole picked from one of them. With all the snaky peregrinations, we got the feeling that if Fifth Machias Stream were straightened out it would reach to Passamaquoddy Bay, fifty-five miles away. Sometimes it wound around itself so drastically, we joked that we might meet ourselves coming around the next bend. After one particular sharp turn, something caught Kurt's eye from his bow seat. "Let's go back," he called over his shoulder. We did, and there, hung up on the roots of a tree stump, was a drowned moose. Still completely intact except for some trailing intestines, it appeared to be a medium-sized cow, entirely preserved by the cold water. "Probably an ice accident," Kurt conjectured, and it was a sad thought indeed. No doubt it happens to a percentage of moose each year when, in late winter, they wander across moving water disguised by thin ice and a covering of snow.

Dead ahead lay the first serious drop with high haystacks. Perhaps it was the remnants of the old Knight's Dam we'd read about. The decision was made to pull out and size it up. A large log loomed ominously beyond those tall rooster tails. One end was sticking up and the other was buried in the streambed. A dead head, as it is known, can be extremely dangerous, especially if it's facing you. This one was positioned crossways to the stream. The "forge-ahead" theme born at the beaver gully was still in force. "We'll just bear left there," Kurt offered, pointing to the end of the log.

The stream voted nay. As the current carried the canoe into the fast water and its velocity increased, Kurt reached left to pull water toward the canoe. I could see the collision before I heard it. *Bam!* and we both shot forward in our seats. Water came over the stern, but in a matter of seconds Kurt had used the butt end of his paddle to unbreach the canoe from its log mooring. On this adrenaline surge, and with no opportunity to pull out, we heaved straight into a new set of haystacks. One of us shouted, "Yeeeha!" but I don't know which one.

Edward Ware Smith, writing for the *Saturday Evening Post* in the 1950s, made Smooth Ledge Falls on Fifth Lake Stream famous. Sonny Sprague had guided Smith there. Today, it is as enchanting as Smith's beautiful writing said it was— "dark, deep water following the falls that have the look of perfect trout habitat from early May to early June." With the roar of the fast water behind us, I contemplated the stretch, wondering if it looked any different to Sonny and Edmund half a century earlier. Kurt took a halfhearted passing shot with a light spinner, but turned only two chub shiners. We'd already lost some time to paddle repairs, still had a lunch stop to go; we'd told the wives not to worry till past dark.

Further downstream, we found a lunch ground that guides dream about: stone architecture on sunny ledges with erratic rocks forming a perfect, natural fireplace. On the menu today was venison tenderloin from the deer Kurt had harvested last fall, and beans—but hold the beans. They're back home with my spare paddle.

Shamefaced, I attempted to make up for it by emptying dunnage from the canoe to dry it out, then building a good cook fire that would grill the meat to perfection. Just then, a black fly found a home in my left eye and began rearranging furniture. I stood up, staggered, nearly fell into the stream, and Kurt yelled, "You okay?" I was, but it took a gallon of Fifth Lake Stream water to flush that bird out.

No tenderloin ever tasted better. Kurt generously observed that Daniel Boone probably didn't always have beans on the trail either. Sensing that my moment of triumph had arrived, I routed through my pack and came up with two supersized Hershey Bars, both melted to a paste. It was hot chocolate for dessert, and only the eagle cruising a thermal overhead saw how funny we looked spooning it up.

With this sugar-charged booster shot, we pushed into the last of the surf before entering the long stretch of marsh water that precedes Fourth Lake. Wearing the canoe at the hips now, we found our stride and balance. Our movements synchronized as though we'd paddled together all our lives. Instinctive leanings left or right happened in silence like some choreographed skit. Talking seemed redundant. Each scene passed in slow motion as pure tableau, digging a deep impression until the next one replaced it. No remnants of the day's strong winds penetrated to these depths of Fifth Lake Stream's meanderings. Its path now was that of a retreating glacier scribbling with a geologic crayon 10,000 years earlier.

As the afternoon sun sank, the stream showed us its signs of proximity to the lake. Silted shallows showed up and the darkest water was confined to the center of the flow. Up ahead, the skies opened. Once again, we heard the wind and saw its strength as it propelled a flight of black ducks past us at breakneck speed. When we struck the mouth of Fifth Lake Stream at Fourth Machias Lake, we were on the lee shore.

I could now tell that the repairs to my paddle were temporary. It began to flex under my lower hand. I'd be lucky to make it last across this lake.

The strong, southerly winds propelled us downlake. One long, silvery beach compelled us to pull in and admire the sculpted dunes that heaving ice had made over winter. It felt good to stretch the legs and walk a bit. No sign of humanity anywhere. Only a flagpole on the beach of a camp on the distant western shore.

Beholding the home stretch before us, my rehabilitated, "Sonnied" paddle finally gave out. "I'm gonna save this paddle to remember this day," I said to Kurt while ruddering with the blade alone.

"I'm gonna remember it anyway," he replied.

Words to Live by No More

There are a lot of outdoor words that have fallen through the cracks of usage. Ever hear of a "chiminage"? It's something that is coming up increasingly in the state of Maine, and it is rarely well received. It's a toll paid for entering a forested area.

If you hear someone using "ite" in a sentence, chances are you won't know what they are talking about. If the speaker happens to be a student of outdoor language and forgotten idioms, he might be talking about a stop he made on a recent float trip. "Eyot," pronounced "ite," is a small island located in a river or on a lake.

In early spring when many of us Grand Lakers cut and split next year's firewood, we run into something that makes the work more difficult, especially the splitting. It's called a "gnarr," and it's a thick, sinewy, sometimes bulbous-looking section of a tree. It looks like a tree tumor, and one might presume that the word "gnarly" is a derivative. Anyone who burns wood for fuel knows all about gnarrs even if they've never used the word. I know one clever woodsmith who fashions gnarrs into ashtrays, and another who uses them to make unique bowls.

The word "gore" has crossed most people's paths, but maybe not in one of its classic usages. Check almost any Maine map and you'll find gores—Misery Gore, Coburn Gore, and so on. Gores are small, odd-shaped parcels of land that at surveying time couldn't for one reason or another be fitted into a township.

In more detailed maps, you might see a small piece of land named a "surplus." It is essentially a surveyor's mistake and may appear as "Bailey's Surplus" or "Andover's Surplus," for example. Most local guides know about a lunch site on Big Lake, prized in an east wind, named "Jones' Mistake." Various versions of the story are afloat, some of which would place it in a surplus.

To sufferers from the buildup of uric acid, gout is known all too well, but probably not the "gowt." An eel weir trap is often placed below a sluice in a downstream grade that forces the water through a narrow passage in a flowage. There's a name for that passage, and you guessed it, it's a "gowt." I once pulled a Grand Laker through a gowt in Horseshoe Pug between Junior Lake and Sysladobsis. I just didn't know it was a gowt at the time.

On dry land, we find narrow passageways that let people, but not animals, through. They might be part of a stone wall, a wooden fence, or the type used by the Department of Transportation in some Canadian provinces. Metal fences keep deer and moose from straying onto the highways, but there are one-way openings to let people through. The name for these openings: "grikes."

If someone from New England asked you if you'd been in a "logan" recently, you might say no, but the next time you fly in, you intend to get some scrod in a fine Boston restaurant. Trouble is, they weren't referring to Boston's famous airport. The culprit of this miscommunication is an old Yankee word for a swamp or a bog: "logan."

I know many people who earn their living with the use of a paddle, but I've never heard one of them use the term "pudding stick." It's a particularly stiff paddle with absolutely no give or play in it. Come to think of it, that paddle I busted on the Fifth Lake Stream float trip was kind of a pudding stick.

"Rime" is the film of ice on the grass or your windshield left there when low-lying fog freezes. It is similar to hoarfrost. When the fog or the dew doesn't freeze and everything has a wet morning coating, that's called "rorulent."

Anyone who has spent a lot of time in the open country has probably heard and often used the term "swale." It refers to a kind of depression in the topography, sometimes wetter than the ground around it, sometimes thick with the growth of alders, or pucker brush. In the fall, we might send the pointer into a swale in hopes of seeing a bird boil out of it within shotgun range. What we don't hear as often is the term "swallet," and no, it's not a female swale. Remember those times you've been walking through the woods and suddenly the small stream you were following disappeared underground and you could still hear it gurgling under there, but couldn't see it? What you're hearing is a "swallet." I have a favorite swallet in a cedar swamp where I like to sit in November and have a Hershey bar. Listening to the underground babbling of a swallet is very relaxing.

My seat in that swamp is nothing but an old cedar stump almost two feet through at the base. I've always suspected it was cut by Sonny Sprague years back when he was looking for a good cedar log for the planking and ribs of a Grand Laker. He may have known that this withered old tree stump is called a "zuckle." When I thought of how many Sonny zuckles I'd sat on, I had to chuckle.

So here's a plug for the old words, the ones that our forebears probably used in daily banter but which since, for one reason or another, have been practically lost. In the same way, many words in our own daily banter will doubtless one day go the way of swallets and eyots.

The Hendrickson Hatch

According to the United States Geological Survey website, which publishes stream flow data, Grand Lake Stream was running in May of 2006 at record lows. One week, it fell to 180 cubic feet per second (cfs), and spring fishermen were awed at the sluggish, summer drought–like conditions. Then, it went to 150 cfs early the next week, and finally, by that week's end, it had dipped to less than 130 cfs.

Most spring fly fishers on Grand Lake Stream are thrilled to see it running as low as 350 cfs during May. Some years, anglers and local business owners are calling Domtar Industries, the controller of the dam gates, lobbying to get the gates dropped and the current slowed. Heavy current keeps fishermen and a spring economic booster shot away at a time when it's urgently needed.

"Low water may be unusual right now, but it's not the worst thing in the world," my sport and a long-time visitor to Grand Lake Stream said. "Once the Hendrickson hatch starts, we might even be thankful for it." He was referring to the dry-fly fishing that usually begins with this fruitful first mayfly of the coveted dry-fly season. With less water in the river, some of the choice spots would flatten out to better reveal surface activity.

To say that there is a "dry-fly season" doesn't refer to any dates or law book language demarking such a period. Its beginning and end are a function of water temperature and time of year. The term "mayfly" includes a broad range of insects, many of which do not only hatch during the month of May. They belong to the insect group, *Ephemeroptera*. Many of the mayfly species, like the Hendrickson, live a day or less; some only minutes. Their bodies tend to be cylindrical in shape and narrow, and their wings are veined. The adult mayfly does not feed at all. Its days are not numbered; rather, its hours or minutes are.

We owe the Hendrickson imitation mayfly to Albert Everett Hendrickson, an avid upstate New York fly fisherman in the early 1900s. Through disciplined stream observation, Hendrickson saw early spring trout rising aggressively to this prolific hatch, which, until then, had been unknown to him. He corresponded with a fishing pen pal named Roy Steenrod, from Liberty, New York, an angler whose fly-tying skills were known to Hendrickson in 1916.

They agreed to meet on the waters of the famed Beaverkill River, and sure enough, when they did, a blizzard of *Ephemerella subvaria* assailed the air and water before them. The trout in the pool they were fishing were suddenly whipped into a frenzy. Steenrod captured a specimen to study over lunch. He tied imitations on the spot, and he and Hendrickson approached the pool with zeal after their lunch break.

For the next several hours, and for days afterward, the two took one trout after another on this new pattern. Steenrod, a loyal friend and honorable person, named his invention for the man who first noticed the hatch and brought it to his attention. It has since become an early spring standard and also an effective attractor pattern under other conditions and at other times of year. We find it just as alluring to landlocked salmon in this part of the world as it has proven to be to trout in other parts of North America, mainland Europe, and the British Isles.

The Hendrickson hatch usually comes in a light or a dark version, the light representing the female dun stage of the mayfly. This stage is sometimes referred to as "upwinged," describing the moments just after hatching. The newly born insect emerges from the streambed and floats on the surface. This is its most vulnerable period. Blood is being pumped into the veins of the wings, which are simultaneously drying. If all goes well, the mayfly can then leave the stream's surface on its own wing power. Just as likely, a big wave or gust of wind puts the insect back underwater where it can be taken by a fish without disturbing the surface.

With such low water in the river, my sport decided to play his luck. He suggested a pool where the river widens. It was the third week of May, and my practiced fly fisherman and I knew the conditions were ripe for a hatch. The water temperature was 53 degrees, and the barometer was dropping as an impending storm system moved in from the southwest. Reaching the pool in the late afternoon, we sat down on the bank only to see the water dimple downstream of a huge, subsurface boulder. "Did you see that?" "Yup," I replied, and my client tied on a Hendrickson and doused it in dry fly floatant. The fish rose again, and he waded one step into the stream, took out his fly net, and scooped up a specimen. "Hendrickson!" he piped, and he moved into position to cast to the rising fish.

It would be a trick to land his dark Hendrickson dry fly upstream of the dimpling surface; mature fish will tolerate no "drag" or unnatural pulling of the fly downstream by a sloppily presented leader. At my insistence, my sport rehearsed several times upstream of the target like a batter practicing in the batter's box. When he was ready, he stepped into position, false-cast a couple of times, then landed the Hendrickson dun about six feet above the dimples. It doesn't matter how many times I've seen this. As the dun swept over the hot spot I involuntarily held my breath. *Bang!* The stream exploded as we were treated to a half-dozen jumps and a short tail dance from this beautiful landlocked salmon.

I was wishing someone else had witnessed this moment when, over my right shoulder, we heard clapping. Another fly fisherman approaching the pool had stopped and quietly observed the whole thing. My client basked in the applause of a peer while I gave private thanks to Roy Steenrod and Al Hendrickson for arranging for this moment back on the Beaver Kill in 1916.

Drummond Humchuck: Soap Day

On a recent spring visit to Drummond Humchuck's place in Township Unknown, I found him making lye soap. It's the second time I've seen him do this, but the previous time I walked in at the very last of it when he was boiling the rendered fat and lye solution in a large kettle outdoors. Before my eyes, soap was formed in this kettle, and in a display of a brand of guts I don't possess, Drummond put some of the solution on his tongue to see if it would "sting" him. Anyone who knows anything about lye would have their hand on the phone to the EMTs. When it didn't burn him, he declared it soap. It had been boiling for six hours when I walked into his dooryard.

Beyond the fact that Drummond Humchuck is a self-made and happy man, beyond the many traits that make him distinctive by any measure, he has an uncanny trait that so far as I'm concerned is metaphysical. Over the many years I've been trekking out to visit him, I have never once caught him off guard. He somehow knows I'm coming and won't reveal how. I've tested this trait by purposely using every guide's trick I know to put him off my approach, and yet, he's always looking right at me, smiling, when I enter his cabin dooryard. He also has the teapot on and two cups at the ready. Whether he watches birds, squirrels, or has some kind of precognitive power—this enigma, for me, is still under study.

This visit, I got to see the soap operation from the start. Even though he knows I'd be happy to buy lye for him, he prefers to make it from scratch out of ash from his woodstove. His setup is curious: a bottomless barrel set on a flat rock with deep, chiseled grooves in it. First, a layer of sweet grass—more like straw—that he'd saved up went into the barrel. Over that he layered a generous amount of stove ash. Then he poured on buckets of water. As it filtered through the ash and straw, it came out brown into the channels carved in the flat rock. This liquid, he told me, was lye. When he was done, he removed everything from the rock and tipped the lye into a basin.

"Got to get the sweet grease now," said Drum.

Today, "sweet grease" is a term you could live your whole life without ever hearing once. In Drummond's world, it's something you have to know. To make soap, you collect fat or cooking grease you'd saved up, even if it's gone rancid. It is boiled for most of a day over an open fire with equal amounts of water. In the end, more water is added, and it is allowed to cool over night. Drummond did all this the day before, and now all he needed was some help lifting the giant kettle of sweet grease from where it was cooling to make way for the smaller kettle and the new fire which would actually make the soap.

"How in the world were you going to lift this if I hadn't come, Drum?"

"You were comin'," he said with crinkled eyes.

His sixth sense almost scares me. The large cauldron must've weighed 150 pounds and was full to the brim. Only now as I hovered over it did I recognize the source of the odor that had greeted me when I arrived. It was the smell of boiling bear fat. Smells like this never leave you once you've smelled them. In that instant I was returned to the day as a small boy when I was present for the rendering of bear fat for boot grease. My older nostrils now were no less repulsed than my young nostrils were then. Positively miasmic. How something that awful can produce something we use to clean ourselves is a chemical miracle. I knew then why this was an outdoor operation.

"How long's a batch like this going to last you, Drum?"

"Two years next week," he said.

With his habits and routines as unchanged as I knew them to be, I didn't doubt for a moment that he knew the exact week two years from now when he'd run out of soap. Each hunk probably lasts the same number of days, and from this, he has calculated the number of days a batch will last.

The final step was where Drummond's age and experience paid off. He needed to know exactly how much of the brown lye liquid to add to the sweetened grease. Too much lye is trouble. It is an extremely caustic, dangerous solution. Too little, and you don't really have soap that will do much good. Drummond used a ladle, and counting, added the amount he knew to be correct. I lost count but it was somewhere in the teens. And, whether he was showing off or not I can't say, but the last ladle was only half full. When this was done and the fire underneath stoked in good shape, I followed him inside.

This is when I always size up my reclusive friend—when we sit to have our tea. The tea, incidentally, comes alternately from birch leaves, basswood leaves, goldenrod, black alder leaves, wild raspberry, or wild strawberry. They all make a most excellent refreshment. Drummond looked good to me, but then he gets more exercise than most of us. His cheeks always have some red in them from time spent outdoors every day, and his eyes lack the cloudiness you find in some elderly people. They're clear, focused, and always thoughtful.

I stayed long enough for the tongue test just to make sure he didn't scald himself. When he pronounced the batch a success, I asked what was next. He signaled me to follow him, and once inside the woodshed, he pointed to four large, wooden trays with low sides. They were hanging on nails. He took two down, and I grabbed the other two.

"Gets poured in these. Long as the nights ain't too cold I'll set 'em out under cover and in a week or two I'll cut the bars. Good thing, too. I'll be outta soap by then!"

I reminded my friend that the guiding season was about to start up in earnest. We both knew what that meant: I wouldn't be back at least until the end of the summer. That's a long time, but I really shouldn't worry about him. He's been at this longer than I've been alive.

Summer

Special Days

The wait is over. The bulk of the season's clientele is now arriving for the guided fishing trips they booked a year in advance. In days past, the town could gauge these changes by the accelerated activity at the guides' lockers. The lockers served, beyond their practical use, as a catchall storage facility, both as a starting point and a meeting place at day's end. Even on their days off, guides found fellowship here. They rented the lockers to keep gear under cover while their canoes were often turned over on the beach for the night. By the mid-seventies they had fallen into disrepair and were torn down.

Up to the 1970s, most guided fishing focused on the West Grand Lake drainage system where landlocked salmon were the preferred sport fish. Big blows were the only thing to drive guides from these waters to Big Lake bass waters, where quiet refuge could always be found from its twenty-eight islands. By the late 1970s, smallmouth bass fishing began to come into its ascendancy. Today, the bass spawn of June is as popular as the spring salmon run was in the days before the lockers were torn down.

Paradoxically, the longest days of daylight go by the fastest for guides, while the shortest days of winter seem the longest. Now, time will quicken even though a workday might last fourteen hours. Certain dates mark progress of the season. June 21 marks

Photo courtesy of Randy Spencer

Here's Shelley riding in Grand Lake Stream's annual Fourth of July parade.

not just the day of the summer solstice, but also the start of legal live bait fishing (from ice-out to this date, only artificial lures are allowed). The Fourth of July in Grand Lake Stream, in addition to being a celebration of the nation's birthday, is an official summer commencement with a parade and party that busy guides don't usually get to attend. Summer vacations, for most families, start around this time, and July and August are when guides become teachers and mentors to children. Some parents send kids out alone with their guide, while some go along themselves. It's just a short hop to Labor Day, but by then, lakes are already "turning over," and the first chill always catches everyone off guard.

Clients, whether they come to fish or enjoy a scenic, eco-tour of the lakes, find it easy to unwind in this environment. Even beyond this, there are days spent on these waters that become, for the visiting sport, life-changing experiences. When they return the following year—and most of them do—they carry that image with them, the image of the experience that changed them. On that most memorable day, everything was perfect. Perfect, of course, varies depending on the person. Perfect for a veteran salmon fisherman might be 45 degrees, overcast, a light rainfall, and a 5 mph southwest wind. Perfect for a smallmouth bass fisherman could be flat calm, full sun, and 85 degrees. Ultimately, perfect is whatever the conditions were on that special day, which is now part of personal lore. It may never be repeated, but revisiting the scene of their epiphany seems enough. Most longtime guests of Grand Lake Stream have had one or more such experiences.

Usually, at some point in the day, the guide becomes the sport's confessor. It's not that we have any special credentials for this job, and none of us that I know of are ordained. It's the

Photo courtesy of Randy Spencer

Rebecca Lekowski shows off a smallmouth bass she caught on Big Lake.

stage set and the props that are responsible. The sport looks over the guide's shoulders and sees paradise. There is peace here, and beauty, and the guide is along for company, cooking, and fishing counsel. It is commonplace in this context for life stories to be told, and most of us are sworn to pacts forged under big skies on remote waterways. The truth, back where many of the sports come from, hides easily in a welter of noise and distractions, but tends to stretch its legs in such a place as Grand Lake Stream. A lot of distillation goes on here; one might even say healing.

Working-Class Hero

The walls of local sporting lodges are adorned with fishing photographs of celebrities from the 1950s: Norman Mailer, Ted Williams, Curt Gowdy, and others. Calvin Coolidge fished out of The Pines sporting lodge on Sysladobsis Lake just twelve miles west of Grand Lake Stream. Oddly, Grand Lake Stream remains today a fishing destination that is both acclaimed and obscure. Many people who were born and brought up in Maine have never heard of it, but float the name past fly fishers in Iceland, Patagonia, Scotland, Russia, the Colorado Forks, the Snake River in Idaho, or along the Rogue River in Oregon, and you can bet it's in their vocabulary.

West Grand Lake is, after all, one of only four waterways in Maine where the landlocked salmon is native (the others are the Union River drainage near Ellsworth, Sebec Lake, and Sebago Lake). For at least seventy-five of its one hundred years as a sporting destination, it was the salmon that brought fishing

Photo courtesy of Dean L. Lunt

Photograph, on the mantle at Leen's Lodge, of Ted Williams during one of his visits to Grand Lake Stream and Leen's.

business to Grand Lake Stream. Since the late 1970s, small-mouth bass have also been a draw.

A political appointee in Maine state government told me one day as we were fly-casting for bass, "Some people in Maine tend to look down their noses at bass fishing." He was right. If fish were segregated into social classes, these folks would place salmon and trout in the aristocracy, and bass would be consigned to the blue-collar working class.

In terms of angling gratification, it's true that fighting a "silver sides" or a "square tail" on light tackle is strong medicine. The problem is, with the end of raw, damp, salmon weather followed by blooms of black flies that can leave you anemic, this coveted brand of fishing takes a powder until autumn (except for the dry-fly fishermen). Not that you couldn't put in the time and come up with salmon or togue trolling down riggers or lead-core line. You'd just be missing the kind of consistent, top-water action that keeps you hyped in the spring. This is when more than a few spring fishermen hang up the rod, pick up the golf bag, and give fishing a rest until fall.

Not the bassers. They're not about to squander one of the most adrenaline-spiked sports of the year just because the aristocracy is napping. Dr. James Henshall, the nineteenth-century doctor, writer, and angler credited with originating bass fishing in America, wrote of the bronzebacks, "Inch for inch and pound for pound, the gamest fish that swims." The quote is often repeated as avid bassers set out with poppers and a six-weight fly rod just as the morning mist lifts from the lakes.

Highly skilled spin and bait casters fish more water in less time. This may seem to run counter to the idea of fishing for relaxation, but the working person who has only an afternoon or an evening to fish can have a big experience in a condensed time frame. Bass fishing lends itself beautifully to the brief outing.

Lauri Rapala learned that early on. Growing up in Finland, he fished tirelessly in the reachable waters near his home. His favorite was Lake Paijanne. Since he was a small boy, he dug or caught bait, rowed out to his honey holes, and fished until the bait was gone. But Lauri was possessed of acute observation skills. Day after day, he watched as gamefish swam into schools of minnows picking off the weak or the wounded. Lauri looked further to see that those weakened or wounded minnows swam funny. It was a wiggle or a wobble undetectable in the healthy members of the school. Time after time, it would be that fish that was destined to be marauded by a hungry predator.

Photo courtesy of Randy Spencer

A modern Rapala bass lure.

School went into session in Lauri's mind. Couldn't he craft a representation of just such a minnow? He got hold of a shoemaker's knife and began to whittle. His medium was cork. When he had a shape and a size to his liking, he sanded the cork smooth, then covered the body of his "lure" with tin foil from chocolate bar wrappers. Then, by melting the negatives from photographs, he was able to waterproof and protect the lure's surface.

Having captured the appearance of a baitfish in his prototype, the job now turned to mimicking the swimming pattern of a wounded minnow. To accomplish this, he fashioned a "lip" and attached it so that it protruded from the face of the lure. When retrieved, this gave the bait the desirable wobble that should, he thought, successfully gain the notice of opportunistic predators. It gained notice all right, but not just from predators.

The year was 1936. Lauri's personal angling immediately took a big turn. Legends claim that Lauri, using his ingenious cork invention, would catch as much as 600 pounds of fish per day in Lake Paijanne. It turned out to be a powerful prototype indeed, serving as a template for what became the Original Floating Rapala lure. The motion caused by the "lip" is now internationally known as the "walking the dog" action that millions of fishermen employ.

Fishing guides probably see more Rapala brand lures in their sports' tackle boxes than the sum of all other manufacturers'. When everything else fails and conditions coalesce to spell hard fishing for even the best anglers, a Rapala will likely be tied on. Most patterns have a lighter belly than the back color, and most of them float, even if their action is only achieved with reeling. This submerges the lure and gives it the unmistakable "wobble" so cherished by Lauri Rapala.

The polishing and fine-tuning that went on over the next decades only served to heighten Lauri's name and the fame of his wobbling lures. Weights were added to achieve greater casting distance and deeper running depths.

Today, the Rapala Group still operates from its home base in Finland, but has an American headquarters in Minnetonka, Minnesota, complete with a fishing pond for product testing. Lauri's three sons run the company. In honor of their father, the sons released a One Hundredth Anniversary Lauri Rapala Lure. It commemorates the year of Lauri's birth and comes in three color designs the boys themselves selected.

Bass fishing in Maine has indeed grown, especially Down East. Icons of the sport like James Henshall and Lauri Rapala have certainly brought the sport distinction. Today, it tends to be bass that teach the sport of fishing to children, giving them their first memories of strong "pull-backs." These children may one day become adult anglers who love the sporting feel of fly-fishing for salmon and trout. They may, in their lifetimes, take up many kinds of fishing, but chances are they'll never look down their noses at a bass.

Weather Wise

Most guides are, by necessity, amateur weather watchers, and they know that the two most important observations you can make are right before sunset and right after sunrise. These unofficial readings of the sky may be the best on-the-fly gauge we have of what is to be.

Probably the easiest of all cloud patterns to identify is cumulonimbus, or thunderheads. They seem to appear out of nowhere and take shape in an unbelievably short time. They can look like the mushroom over Hiroshima or any other celestial harbinger of doom. They swell from their beginnings in relatively low altitudes to tremendous heights, and then fan out at the top into the classic anvil form. When the bases turn dark, trouble will soon begin. Right below these dark bottoms there may be puffy, ragged clouds blowing every which way. This is the warning of heavy rain, possibly with hail, on its way, and soon.

The next easiest formations to recognize are termed mares' tails and mackerel skies. They are long reputed to "make tall ships carry low sails." Mares' tails are those high, thin, wispy clouds that usually contain ice crystals and foretell moisture approaching. Cirrus is their scientific name, and one of their hallmarks is height. Look for these filament-like strands at altitudes of 18,000 feet or higher, or look out the plane window next time you're flying and see them below you. Their close relatives are the cirrocumulus patterns of white, patchy clouds in sheets or layers, otherwise known as mackerel skies, and again, rain is most likely on the way. Cirrocumulus is the pattern responsible for the ring around the sun that likewise tells us to have the rain gear handy.

The National Audubon Society Field Guide to North American Weather suggests an afternoon reading at three o'clock. This is when the sun is usually at its strongest and the day's temperature peaks out. Most of the clouds that predict moisture give a generous lead time of up to eight hours, all except cumulonimbus. There, you're lucky if you have eight minutes.

Here's a refresher on the old thunder and lightning distance calculation we learned as kids. Lightning is at the leading edge of the storm. It is what makes the boom. Thunder does not exist by itself—it is a product of lightning. The speed of sound is about five seconds per mile, so between the time you see the lightning and hear its report, you can measure the storm's distance from you. If it is two miles away, using the five seconds per mile scale, you will be able to count to ten (using the one-one-thousand, two-one-thousand method) before hearing the thunder. If it's one mile away you'll only be able to count to five.

If you end up going to shore to escape a storm, take shelter in a thick growth of small- to medium-height trees, definitely not the towering spruce, pine, or hemlock near the shore. If you are caught in the open, go to the lowest point, but not if it's a stream. That can conduct current in the event of a strike.

Speaking of current, that's the reason to bring all the boat cushions ashore and sit on them wherever you make your shelter. In default of cushions, use anything, including dry rope, sleeping bag pad, pack—anything. You've got to be off the ground in case of a hit. People should be separated a healthy distance from one another so that if lightning strikes one, the current will not transfer to others. Finally, if one person is unfortunate enough to be hit, they should not be touched for at least five seconds.

"When dew is on the grass, rain will never come to pass." "When grass is dry at morning light, look for rain before the night." Now it's true that axioms that contain the words, "always" or "never" are bound to be disproved. But when you think about it, dew really does show up on nights that are clear and calm, not when it's overcast or windy. Dew is condensation resulting from rapid ground cooling. This simply won't happen if the night is windy or cloudy. So if there's no dew, those same clouds that prevented condensation overnight will very likely produce precipitation before the next night.

"If smoke falls to the ground, it is likely to rain." If you're around campfires a lot, this one is going to dawn on you sooner or later. If rain is on the approach, the humidity is high. If the humidity is high, water molecules connect to smoke particles and make it heavier.

"East is least, west is best, south prepare, north beware." This rhyming adage pertains to fishing winds. It is sworn by and sworn at, but the grain of truth that gave rise to it may be located in low-pressure systems. They move counterclockwise in Maine, and so our weather events tend to come from the south and southwest. A falling barometer attends these events, and the fishing is likely to light up as the pressure drops. "North beware" could be construed to mean wind, or just lousy fishing in high pressure on bluebird days. In a fishing context, east has been associated with, well, nothing. It could be a later tier of a high-pressure system or an early tier of a nor'easter, but for me, this part of the proverb is the most flawed. I have repeatedly seen sports do well on an east wind. So it goes with the old weather sayings.

The late Jim Cochran, beloved to his clients and guiding colleagues for his directness, was especially adept at calling the weather before it happened. One midday at a lunch site with four sports, we all saw the classic cumulonimbus formation fast approaching our position on the lake.

"Get out your rain gear!" Jim said.

"Oh no," moaned the husband of the couple he was guiding. "We left them in the cabin."

Jim smiled and said, "Good. They'll stay dry there."

The wife then faced off her husband and said, "What do you mean, *we?*"

Jim slunk away to his canoe for some spare rain gear. Of all the flawed forecasting formulae, here is the most tested old chestnut in the guiding game: Bring your rain gear if you don't want it to rain; forget it if you do.

Hard Rain on the St. Croix

Jim Fowler from Easton, Massachusetts, has planned an annual August trip to the area since the late 1990s. In our early trips together before I knew Jim very well, I carefully chose our destinations to assure good catch rates. Most guides have places that are good to them time and again, and I relied on these. Later, I got the sense Jim might be willing to forgo the tried-and-true and range around for new adventures. When I brought it up, Jim was game.

After mostly fishing the local lakes, he agreed one day, in the face of a dismal forecast, to give the St. Croix River (*Skutik*) a try with me. This is the international border water between Maine and New Brunswick, Canada, which we access this day at Woodland Lake. Woodland Lake is, in truth, a wide portion of the St. Croix where the current diffuses. It is fraught with stumps, waterlogged pulp from river-driving days, and menacing rock pilings just under the surface of the dark, tannin-colored water. A perfect, man-made smallmouth bass lake would look exactly like this.

As we leave the launch in a pelting rain, a grinning Jim points out that the red dotted line on the map is invisible in the actual river. It's the international boundary, which for the most part runs up the middle, but at times takes curious, illogical tacks. Headed upstream from Woodland Lake toward Grand Falls, the land on the starboard side is mostly Canadian, on the port side, American. Except for sometimes. A closer look at the boundary reveals brief stretches in the narrow river where certain trees and bushes on the port side are actually Canadian. Sometimes, the reverse is true where one hundred yards of starboard shoreline is American. I explain to Jim that in theory at least, if we washed up on the Canadian side with a lame motor or landed there to disgorge a lure from a spruce tree, we could be detained and have everything confiscated. Border Patrol officers now routinely scout these environs.

Just below Woodland Lake in the town of Baileyville, Maine, is the Canadian-owned Domtar Industries. It purchased the facility from Georgia Pacific in 2001 and ran it as a pulp and paper operation until 2007. Papermaking ceased that year and now it just manufactures pulp. Between here and the International Bridge at Calais, the eight-mile stretch takes a 90-degree turn westward, then turns sharply again almost due north until it reaches the bridge that connects Calais to Saint Stephen, New Brunswick. From here it is clear sailing to Passamaquoddy Bay and the Gulf of Maine.

Jim and I pick our way through the obstacle course of hull crushers until we feel the southerly flow of the St. Croix against our bow. Jim, facing me, is craning his neck back and forth between two countries as if watching a Ping-Pong match. High atop a Canadian embankment only thirty yards from the canoe, a group of overnighters with RVs give us a wave. Farther on, a Canadian flag waves proudly, if soppingly, from a dock reaching into the river. I pipe up a verse from "The Maple Leaf Forever" to impress Jim, but it flops. The second verse, however, brings half a smile.

Smiles don't come easy in a hard rain. Water was collecting so rapidly in the stern, I had to pull the plug in the transom to let some out while we were under way. As we progress north, the river narrows and the current accelerates. We stop a few miles up, within sight of the unnavigable fast water that separates us from Grand Falls.

"Jim! I'm going to do a one-eighty—nobody move!" This turn can be perilous if done poorly. The current hits the canoe broadside during the turn and the slightest rocking or shifting of weight can be disastrous. We pull it off, and Jim takes to the casting seat. His hood is pulled up as is mine so that communications must be ramped up a few decibels. "Go in close to shore under those tree limbs, Jim!" We're on a fast, down-current drift, ruddered by my paddle off the stern while Jim peppers the Canadian shore with a Mepps spinner. His son and also my sport, Craig, have convinced him to have confidence in this lure. It makes no liars this day as Jim is landing a smallmouth at least every fourth or fifth cast. These are river fish, strong from fighting current and therefore better able to challenge the angler to keep them hooked. The trouble, Jim notices, is that we're missing many promising targets due to our speed. "Don't worry about that, Jim," I shout. "We'll come back after lunch."

For the first couple of hours, Jim cuts his teeth on splashy smallmouths of the twelve- to fourteen-inch class. Then, some of the older, stronger bass got curious, and it is no small miracle that people can forget about a torrent falling on them because of what's going on at the other end of their fishing line. Any other time it would be high anxiety. While our skin remained dry under good Gore-Tex, nothing else could've been any wetter unless we had capsized. The brooks, runoffs, and rivulets that entered the St. Croix on both sides were churned up and muddy while more and more detritus swirled past the canoe. I winced to think of conditions at the lunch ground and could only pray for a reprieve by then.

Of the three lunch sites within easy reach, I chose the one with the thickest stand of pine, spruce, and hemlock so I could use it for shelter and spare my sport a Niagara banquet. Jim helped me unload the nearly floating picnic basket, woodbox, bow bag, and other items, which let us see just how much water we'd taken on. We then moved the picnic table away from the river and placed it under a dark conifer canopy. It helped until the wind shook the limbs loose of their soaked foliage all at once. Jim, in fine fettle at sixty-five, never breathed a sigh of discontent and only asked what he could do to help as I cleaned and filleted the two bass he kept for his first course.

Can you cook a three-course meal over an open fire in a deluge? As tribes learned ten thousand years before us, birch bark is full of pitch and oils that will burn even when wet. It can be difficult in a rain like this one, but birch blowdowns can usually be found without walking too far. As I prepared the lunch ground, Jim was on the move finding a dandy that illustrated how this tree earned the sobriquet, "widow maker." Birch trees usually die from the top down, and those rotted, high limbs can topple to ground at most inopportune times. All of this one's top wood was long since downed, and finally, the rest of the tree had fallen. We ripped off the outer, rough layers until we saw bone-dry bark, which we peeled away like so many layers of paper. We stuffed it under our rain jackets.

Jim truly earned the handle "sport" this day for all he endured just to catch some fish and have a shore lunch. Alhough it took a little longer than usual, we had a hot, fortifying, midday meal, loaded up, and yanked the stern plug on our way back upriver. Jim boated another twenty-five smallies on an afternoon when other anglers might've heard the call of a crossword puzzle in the cabin. We joked that I had picked up a fisherman and was sending a drowned rat back to his lodge. In fact, we still joke about it, and then laugh the last laugh for rescuing a great fishing day while reaping our own wet and soggy fishing saga on the St. Croix.

Samuel D. Champlain

As ship navigator on a French-sponsored voyage to investigate the prospects of colonizing a "New France," Samuel de Champlain sailed past what is now known as Head Harbor, Campobello Island, and into Passamaquoddy Bay in April 1604. A consummate navigator, geographer, cartographer, artist, and writer, Champlain was a sailing placard of the French

Renaissance. He swung northward into the St. Croix after passing today's Moose Island (Eastport) and Pleasant Point (Sepayik Passamaquoddy Reservation) on his port side. A few miles north, he beheld the mouth of the great river at today's Saint Andrews, seeing how it formed a cross at Oak Bay where the Waweig River flows in from the westward side, and the St. Croix (then dubbed "The Skoodic" by Champlain) flowed in from the eastward. This configuration gave him the idea for "Croix," or cross. In the future he referred to inhabitants of either sides of its banks as "Crucians." The river, it should be noted, already had a name: "Skutik," meaning "burnt land along river."

From his journals it is not established how far he ventured up the St. Croix, but he did chronicle his explorations of Salmon Falls, today called Milltown Falls just above Calais. He was notably impressed there by the Indian encampments. The timing of his journey coincided with the annual harvesting of migrating alewives as well as other species. At the Falls, he observed, there were "enough alewives with every tide to feed entire cities." Following them were salmon, shad, and bass in dizzying numbers.

The Falls, though somewhat altered by decades of logjam blasting during river drives, remains today a precipitous drop of treacherous white water omitted from DeLorme's designated St. Croix canoe trip. The suggested trip is from Vanceboro to Kelleyland. Either this site, Milltown Falls, or Grand Falls upstream was the likely end point of the alewives' migration, since they are not anatomically equipped to jump and negotiate steep grades like Atlantic salmon.

Champlain's attempted settlement of colonists at St. Croix Island (*Mehtonuwekoss*, or "little out-of-food place") was short-lived, but European settlers would sail west soon. Shamanism and the old ways of the tribes were subsumed under Catholicism, peddled by "Black Robes," the ominous moniker for proselytizing Jesuit priests. It was not until 1839 that the St. Croix was decided upon as the demarcation between Canada and the United States. At one point, its name was almost changed to "The Tweed," an Anglo-Saxon namesake of the one that separates England from Scotland at its entrance on the North Sea coast.

Hymn to the Silence

What first caught Gerry Flanzbaum's attention was the quiet. "If I don't catch a single fish all day, it will be worth it just to see this, and hear this," he said. He wants to drift and listen. Trying to identify each sound—woodpecker, loon, fish swirling—concentrates the mind in a healing way, he said. At this moment there are no European flights at 30,000 feet; not even a distant outboard motor. Studying the live, environmental soundtrack from the casting seat, an elbow on a knee, Gerry resembles Rodin's *The Thinker*, a silhouette against the horizon's early light.

I point my paddle at a nearly fallen birch protruding over the lake from shore. It probably went down in one of the big blows the previous winter that took several ice shacks. There are lots of these new blowdowns around all the lakes this summer. You can always tell a recently wind-damaged tree because the color of the wood at the break hasn't darkened yet.

From years of fishing together, Gerry knows what I mean by pointing the paddle. He can afford to study the target for a long time on this windless morning. On most other days he might have one passing cast at best before the wind puts him out of range. He composes his first cast, and it goes haywire. "Out of practice," he mutters under his breath.

We both forgive the errant pitch. Gerry just came in on a floatplane after flying from LaGuardia to Portland, then driving a rental car to Bangor. He's working against jet lag, road jitters, and sleep deficit. At sixty-eight, he never sleeps well the night before departing because, he admits, he's too excited. How things have changed since the days of the earliest guides. Here I am on a remote, eastern Maine lake guiding a man whose day started at three o'clock in the morning in New Jersey!

The next cast redeems him, and he plants the lime-colored, striped Dying Quiver just at the point where the birch log touches the lake. He knows enough to do nothing just then but reel up slack. Guides traffic in moments, and this one is promising. It is a propitious place for a smallmouth spawning bed: gravel bottom, shelter overhead, and the right time of year. The suspense is almost paralytic. Gerry makes the first twitch, and that's all it takes.

The glass-smooth lake shatters into shards of watery violence. A head rears up, thrashing, shaking; rings push outward until they reach and gently rock the canoe. The first fish of Gerry's long-planned trip is hooked. We know it is a male since he struck from the spawning bed he was guarding. The female, having made her deposit, is off in deeper water. The smallmouth shows magnificently again and again until once, he swims too close to the boat and sees it. This gives him a second wind, enough to turn the tide and give the fish the advantage. Gerry's jet-lagged mind is racing. Has he set and tested the drag on his reel? No, he has not. On this go-for-broke run made by the heavy bass that has everything to gain by doing it, the line snaps, and just that fast, the world returns to deafening silence, all except for the confabulations of a bullfrog registering his approval from an adjacent bog. The laughing screech of a pileated woodpecker flying over the canoe doesn't help.

Gerry resumes his Rodin pose, and I react quickly. "Now remember what you said about not catching a single fish all day. We're still having fun, right?" Gerry finds a grin, but it has teeth in it. Out of the tackle box and off the bench comes his second-string lure. It's got lime in it, but some orange, too, and an added zebra pattern on the sides.

"Bright day, bright pattern. I like it," I bolster.

Gerry and I are often like-minded on lure selection. Better to fish a pork rind with confidence than the newest cable TV miracle lure with flagging faith. There is no shortage of shoreline—boulders, blowdowns, shadows from overhanging hemlock limbs. Gerry likes the shadows. The next cast has a feel of imminence. This time, there's no suspended state, no wait for the first twitch. Instead, a dorsal fin darts from under the hemlock branch and meets Gerry's second-string Quiver at the splash point. Only one predator in these waters presents with this sidewinder, lightning strike while showing fins.

"Gator!" I call, as Gerry stiffens for a pickerel fight to spur the day's drama. This one's a wily adult, and it's by no means a given that its fate is sealed. It shows several times, and when it teases its opponent by coming within netting range, it gives the rim of the net an impudent slap with its tail and takes off with the horsepower of pure predator adrenaline.

The counterpoint of such explosive action plays against the morning's tranquility. Gerry's jet lag has flown. He loves pickerel, and his shore lunch now has an hors d'oeuvre foreign to all of the delicatessens back home. He has settled in and found his fishing mojo, missing since he left last year. This has the predictable effect of freeing the mind, allowing it to take flight while hand-eye coordination takes care of everything else.

Gerry has loosened up; his "confessions" begin. There are times when he rambles on, surprising even himself at what passes his lips. He really isn't talking all that much, though. The silence keeps trying to butt in. At the end of the day, that's what both of us had noticed most. The silence.

Humbled

Who was it that said, "It wasn't until after I already knew everything that I actually began to learn?" I know it was golfing legend Sam Snead who said, "I never learned anything from a golf game I won." I like that, too, and in the guiding game, most of us would agree that the guide who can't learn from a sport is finished. Just try carrying yourself around like an expert as if you've seen and heard it all. That's precisely when Bill Bacon breezes into town.

His sporting lodge host told me over the phone that my sport for the next four days was from Houston, Texas, and this was his first visit to Grand Lake Stream. That news inflated me. Oh boy, I thought—I get to be Aristotle for the next four days with my own Socrates sitting at my feet.

Some days, I can get my foot into my mouth in record time. After we shake hands in the lodge parking lot next to my Grand Laker, this is what I say to Bill Bacon: "Well, Bill, coming from Texas, you probably don't get much smallmouth fishing, so I'm betting you'll be impressed with how different these fish are from largemouths."

Yup, that's what I said. The Devil's River, running into Lake Amistad in Del Rio, Texas is—I soon learned— renowned smallmouth water, and of course Bill Bacon makes the six-hour trip from Houston for float trips down "the Devil's" at least twice a year. There are five- and six-pound smallmouths in this body of water, which, in photos, appears to have a clear, aqua color. The Texas smallmouth spawning period may last up to five months. Folks there are fishing the spawning beds while we're setting the ice shacks out for the year's first winter fishing. The second spawn there happens at about the time we're praying for a little Indian summer to visit eastern Maine in October.

These float trips on "the Devil's" are done with an outfitter and a double-end canoe, up one side of the river in the morning, down the other side in the afternoon. With a growing season that long, it's no wonder that the Texas smallmouth record exceeds seven pounds! That bronzeback was caught by Tim Teague in 1998 in Lake Meredith, about forty-five miles northwest of Amarillo. It weighed in at 7.93 pounds, a fish the likes of which we are not likely to see in Washington County anytime soon.

All this I learned before leaving the lodge parking lot. Humbled, I quieted down in a hurry, dislodged my foot, and listened. While briefly assigned to Loring Air Force Base in Limestone in 1972, Bill had chances to fish Maine bass waters. He made encore trips later in his career, and attested that we have a brand of fish that is considered, even by adept Texas bassers, to be the "hardest fighting fish" they've encountered. Maybe it's because with only four and a half active months, our fish tend to be a little more irritable at the other end of the eight-pound test. That's a short time in which to get a lot done.

Although past his sixtieth birthday, Bill casts the way a man half his age might if he'd been at it for a lifetime and had been taught by pros. He carries no less than five rods, and, on request, can do a sixty-second commercial for the tackle he considers top shelf. "As far as I'm concerned," he offers, "when it comes to reels, there's Shimano, then there's everything else." G Loomis is his rod of choice, seven-foot, medium weight.

He handles these rods like extra appendages, deftly setting one down and picking another up as ever-unfolding new situations dictate. They're all rigged differently according to how Bill is reading the water at any given time. His cast is so subtle, if you were sitting in a separate boat looking on from behind, you might not notice it. His elbows barely leave his rib cage as his wrists give a sharp snap that sends his rubber tube bait with a bullet weight almost out of sight. When he's fishing a Rat-L-Trap, he reels so fast you wonder how any fish could muster the swimming velocity to catch it. But catch it they do! Bill Bacon probably executes more casts in an hour than most bassers do in half a day. These are not haphazard casts. They are surgical, designed to extract bass from places that would otherwise be safe havens, even in the heat of midday when catch rates can droop.

As active and rapid-fire as his style of fishing is, it all spells relaxation for Bill Bacon. He's just come from the U.S. Open Sporting Clays championships, which were held on the Eastern Shore of Maryland's Chesapeake Bay. Bill is the now-retired chief executive officer of American Shooting Centers, the largest clay target shooting enterprise in the country. And that's only his current career.

Bill flew B-52s in the Air Force for twenty-seven years. A veteran of three tours in Vietnam, one in Desert Storm, and 5,700 hours of combat flying time, Bill knows the difference between being "on" and relaxing. After learning a little bit about Bill life's story, it was even relaxing for me to see Bill relaxing.

By noon of our first day together, I decided to show Bill four different lakes, one each day of his trip. This was partly self-serving. I now knew I could learn volumes from this freshwater master. He would show me ways to find smallmouths when no one else could. I would learn new techniques, see new baits virtually unknown in Maine, and, in the end, I would have increased my capacity to help other fishermen pursue their passion. Bill did not disappoint.

Without once alluding to it, the veteran aviator and southern gentleman was guiding me, and he knew it. When he changed lures he explained why, and then showed me his unique way of rigging certain baits. When retrieving hard-fighting smallies, he had an effective means of reducing the chances of losing them on jumps. Bill thrust the tip of his Loomis rod underwater, which had the effect of forcing a fish on a short line to keep his nose down. On the second day at lunch, Bill, without bombast, demonstrated a faster way to fillet bass with just two swipes of a razor-sharp fillet knife. Bill also brought along his own private stash of seasonings, asking if I would mind sampling them. They made the fresh smallmouth fillets surge with taste. From that day forward, I have used these same seasonings, one of my trade secrets, when cooking smallmouth bass. If I show up without Bill's spices to "kick up" the fish hors d'oeuvres, my regular sports sport long faces.

Bill has returned every year since that first year. Thanks to Bill, I've adopted another chestnut that I hope can keep me from setting new foot-in-mouth speed records. It comes from that eighteenth-century Whig and turner of flowery phrases, Lord Chesterfield: "Never seem more learned than the people you are with. Wear your learning like a pocket watch and keep it hidden. Do not pull it out to count the hours, but give the time when you are asked."

Diz Dunbar

The wind is coming out of the southwest at eleven mph—that is, if you believe the morning forecast. In truth, it's coming out of the south, southeast, and southwest at a steady twenty to twenty-two mph. All commercial watermen know that on the water, the wind seldom comes from only one direction as depicted on the tidy TV meteorological maps. Diz Dunbar knows, too, but he is not thwarted. His fly rod is cocked with the safety off as he studies the passing islands and miles of mostly undeveloped shoreline.

"What would a place like that cost?" he asks as we pass a camp set back about one hundred feet from the water. The oft-repeated question means he is picturing himself spending time in a place like that. He's taken by the wild, rugged country. It brings back fond memories, and he has lot of those to draw on—on his next birthday he'll turn eighty-seven. He lives in northern Virginia, but spent most of his adult life in Los Angeles in the insurance business.

"Hard to say, Diz," I call out over the outboard. "Not many are willing to sell."

The day is new and I sense that there's a story in Diz that may come out. If I play it right, it will happen of its own accord, emerging one cast at a time. When the canoe glides into a quiet, leeward area, Diz readies himself by shifting his position to the forward fly-casting seat. He's already tied on his first choice—a leggy, lime-green and yellow dragonfly imitation flecked with black. He doesn't cast right away; rather, he studies the habitat intently. "How deep?" he wants to know, and he locates the sharp drop-off between shore and the canoe. "Seven feet under us, seven inches where you're going," I answer. Finally, he lengthens his line, hauls, and the popper fly is now whistling overhead as the fly line unfurls. With two false casts he lays out seventy feet of fly line, and I know from this first effort that Diz is no novice.

Bam! On the second cast, Diz hooks a smallmouth that hasn't been told he's only twelve inches long. He fights like an older, heavier fish, and Diz delights in the battle. The fish is netted, admired, let go, and as the dragonfly is once again airborne, the timbre of Diz's voice suddenly changes. The story begins to unfold.

"When I volunteered to be a forward artillery observer, I had no idea what I was getting into," Diz blurts out, relevant to nothing.

Aha! I knew there was deeper water to be explored today. Which cast, I wonder, which bit of shoreline brought this on? Or was it that first fish? I determined to keep paddling Diz into casting targets that might preserve this mood. I said, "You volunteered for that?"

"They told me I had a fifty percent chance of either being killed right away or sustaining serious injuries, and let me tell you, the training was nothing like the real thing."

Bam! Diz executes this second fish fight with the hand of a fisherman long on experience. Something reminds him of something and he blurts out, "New Zealand."

"You've fished there, Diz?"

"Yeah, nine times." And not only there, he goes on, but in Chile, Alaska, Montana, and Wyoming, too, and now I know that today's bassing jaunt is a stroll in the park for the octogenarian in

Photo courtesy of Tim Parker

Traditional streamer flies used to catch salmon and smallmouth bass. These mimic the movement of minnows or smelts.

my bow. The second netting apparently moves him to make more of the past present.

"I was at Omaha Beach twenty-five days after the Normandy offensive. It was nothing you'd ever forget."

Words like this drop into a deep well of silence. They're looked at and weighed for how they must sound to someone who couldn't possibly know. Other words follow, equally searing when spoken in this serene setting.

"I was in the Battle of the Bulge and I was with Patton's Third Army on the drive to Berlin." He gives the dates, the casualty figures, the numbing temperatures, and amounts of snow. His memory wows me, thirty years his junior. Any listener who thought Diz was bragging would be far from the mark. He speaks instead in the voice of someone amazed and humbled by his own survival; someone who has witnessed the worst horrors imaginable, then had to find a place to put those horrors and live on.

Bam! Number three. Diz had put his bug down next to a beautiful piece of structure—a pine deadfall all but completely submerged. He waited a long time before moving his popper, and when he did, that was it. This fish didn't have to be told it was big. "Wooo!" Diz exclaims as the seventeen-inch smallie dishes up a tail dance.

In the calm after this storm, Diz mentions the best friend of his youth, killed by a mortar that landed right on top of him. "The same thing nearly happened to me," Diz adds. "An eighty-millimeter round landed right next to me, but it was a dud. I just sat there and stared at it."

How many long nights, I wondered, had Diz pondered why his friend was killed but he wasn't when the "dud" fell in his favor?

Diz was always in the forward positions in the big war. He had to be to do his job plotting artillery strikes. He was in many of the most devastating battles of the war—in fact, in the history of warfare. I may have sensed a story in Diz, but he trumped all expectation. Here was the old veteran quietly casting his popper fly with such grace, reflecting simultaneously on his recollections of war-torn Europe.

At some moment I grow self-conscious. I'm in the presence of a legitimate American war hero. I hope I haven't misspoken or opened up old wounds for Diz. He seems content to reminisce in this particular place at this particular time. It must seem safe, I reason; it must be the right setting to invoke those memories in this way. He has found a way to smile back on what he has lived through, even while relishing the present moment.

No day in my guiding experience ever went faster than this day with Diz Dunbar. Sometime in the late afternoon Diz says that his rotator cuff is singing. "Well, you've pitched twelve innings," I reply, "and your ERA is way above the curve." Diz chuckles, casts again, then chuckles some more.

"What's so funny, Diz?" He says he was thinking of his trip a couple of years ago to the D-Day Museum in New Orleans. He had gone through several dialogues with himself previously, not sure whether he wanted to revisit such unpleasant memories. He was finally talked into making the trip.

"And so, how was it?"

"They made me pay to get in!"

We both laughed.

Fishing for Ancestors

Ragan Elsemore comes by her confidence around Grand Lake canoes and the local lakes honestly. That's not only because she's been a biologist aboard New Bedford scallop boats, or because she's worked in marine science at the Wood's Hole Oceanographic Institute on Cape Cod. Nor is it just because she's a former competitive swimmer or because she's crewed and taught on the *Lady Maryland*, a replica of a Chesapeake Bay schooner operating today as a living classroom out of Baltimore. Beyond all these credentials, her confidence on local waters may come from her unimpeachable pedigree. She is the great-granddaughter of Eben Everett Elsemore, one of the legendary pioneering figures of the guiding profession in Grand Lake Stream.

The Elsemore family moved to Grand Lake Stream from nearby Plantation 18 when Eben was three. They saw the transition from tannery town to sporting town, which included the emergence of the first township government. George Elsemore, Eben's father, figured prominently in the village's fight for new status and greater recognition as a township with an actual budget for education, roads, and bridges. He was elected Sealer of Weights and Measures on January 15, 1897, and even put in a bid to become the town's first tax assessor.

When he was twenty-six, seven years younger than Ragan is now, Eben married Lizzie Kelley, daughter of the station manager at the railroad depot in Kelleyland (now Baileyville). They eventually moved to the west side of the stream, known then and now as "The Tough End."

Both Eben and Lizzie were eminently suited for their first employment as a couple. James T. Maxwell of Saugerties, New York, had built a seasonal home in town in 1909 and later added another on Sysladobsis Lake. By the time the young Elsemores went to work for the Maxwells, they had begun what would eventually become a sizable family. Lizzie bore five children from 1907 to 1920. In order, they were Dexter Everett, Franklin Fenno, Annie Loretta, Charlotte May, and Vernon Cyril. Each year, the entire family made a seasonal move to work all summer for the Maxwells. Lizzie and her daughters cooked and Eben guided the many sports who came to the Maxwell place while also managing the grounds and looking after the boats with the help of his sons. Eben also found time to lead the first teams from the United States Geological Survey through the area in the early 1900s to do the arduous work of wilderness cartography, much of which survives today on regional topographical maps.

Mix an impish sense of humor with a mastery of storytelling, add a large arsenal of tricks, gibes, and endearing social skills, and you've got a highly marketable guide. According to surviving family and friends, Eben Elsemore was possessed of these attributes and many others. In 1914, he won first prize for "most outlandish costume" in the "callithumpian parade." Strapping his lower leg up to his thigh and attaching a homemade, prosthetic leg to his knee, he marched the entire course as a peg-leg peddler. He then stripped off his layered clothing to a howling crowd. What was left in the end was "the gaudiest pair of overalls in Washington County," according to an old clipping a family member had found and saved. And, like all great storytellers, Eben was not a one-horse show. Days could be long, especially if the fish weren't cooperating. He reputedly could launch into the first measured lines of the next spellbinding story before the laughter from the previous one had abated. Then, at just the right moment, Eben broke out his fiddle and accompanied himself while singing to his eager lunch ground audiences. He also played regularly at town dances held in the old Sutherland Store.

A guiding career that spans over fifty years lives well beyond itself. Hundreds, perhaps thousands of lives are touched, many of them from far-flung parts of the world. Often, the surviving family of a guide who has passed on hears from these people for years. Eben Everett Elsemore represented the best of the guiding profession he helped to grow in Grand Lake Stream. He died in Calais, Maine, on December 19, 1971, at the age of ninety-one.

Now, on this summer day, his great-granddaughter heads up into the estuaries that act as nurseries for the many varieties of forage fish that feed the popular gamefish, smallmouth bass. Ragan began her journey several years earlier by visiting Elsemore Landing on Pocumcus Lake, a popular camping site named for her great-grandfather. This trip, she hopes to learn the feel of days spent in the graceful crafts that were maneuvered by her great-grandfather as a guide, seventy years earlier. I caution her that I could never live up to his legacy.

Ragan wants to be adept at catching bait on the first cast, but she learns fast that it's more about finesse and patience than immediate gratification. These moving schools need to be found, tempted, lured close to the boat, then "lifted" out of the lake on tiny hooks with only a morsel of bait. When she finally succeeds, it whets her appetite for more.

As the Grand Laker follows angular, Magellan-like courses to avoid sunken islands and rocky shoals, Ragan, the earth science teacher, is transfixed. Maybe it's the bald eagle that leaves its perch with one tremendous wing swoop, then soars easily on a thermal high above the canoe. Or is it the eagle's young ones, already huge and perched near the nest? Maybe it's the unsullied shoreline, or the countless islands rising up like wooded oases. When the canoe finally stops, it's not long before these mental meanderings are replaced by the raw excitement of a smallmouth feeding frenzy. Ragan's rod is bent double by the first fish, which, once in the net, is declared a "luncher." A second soon goes on the stringer, and I know that with Ragan aboard, this party will never starve. Even though this particular fishing drill is new to her, her water sensibilities give a profitable edge to her inexperience.

The scientific side of Ragan wants to embrace every natural aspect of the outing, and at times the canoe becomes a classroom. Why are spiny-finned fish illegal as baitfish; why was a slot limit introduced; why are the bass behaving the way they are at this particular time of the year, and how does their behavior change at other times—these are her questions, and the answers only serve to pique her abiding interest more. In the quiet moments between teeth-clenching bass fights, her contemplative expression returns.

Ragan said, in the end, that the day lasted only three minutes. Between fish battles and photo ops, the morning flew by in one; the time spent picnicking on fresh fish, guide's coffee, and brownies consumed another; and in just one more fleeting minute of landing fish all afternoon, it was time to head for shore.

A full acknowledgment of one's ancestry probably requires boatloads of intuition and imagination. I like to think Ragan may have actually found something of Eben Elsemore in his old haunts. I like to think that in those reflective interludes, she may have seen what he saw, and felt what he felt. I like to think that she may have shared something special with the great-grandfather who died six years before she was born.

The Net Experience

The Grand Lake Stream Historical Society houses many representations of the local guiding industry, especially from the early and mid-twentieth century. These were the years Edmund Ware Smith was writing about in the *Saturday Evening Post*. News of Maine's sportfishing was traveling at the speed of rail, as early hunting and fishing expos wowed outdoorsmen throughout the East.

When Grand Lake Stream was harder to get to, people stayed longer. They also tended to come in larger groups than are typical today. Cost sharing made those two-week sojourns more affordable for each participant. The sporting lodge business was driven and sustained by these large parties of sports.

They were pampered as much as a visitor might be given the rustic, sometimes harsh environment and weather. They went out on the lakes with ten and twelve guides at a time. Experience for these fishing clients, then as now, was of little consequence. City slickers and dandies came, along with veterans of roughing it in the Maine woods. Sometimes, if we can believe the old diaries, everyone caught fish all day long. Naturally, the big ones got bigger in the retelling.

"I believe mine was seventeen and a half, wasn't it?" says the yarn spinner, nodding to his guide.

"You lie, and I'll swear to it," was, and remains, the well-weathered response.

Most of the photos of guided groups from this period were taken at lunch. "Banquets" would better describe these midday feasts. Today, I experience the banquets represented in those museum pictures when I'm part of modern-day incarnations of them, such as "The Kotok Party."

David Kotok, an internationally acclaimed economist, has fished local waters for nearly two decades. Guides and other fishermen can identify his fly-rod skills from a distance. On point in the bow of a canoe, he probes shorelines and islands with colorful bass hackle. Not content with any fishing formulae, he's on the move with his Passamaquoddy guide, Ray Sockabasin, scouting the larger rivers, smaller streams, flowages, ponds, and lakes.

At least once per season, Kotok invites a cast of financial luminaries along with other friends and guests to share in a three-day, outdoor caucus punctuated by fighting fish. Everything is done according to guiding traditions established over a century earlier. At banquet-sized picnic tables, bank presidents, financial writers, members of the Federal Reserve Bank, college professors, and financial advisors discuss a little shop and

Photo courtesy of Randy Spencer

Gathering of guides for the annual Kotok party at Grand Lake Stream.

a lot of fishing. Across the ranks of the distinguished assemblage, commentary bubbles up about the profits realized from such a "meeting." The world left behind comes into sharper focus as these remote, wilderness lakes provide a kind of special lens.

At the preordained meeting site for lunch, David's entire group gets to see how it must have been in those earlier days. In fact, on this trip, there are two guides in the party of thirty-three who were guiding in the 1950s for Leen's Lodge. Stan Leen attracted famous fishermen from all over America to his "Waldorf of the Wilderness." Today's sports have traveled as far as those visitors did almost a century ago to stay in the same lodge, hosted today by Charles Driza. Some have come many times for the Kotok gathering, some are here for the first time. The difference is always evident to the guides. First-time guests arrive at the lunch ground wearing a conspicuously different expression than the one seen at breakfast. The wilderness lakes have wielded their power to soothe urban angst and open the brain's circuitry. Eagles soared, a bull moose wallowed in the marshes; even the fish cooperated, or conspired with the guides to show the Kotok Party a déjà vu of Grand Lake Stream's guiding heyday.

Perhaps photos of this modern-day banquet will be added to the local archive that has chronicled the history of the guiding profession so well here. They're a perfect fit. Grand Lakers lined up on shore, happy travelers making new friends—these photographs retell the story of sporting days that continue in a time when every influence should have eradicated them. Changes will, of course, be discerned: Many of the outboard motors have gone from 2- to 4-stroke; the clothing worn by guides and sports has morphed from canvas and rubber to Gore-Tex. But the sparkling lakes, the smiling faces, the shore banquets, and the essence of the experience all look the same. These travelers of our time learned, just as those early sports did, that in the end, it's not only about the netting experience. It's about the net experience.

Without a Paddle

K Bolduc's initiation into the quiet, contemplative world of canoeing began in 1969 when she was eight years old and her parents sent her to Girl Scout camp. She loved it so much, the following summer she lobbied them for a four-week stay instead of the usual two. Forty-one years later, she is one of the most experienced wilderness trip leaders and Junior Maine Guide instructors in the state.

When K began a sixteen-year career at Camp Pondicherry in Bridgton, Maine, as an instructor of Junior Maine Guide candidates, she acquired a special paddle to commemorate the event. It was 1977, and from then on, it was always aboard, either in her own hands or in those of a trusted bow person. The names of the lakes she canoed were inscribed on the paddle along the way. Her goal was to one day be able to say she had canoed all the major lakes in Maine; the paddle would bear witness.

After the sixteen-year stint at Pondicherry, her journey as a Junior Guide instructor led her from Bridgton to the Belgrade Lakes region, where she has worked for the past fifteen years as trip director at Camp Runoia. She leads six to eight trips per summer, also pulling duty as examiner at "test camp," which all Junior Maine Guide candidates must attend to complete the program.

The Junior Maine Guide Program is a state-recognized wilderness program for boys and girls, ages nine to eighteen. Sponsored jointly by the Maine Youth Camping Association and the Maine Department of Inland Fisheries and Wildlife, it is a one-of-a-kind program unique to Maine, begun by legislative act in 1937. Kids get involved with the program through a participating camp. They are led, usually in groups, by certified instructors to wilderness lakes and streams where they learn canoeing, camping, and survival skills.

That was K's job. Her work has been her passion—teaching and mentoring young adults throughout her career as a trip leader. Those trips most often took her to the Mooselookmeguntic and Richardson Lake regions earlier on. In more recent years, they have led her to eastern Maine, and no canoe trip to eastern Maine would be complete without what she came to call "the West Grand trip."

It was 1999, and with her cherished and by then heavily inscribed paddle in hand, she led a group of eight girls and two dogs out of the Bottle Lake Landing and onto a windswept Junior Lake. Bottle Lake is about fourteen miles northwest of Grand Lake Stream as the crow flies, but canoes usually don't travel the way the crow flies. What lay ahead, according to K, were "six days of wilderness paddling during which the girls would practice their canoeing, compass work, outdoor cooking, shelter building, and many other skills needed for their test camp experience."

Her own narrative best describes the experience:

"The first day was a tough one, as we had a lot of headwind and a few weak paddlers. As Junior Maine Guides do, we pushed on, staying close to the shore. We headed for Bottle Island in Junior Lake, and when we saw it was already taken by overnighters, we decided that we could make it to a site that we refer to as 'Indian Point' at the end of Junior Stream. As the afternoon dwindled, we successfully made it to the site and set up camp. The girls cooked a great dinner, set up the tents, and headed off to sleep. The next couple of days were spent working on their ax skills, making maps, and practicing in the canoes. Our last night was an early one as we were going to adhere to an old saying that I had learned and practiced as a camper: 'Up with the sun and down with the sun . . .' Before dawn, we quietly cooked breakfast, loaded our boats, and were off to the other side of Junior Lake."

They camped on the site known to guides as the Junior Stream lunch ground. On Passamaquoddy Reservation land, it boasts, for those with permission to use it, an easy landing, a canopy of softwood trees for protection, and a bluff with a view down Junior Bay. It is a valuable holdover spot in high winds—both the northerly blows of high-pressure systems and the southerly gales of impending weather. The call for a cleanup sounded, and everyone in the group scurried about, policing the area. In the general flap of the moment, K didn't notice that the one paddle that had always been in her canoe during twenty-five years of canoe tripping was not aboard. It was not discovered as missing until days later when the vans were loaded at Bottle Lake launch.

"I returned to camp and for several days, continued to check under the van seat, in the trailer, and even called the family we knew at the landing of Bottle Lake to see if it had shown up or if I had lost it on the shore. No one had seen it."

In the years that followed, K continued leading and instructing Junior Maine Guide kids to Washington County waters, but she felt a lingering sadness over the loss of something meaningful to her, something symbolic that had represented the many places her career had taken her. "Each year since then, I returned to the same sites and to the same landing, forever turning my head when I saw a flash on the shoreline or to what turned out to be a colored board on the bottom of the

Photo courtesy of Dean L. Lunt

My friends and owners of The Pine Tree Store, Kathy and Kurt Cressey.

stream, in hopes that I might be reunited with a paddle that held a bit of my canoeing history. I would take walks around the shoreline after the kids were settling down, just in case it had been washed up, and I might just by chance, be lucky enough to actually find it, or for it to find me."

The paddle's journey back to K began the same summer it was lost. Later that season, Dr. James Eschleman and his wife, Louise, pulled their boat up at the Junior Stream site for a picnic and a rest. Browsing around, Louise came upon the paddle, eye-catching with its many painted inscriptions. As local camp owners, they knew that the number of people who pass through Junior Stream during the summer months is very high. It seemed a shame to leave the obviously unique paddle there, so they stowed it on board, and later that summer, stowed it again when they packed to return to their home in Norway, Maine.

After a year of admiring the paddle and wondering about its history, they decided to bring it to the Pine Tree Store in Grand Lake Stream on the likelihood that the paddle's owner would someday stop by there. The paddle was displayed in various places, sometimes directly above the cash register where people would admire it and ask questions about it, but it went unclaimed for two years.

One day, storeowner Kurt Cressey noticed among the many inscriptions on the paddle, references to the Junior Maine Guide program. Using the Internet he came up with the Junior Maine Guide website and dashed off an e-mail describing the paddle in his possession.

The Junior Maine Guide network lit up like a Christmas tree. The paddle, which was legendary within that crowd, had become more famous with its loss. In record electronic time, a message flashed on K Bolduc's computer screen at her home in

Raymond, Maine. "Your paddle has been found!" A wide, teary smile stretched across K's face.

She sent a note to Kurt at the store, saying, "Thank you to all those who enjoyed the mystery of the paddle, and I am glad that it has found me. It helped bring smiles to many young campers and has been a bright memory of many canoe trips that have brought me joy throughout my life."

After a four-year separation, K and her special paddle were reunited during the summer of 2003.

K Bolduc, always an inspiration to her students, is now re-learning her canoeing skills after losing her sight in November 2007 following surgery for a pituitary adenoma. She continues to run the JMG program at Camp Runoia in the Belgrade Lakes region, teaching campcraft, canoeing, woodcarving, and wood-burning skills. Happily, K has regained a small portion of her vision and plans to again begin leading some canoe trips.

The Uplander

Take someone from the sprawling cities, someone whose feet are accustomed to the hard, level surfaces of the vast indoors. Place that person on Maine ground and watch their bewildered feet trip and tumble as if they were intoxicated. It's a fish-out-of-water reaction, and likewise, nothing puts stupefaction on a face any faster than when the uplander finds himself on the bounding main.

The freshwater fisherman goes to sea.

Passamaquoddy Bay, off the Maine coast at Eastport, is not starting in the toddler pool for Frank Burnell. There is trepidation, a knitting of the brow, an intensification of the senses. Is he going into battle? He looks it. Why does his image bring Ahab to mind, standing on the prow of the *Pequot*, peering into the foam, aware that danger lurks there?

We are fishing as friends today, not as client and guide. This uplander is well used to the "personalities" of the lakes. With their ever-changing moods, storms come up fast, and with them, waves and whitecaps that can soak you before it ever rains a drop. The mirror-calm days lull you into a dream-state. But this—the sea—is like the lakes in relief. A macrocosm of watery moodiness. The terrors are more terrible and the dream-states too deceptive for your own good if you're lured into an idleness of mind.

The extremes of the tides alone would be hair-raising enough to the inland dweller. The pilings are still darkened and wet from the last high tide up to the height of a two-story building. These are not the most severe tides in the Gulf of Maine. Those may reach well over forty feet while these will only top twenty-one feet today. Even though no significant wind is blowing, the water seems to breathe. Its swelling and subsiding gives the impression of sitting helpless on the chest of some Goliath, hoping he's not mad.

When the boat slides into the salt water, it floats better. It sits higher, like the mating male loon when adjusting his flotation to flaunt his white feathers. Above the lapping waves and the sounds of marine industry are the voices of the gulls. Sometimes they appear to be laughing; other times they seem to be forming words:

"Go out?"

"Where?"

"Why?"

Right off the launch at the Eastport / Deer Island ferry landing, we encounter rafts of seaweed. With all manner of flotsam trapped within, they circumambulate with the rotation of the whirlpools. I tell my friend that I have seen lobster traps, tires, a TV set, and a telephone pole in them. It's these whirlpools that bring the uplander the most anxiety. He talks to allay his fears. Do they turn clockwise above the equator and counterclockwise below, he wants to know. Yes, that would be the Coriolis effect—but our freshwater friend is too fixated on the fear these whirlpools inspire to care about the science. They worry him. They signify great forces below—great forces acting under what or whose power? Old Sow, the famous whirlpool between Eastport and Deer Island, New Brunswick, has been known to swallow boats, logs, and only Neptune knows what else. So what might it do to the measly little speck of gelcoat the uplander is fishing from today?

This gets to the heart of the matter—that the sea is an awesome power. Its rhythms may be influenced by the moon, but definitely not by man. That's the problem the sea poses, especially to the uplander: It presents him with the clear and present indifference of nature in liquid form, and here we are, floating on her bosom!

The teeming life of Passamoquoddy Bay is eventually enough to wean his mind away from worry. A pod of porpoises swims by in synchronous grace. A sea dog pops up to remind us how he got his name—his seal face looks just like a puppy's. An eagle drifts past, dwarfing everything else on the wing. We're moving toward slack tide and those mysterious forces from below seem sluggish now. Amid the calm, a crashing of white water erupts and two bluefin tuna, probably weighing three- to four hundred pounds apiece, break the surface and arch back into the water leaving the uplander and me agape.

The task at hand calls for pounding the bottom with heavy jigs that are hopefully enough to entice fish—cod or pollock—to make a strike. The problem is dogfish (small sharks) that have apparently infested all the usual honey holes. They strike all right, but they miss with their mouths and come up hooked amidships or astern. Their whole upper body is therefore free to fight, and fight they do. The cumbersome cod rods get a work-out on these gray, dry-skinned Jaws-wannabes. I had recently learned that they are called "poor man's lobster" by those who have a fondness for their tail meat. (If you try it, watch out for the sharp spine hidden by the adipose fin!)

We drop lines an hour before slack tide. Two hours earlier and two hours from now, we would be drifting at the equivalent speed of a small boat with a five-horse outboard, wide open. If you chance to get hung up while bottom-fishing with this tide, you have to throw your rod's bale immediately and get the boat turned around fast. Then you have to throttle up to about 2,500 rpms just to get back to the problem spot. The tides of Passamaquoddy Bay cannot be taken lightly.

Besides the high probability of seeing a whale, porpoises, bluefin tuna, seals, eagles, and ospreys, one of the best sporting reasons for being here, up until just a few years ago, was cod. They inhabited grounds literally a stone's throw from shore, in 200 feet of water. By "shore," we mean Moose Island where Eastport is located, and Campobello Island and Deer Island, both part of New Brunswick.

Today, only a few keeper cod come calling, but mazes of mackerel make their appearance under the boat as usual in mid-August. It is nearly impossible not to catch them. The "tinkers," soaked in brine and canned in mason jars, make a special winter hors d'oeuvre. Once the bottom structure drops away and we're over depths of 150 to 200 feet, the dogfish strike again, and some are able to pin the rod to the gunwales and cramp our forearms. When a cod does get hooked, there's a subtle difference in the way it fights on the way up—less bobbing, more consistent downward pressure.

At three o'clock, we change tactics and take to the flounder grounds just off the mudflats of Deer Island. Using light tackle, their strike registers as a slight vibration at the rod tip. Half a dozen keepers are boated along with too many sculpin, the thorny intruder who likes to leave a nice flesh wound as a parting gift. On the way back toward Eastport and the Deer Island ferry launch, the outgoing tide is ripping now. Large, smooth areas of salt water boil as the seaweed collects at their edges. The hull of the boat lurches in combat with the current, and the uplander is made aware once again that this ocean has cards to play that he hopes never to see.

All in all, this was a day in which it was easy to be seaworthy with its bright, cloudless skies, minimal wind, and arresting natural beauty. It was a photographer's dream, populated by all the creatures, great and small, that any uplander would love to see. Today, we are indebted to our saltwater hostess. Her kindnesses were enough to lure us back here again, perhaps on a day when she'll show us a different mood.

King Cod

Perhaps no fish has been as pivotal to world history and to the economies of western nations as the cod. Cow-eyed, openmouthed, with a single whisker goatee, he is the unassuming bottom-feeder whose meat has been sought after and fought over by every major power in this hemisphere. One of the most authoritative texts on this once-prolific omnivore is Mark Kurlansky's *Cod: A Biography of the Fish that Changed the World*. In it, he reveals how and why the vast populations of cod should have lasted forever, but didn't. Cod are amazingly resistant to both cold and disease, and they have adapted, through the course of their evolution, from tropical to arctic waters. Cod swim with their mouths wide open, and like a vacuum cleaner, swallow anything in their path that will fit. This includes their own kind. The downside of this is that it makes them easy to catch. For this reason they probably have not been considered a gamefish by sports who want flare and splash with their catch.

There are those of us who would contest this. Hook a legal cod (twenty-two inches or larger) on rod and reel in 120 to 200 feet of water, boat the fish, and do this repeatedly for several hours, and you likely will need either a masseuse or a chiropractor the next day. It is fiction that cod don't fight. Because of the haphazard nature of the strike, they are often foul-hooked through the dorsal fin or even tail, and you'll break a sweat even in Passamaquoddy Bay's crisp, cool, salt air.

It's easy to see why cod gained such market popularity. It has almost no fat and is more than 18 percent protein, which is uncommonly high for fish. Just about every part of the cod is edible, especially the head, the meat of which is considered by connoisseurs to be most delectable. The cod's air bladder or "sound" is rendered to make isinglass, the clarifying agent used in beer and wine making. Cod roe and milt are prized by some Asian cultures, and the history of cod liver oil is familiar to anyone who grew up in post–Great Depression or post–WWII America. Today, it is a health food store staple used to relieve pain and joint stiffness due to arthritis. It's higher in vitamins A and D than fish oil, but also has the valued omega-3 fatty acids that promote a healthy heart and circulatory system.

Of the two hundred species of cod, the one we fish for in Passamaquoddy Bay is the Atlantic cod. This is one of the five "gadiforms" or coldwater bottom-feeders, the others being hake, haddock, whiting, and pollock. People can, and do, fish from the Eastport municipal dock and catch harbor pollock and mackerel relatively easily. Occasionally, someone hooks a small cod, or "scrod." This delicacy has been a fixture in New England fish markets and restaurants since the mid-twentieth century.

Of all the gadiforms, cod are the largest and have the whitest meat. It is distinguishable from haddock by the lateral white stripe along both sides, while this same marking on the haddock is black. There is even a legend that holds cod sacred because, the legend maintains, it was this fish that Christ multiplied to feed the masses.

Among its many amazing traits, none is more impressive than the cod's ability to manufacture "antifreeze" in order to inhabit glacial waters. Another is the cod's reproductive prowess. One female forty inches long is worth three million cod eggs at spawning time. An uncaught cod can live twenty to thirty years! It was overexploitation by trawlers that turned the tide on this history-making fish, whose most menacing carnivorous predator was man. Things went so far that the late measures finally taken by governments wreaked havoc on the productive lives of fishermen from Gloucester to Newfoundland.

If any species could rebound from such desecration, it must certainly be the cod. Sportfishing does not constitute a blemish on the downfall of the fishery, and even today, some good cod action is available to the small boat angler. The most common methods of angling are with latex "bugs" on a handline, or jigging twelve-, fourteen-, or sixteen-ounce jigs. A good supply of mackerel or harbor pollock will be caught by accident on the way to or from the bottom.

A Fishing Journal

Richard Miller sat with his feet up on the screened porch of his rented cabin at the close of another guided fishing day, his frayed fishing diary open in his lap. This thing had seen better days. Water-stained and ink-blotched, he had carried it to northern Quebec, Colorado, Tampa Bay, and Grand Lake Stream, among many other fishing destinations.

As I sit in another rocker across from him, listening, I see that just holding the diary puts him in a pensive backwater.

"I only took up fly fishing as an adult," he said. "Where I come from [New York], it began to be talked about as the hip thing to do. People in my circles were beginning to take fly-fishing lessons from schools at L.L. Bean or Orvis. They started buying all the gear and booked trips to fly-fishing hot spots so they could say they'd been there when they got back to the city. I jumped in hook, line, and weighted nymphs. I've thought about this a lot since, and to be totally honest, my heart wasn't in it. What I was really interested in was being able to keep up with the conversation on the golf course when it shifted to lakes and rivers and the cool places you'd fished. It's a strange thing to keep doing something when your heart's not in it. I say that now, but I wasn't thinking about it then. I was doing all these things out of some other impetus. I don't know. What makes us behave like that sometimes?

"Then, on one of these jaunts, I went fishing for brown trout in Colorado. Unexpectedly, something happened that would rewire my entire outlook with regard to fishing. On that trip, I went with my usual buddies, all of whom were far more advanced fishermen than me. The thing was, we each had a separate guide, and mine was the best I'd ever had—Kyle. While we were fishing, he was teaching me where the browns tend to lie—they love cover like logs and boulders and other structures in the river. It was not a clear day and I couldn't see them, so I had to take his word for it and go on untested faith in him.

"I made my imperfect casts to the targets he showed me, each time trying to land my fly upstream of the supposed hot spot. He counseled me to avoid drag in my leader, let my fly line unfurl instead of trying to force it, and mostly just relax. After a while, I began to bring up those brown trout. They didn't all strike, but I was learning what a predictable haven for them looked like. Kyle spoke less after that, and I began to cast to places because it looked like a fish should be there. These were the most exciting moments I'd had in my brief few years of fly fishing.

"On that three-day fishing adventure, I landed a lot of brown trout, the biggest one measuring twenty-one inches! That happened just at dusk. Kyle had told me that the mature browns love the cover of darkness since they do most of their feeding at night. We didn't even start fishing that day until four o'clock in the afternoon. As the shadows lengthened, the strikes came more frequently. I was nymph-fishing at first, then I went to dry flies. I'd pricked, hooked, and lost, and landed a dozen trout by seven-thirty. Then, just out in front of a big 'dead head' in the river, the water eddied around in a curious way. I kept seeing a fish rise in that spot, though very subtly, not making much of a splash at all.

"Kyle cautioned me against drag as I let the Light Cahill dry fly drift past that spot. When I was ready, to my own amazement, I laid down the line perfectly, upstream of the fish, and watched the fly almost make it to the place I'd been watching. It never did. There was no big splash. It was more like a subsurface sip. I'll tell you, all hell broke loose.

"How do I remember all these details? Because at the end of that trip, Kyle handed me a gift. It was this diary. He told me I was ready to start keeping a record of the places I fished and the fish I'd caught and lost. I've done that faithfully for nine years now, and along the way, I've noticed a change.

"My fishing interests have now almost superseded all my other interests. What I write in my diary are details. It's not just a fishing report—lengths and weights and that sort of thing. It's a weather journal, a description of the flora and fauna I've seen on an outing, the tricks and tips I've learned either from my own solo efforts or from a guide. The friends who've accompanied me, the new friends I've made along the way—it's all in here, almost like an autobiography. Now, it's a ritual I have at the end of a day of fishing. Right then when it's fresh, I sit down and reconstruct the whole experience, sometimes even poetically if that's the way it affected me.

"You know, the days that went bust, the times I've been frustrated when nothing seemed to go in my favor—it's been writing about those days after the fact that has often given me a deeper insight into exactly what was happening. My diary has given my fishing an extra dimension. Now, I fish first and reflect afterward. Now, I contemplate my experience, distill it, write it down, and learn from it."

Photo courtesy of Randy Spencer

Richard Miller with a catch.

Old Bushmills Anglers & Sportsmen's Society

Richard belongs to a group of five fishermen who come to Grand Lake Stream each June. They long ago named their group, "Old Bushmills Anglers & Sportsmen's Society," or OBASS. They must have had good reason to invoke the name of the Irish distillery that's been making premium whiskey since the thirteenth century, but that information stays locked in the vault. In the meantime, it serves as a singular identifier and easy acronym for T-shirts, hats, and other insignia wear.

OBASS loves to golf as well as fish, and comparisons are inevitable during days on the lakes and lunch grounds. For example, it has been suggested that with fishing, it's easier to shed the raiments of career, profession, and persona than it is with golf. Did somebody say that fishing brings out honesty and genuineness more readily than do the links? It's a dangling conversation, and the jury is still out on this and other matters that are turned over and examined closely by OBASS with each fishing foray into the north woods.

Michael Barocas, a career investment counselor, composes his casts the way an artist studies a model. A mental measuring takes place with accountings for crosswinds, currents, the weight of the lure, and timing. If the boat is moving, he may lead the target by a few feet in order to hit a bull's-eye only his eye sees. One imagines that he orchestrates his golf shots exactly this way. His reflexes, from years of surf-casting for striped bass off Montauk Point on Long Island Sound, are honed to instant response when a pull-back occurs. Michael is at the forefront of the most thoughtful, patient sportsmen who bring their skills to the bountiful bass waters of Grand Lake Stream.

The "Ballad of the Three Steves" takes on new verses each year as different guides fumble trying to distinguish one Steve from two others in OBASS. When in doubt, they just say "Steve," and have a three-fifths chance of being right. The Steves themselves absorb this in good humor, for each one is indeed distinguished and distinguishable. Steve Wohl, an estate attorney, is only exchanging one body of water for another on these trips, because he lives on fishable water year-round. More than most, he has an angling acumen that is always adjusting to the conditions of the moment. It is most evident in his sight-casting to those telltale bleached orbs betraying a bass spawning bed. He dials in these targets like a winged predator with telescopic vision, and he is able to cover fertile fishing grounds with volleys of line-drive casts. For years, this Steve was known as "Togue Man" for catching the largest lake trout OBASS had ever seen.

That was until Steve Kaufman, a real estate magnate, trolled a fly in June over a sunken shoal formation called "Half Moon." The craggy, underwater crescent was known to guide John Arcaro for holding togue of epic adiposity. Perhaps on chance, Arcaro thought, one still lurked there in June before making its migration to the depths of cooler water in summer. One did indeed. When John saw this Steve's rod bend double, the thought crossed his mind that the tandem streamer fly had made a lunar landing on one of Half Moon's jagged rocks. With the pull-back weight of one of those boulders, the togue left the ledges and headed for refuge in deeper water. Steve held his own against a fish bound to be free and fighting as if its life depended on it. While interjecting his quiet counsel, Arcaro turned the canoe when it served to support the fighting rod and backed it off when stress came to the breaking point. The hopeful Togue Man–elect watched, as entranced as his guide, as a trophy trout exploded the calm of an otherwise tranquil lake. The rod, the line, the leader, the knots, the angler, and the guide all held their own until this shimmering, speckled gamefish made a daring pass within pole-netting range of the canoe. Arcaro was a stroke ahead of the eye-popping prize that swam, unwittingly, into the fish-friendly rubber mesh and was airborne in the next instant. The new Togue Man reigns supreme as of this writing.

Steve Kunreuther, a promotional and marketing expert, proclaims no fishing prowess to any guides or to his OBASS mates. He brings a sporting modesty to these outings, offering up each new day as a blank slate to be sketched with adventure and learning. A guide feels blessed to witness such openness. Everything that happens will be big, exciting, a first, a record-setter! Learning one year to fish rubber crawfish in gravelly shallows brought rewards that rivaled anybody else's lunch ground narrative. "It seemed like almost every cast I had a fish on," he effused while everyone else looked at this Steve's guide for cracks in the concrete. A different June, guide Sue Hurd took him to islands she knew could harbor smallmouths in numbers. It was his first experience at seeing schools of bass to cast to, usually resulting in a frothy fish fight. His reactions and exhilaration for days to come provided the gratification all guides covet.

The OBASS brotherhood, whatever its mysterious affiliation to the Old Bushmills distillery, is a modern example of triumph over the headlong rush. At least once a year, its members replace overscheduling with serenity, fractured attention with pure contemplation. As with Richard's faithfully kept diary, the ever-fattening OBASS journal reflects the regenerative power of this wholesome tradition, one that has kept the bonds of OBASS strong for more than thirty years.

Arline's Epiphany

It might be easy to suppose that guided fishing is mostly a men's club. It's certainly true that most of the clientele are males, but by no means all of it. Two shifts occur during the guiding months of the year that bring different fishing customers with different agendas.

The ice-out fishermen are a rugged bunch. They're not going to be stopped by weather, and at that time of year almost all of it can be bad. Icy wind, driving rain, and high, freshwater seas can pummel these early May anglers who are dressed in multiple layers beneath their foul-weather gear. If you're a lady and you feel no compulsion to have an Ernest Hemingway–type experience in the outdoors, don't come then.

The die-hard sportfishermen comprise most of the business through the months of May and June, though we now see far more women in June than we used to. May and June has traditionally been the time for father-and-son trips, old army outfit trips, college chum trips, and business buddy trips. This gives way, once summer begins in force, to family vacations. Now the disposition and substance of these outings change. Gone are the furrowed brows of conquest, the intrepid challenge against the elements, the intense concentration of matching wits with wily sport fish.

Some of the oldest photographs taken of fishing parties in Grand Lake Stream after the railroad came to Princeton depict women in gingham behind long stringers of fish. This was a far coarser environment than now, and far more arduous to reach. And yet, with their tiny waists under tight corsets and their long hair piled up high, there they stand in the 1890s in front of large canvas tents lining the stream. Ladies, there is precedent for your presence here! If you've never tried anything like this before, consider Arline Ritz.

To say that Arline looked stunned on her first day would probably not be a stretch. She was, after all, sitting right in front of me, facing me, and I couldn't help but notice. Her facial expression seemed frozen in a stare. Several times that morning, she opened her mouth as if to speak, then shook it off as though whatever it was she was going to say sounded dumb to her en route from brain to lips.

She and her husband, Don, had taken a road trip from Philadelphia to the Maritime Provinces of Canada, and on the way home, made a side trip to Grand Lake Stream. The couple had booked themselves into Leen's Lodge, and on a lark, decided to stay a few days. They decided to book a fishing guide.

That first morning, we traveled about six miles over woods roads to come to a boat launch on a river. I told Arline and Don, who were surprised to think we'd be fishing on moving water, that we were only going to use this waterway as a passage into a lake. For Arline, every step on this ground was taken as though on eggshells. When the canoe was loaded, she was slightly relieved to find that she'd be seated in the middle, close to me, "just in case."

We picked our way through subsurface boulders, upstream into slower-moving water. I showed Arline the green paint on some of these rocks where other boats had forged instead of picked. A bald eagle swooped low overhead and Arline cupped her eyes to frame it against the azure sky. She followed its flight out of sight. The flow narrowed and I said, "It's awful bony in here. We might nudge something." As I stood to pole the canoe through the flowage, a rock harmlessly glanced the aft portion of the canoe and Arline lurched in her seat.

"It's okay," I said, trying to soothe. "No harm at all, happens all the time," but Arlene was clearly uneasy.

When the lake came into view, broad, silver beaches riveted her. She started to speak and stopped several times before finally saying, "Who put that sand there?"

My reply—"God"—fell on Arline as the last thing on earth she expected to hear. If I had said, "The Hilton chain," it might have made better sense to her, but the answer I gave meant that

Photo courtesy of Randy Spencer

Turn-of-the-century lady sports showing off their catch.

she was officially far from the only world she knew—the world of man-made everything.

Five minutes later, I saw a bear running out of the woods and down to the shore to my right. The bear went straight into a strong swim producing a good-sized wake. I pointed my paddle blade, and both Don and Arline turned in their seats to see. I slowed the canoe so that we wouldn't come too close, but even so, I couldn't tell whether Arline might be imagining the bear jumping into the canoe and making short work of all of us. She never spoke, and negotiated this event better than I expected. From that moment on, the day, working like a spinning wheel, spun a tapestry of more scenes, one flowing into the next, without need for commentary or captions. Like a child, she was beguiled by this magical web that divested her of words.

At lunchtime, we landed at one of the sand beaches that so enthralled Arline. As I readied the picnic site, she approached the lake cautiously, then reached down and pulled off her shoes. Don was off in another direction, casting and retrieving a floating lure. She touched her toes to the water, retracted them, then rolled her pants up to her knees and walked in up to her ankles. She walked down the beach, then back to the lunch site, slowly taking a seat next to where I was working. As her stare was fixed on the lake, I noticed her chin quivering. I came around, sat down beside her, and placed my hand on her shoulder.

"Is everything all right, Arline?"

"I don't think you'd understand," she replied, shaking her head.

"Try me," I said, giving her a pat on the shoulder.

"I don't know what's happening to me. I feel something, different. Very different. I'm a city girl. I've been in Philadelphia all my life. For me, a nature walk is a trip to the pet store. I have occasionally watched some of the fishing shows on cable TV with my husband. I know who Jimmy Houston is, and I've seen him kiss fish. I thought that was strange. But I never, *I never*, knew it could be like *this!* These lakes look and feel magical. They change you—something is happening to me and I don't know what it is. I've never heard such quiet! You know, when we saw a hawk fly right in front of us as we drove out a *dirt road* to come here—probably just another day at the office for you—well, I've never driven down a dirt road or seen a hawk on the wing in my life! Then we got to the lake and there were no houses! I know this must sound strange to you, but I've never seen a lake with no houses around it."

Arline choked back some tears when we both saw Don approaching.

"I know, I know," I offered clumsily, and stood, my hand still on her shoulder.

Don held up a pickerel on a stringer and said, "Do you cook these things?"

It was a quiet lunch, as they sometimes are when the power and beauty of the day makes conversation peripheral. The fishing that afternoon did what it was supposed to do on such a day—provide punctuation. I could feel a friendship forming—not as everyday an occurrence as one might think—even in such a context.

It would be wrongheaded to say that the epiphany that happened that day was Arline's alone. The transformative experience she was trying to express had been mine, too, many times, and now she was helping me revisit this phenomenon at its origins. Don and Arline would soon leave Grand Lake Stream and shortly after, the season would wrap up. No guided fishing day that season occupied my thoughts the way this one did. Then, one day in late September, a letter came postmarked from Philadelphia.

"I've been thinking a lot about watching you paddle your canoe—a canoe, by the way, I've never seen the likes of. I can't swim, but I've never felt so secure in my life. Who makes a canoe that can make you feel like that? You said his name was Sonny, and now that name is etched in my mind along with so many other things. Sometimes you paddled and never took the paddle out of the water so that it didn't make a sound. You said those were 'Indian strokes.' I looked over the side and was amazed at how clear the water was. You said you sometimes drink it, and I wondered if I could ever be brave enough to do that. Where I live, no one would ever drink any water from anything except a filter system in their kitchen or from a store-bought bottle. I know I'm rambling here.

"Remember—after threading our way through those rocks, you started the motor and we slowly ambled out into the larger part of the lake? I turned in my seat to see where we were going. There were bright, sandy beaches around the shoreline and I asked you about the sand. It sounded stupid as soon as it came out of my mouth. We saw islands that seemed to just rise out of the lake here and there without rhyme or reason. But I asked myself, does an island need a reason for being where it is any more than anything else does? No; it's just there, and that's enough. More than enough!

"We went through something you called a 'gut,' and by then I had figured out just to accept whatever things were called, even if I didn't understand. You pointed ahead of the canoe at a shape in the water. It was swimming across the 'gut' in front of us, but we were too far away to tell what it was. Out came your binoculars and I couldn't believe the words that passed your lips. 'It's a bear!' I had visions of you with a knife in your teeth, jumping out of the canoe to do battle with this bear like Davy Crockett. When we got up to it—my God—I've never been so amazed. It was the speed at which the bear could swim! Second, that he disappeared into the woods so FAST! You said to snap a picture while the snapping was good, and when the bear got to shore, I understood what you meant. He never slowed down when his feet touched land. He literally ran right out of the lake and into the woods so fast, a picture wasn't possible. I saw a BEAR! A BEAR IN THE WILD!! At first I was thinking of what my friends would say to every single thing that happened, and you told me they wouldn't really understand. As the day progressed, I thought less of that. I was inspired by my surroundings: the wonderment of nature, the serenity of the lake, a fish jumping out of the water to break the silence, and the awesome sound of silence itself. I knew you were right; they wouldn't understand. It would be futile to try and make them. As it was, they were already calling me 'Nature Girl' before I even left, slightly mocking me for my venture away from civilization.

"When we came around what you called 'the main island' and the expanse of the lake lay before us, I wondered how in the world anyone would know where to fish, much less where they were at any given moment. You said that the limbs of certain trees are larger on the south side, especially near the lakes, and I began to notice this. You said sometimes the birds would show us where the fish were. That's when I thought you were working from a script, knowing that city people would believe anything in a place like this. But then a bald eagle swooped down and picked up a small fish right before my eyes. I couldn't speak for the longest time. Right after that, two or three terns began dive-bombing the surface, and that's where you dropped the anchor. Don had a fish within two or three casts. I asked for a little instruction on my casting, and to my utter amazement, I, too, caught a fish right away! After that, the fish got bigger.

"When you chose six or seven white perch for lunch, you have no idea what was going through my mind. I was scanning the whole shore for pavilions, patios with grills, something that looked like a likely place to have a picnic. When we landed on one of those silver beaches I looked even harder, but saw only rocks and trees. Since there was no dock, I wondered how Don and I would get out of the canoe, not being the most limber ducks in the world. You brought the canoe in sideways, got out, handed me a paddle for support and put a cushion in the shallow water for me to step on. Sir Walter Raleigh in the Maine woods! Then you led us up a short path until we came to a fireplace and picnic table! There, at our oasis in the forest, we learned the meaning of a 'shore dinner.' A whole dinner cooked over an open fire, and you never used a potholder!

"I know, I'm really rambling now. As I told you, I'm a city girl. I know you know that something happened to me out there. Well, it has changed me. I know that now. I guess maybe you've heard all this before, and it's probably just a big cliché. I still needed to write and say these things. Also, that we'll be back next year. Does that surprise you?

With best regards,
Arline and Don Ritz"

The Ritzes did come back for five consecutive years after that first trip. Sadly, Don passed away in 2007.

Perch Bums

Perching is a pastime dear to the hearts of Grand Lakers. The meat of white perch, if voted on, may in this town be preferred to that of salmon, deer, or lobster. The limit per angler for this prolific fish is twenty-five, affording good opportunities for that sociable favorite—a fish fry.

The white perch, or *Morone americana*, is not a perch. It is of the bass family, and its features are most reminiscent of the striped bass. They travel in schools, and at spawning time in the spring, these schools sometimes mass into long columns heading toward the mouths of streams. On a calm lake, this rare sighting can be almost unnerving. The moving mass of double-dorsal-finned fish creates "nervous water" on the surface, belying in the imagination some nightmarish lake serpent.

In late summer after the lakes have "turned over," white perch head for the deeper water they will inhabit for the winter. One way to locate a school without a fish finder is to troll a shiny spinner on both sides of the boat. When fish strike both baits, that's the place to drop anchor. At times, the first takers strike deep, just off bottom. Preferred baits are worms, minnows, and sometimes cut bait. Once a school is engaged, it's possible to take fish just under the surface. The run of size may be in the eight- to ten-inch range, but "humpbacks" can reach fifteen inches and two pounds. For their size, white perch acquit themselves nobly in their fight to thwart the net. They provide a perfect opportunity for children to learn basic fishing skills.

On a late summer day that dawned cloudy, blustery, and sharply cooler than the dog days of the previous week, Bobby, twelve, and Brad Farrell, ten, of Vermont were awake by six-thirty. They knew that all that stood between their camp and the guided fishing day promised to them by their mom was a long boat trip down West Grand Lake to the special, remote lake whose name I won't disclose—guide's secret. A northwest wind had whipped up the lake in good fashion overnight, and now the rollers were breaking on their beach as they quartered the wind and headed out of Farm Cove. Across the cove and through The Gut, the going wasn't too bad. Once out into the open lake and turning south, a following sea of three-and-a-half-foot waves was more than enough to wake everybody up.

Once in town, the day began at the Pine Tree Store with a powwow.

"Listen, boys, we've got weather here. It's going to blow today and maybe rain, and you could put this trip off if you wanted to," I said.

These words might as well have been spoken in Swahili for all the sense they make to Bobby and Brad. Why would somebody "put off" a fishing trip, an adventure in the Maine woods, for *any* reason? Weather? Who cares what the weather is doing as long as we're fishing? Satisfied, I secure the load for a long ride over rough roads and off we go in a blaze of dust, Mom waving good-bye until we're out of sight.

On the way, the boys get to see a logging operation in full swing—mechanical harvesters, skidders, loaders, and trailers. Brad points out that he could fit inside one of the hubs of the skidder wheels. By the time the off-road destination is reached, the sun is warming up the day a little, and the boys discover high bush blueberries in full ripeness right next to the boat launch. In nothing flat, all the gear is stowed in the Grand Laker. Everyone has a favorite, "lucky" rod plus a backup. You don't want to take any chances on a trip like this.

The journey begins by heading upstream through an enormous culvert, which doubles as an echo chamber. We try a three-part harmony inside the tunnel and then listen to the notes trailing afterward. "Wow, neat!" So we do it again and again, wondering what it must sound like to someone standing up on the road. Weeds choke the narrow stream at the start, so there'll be no motoring for a while. The Grand Laker threads a course through rocks and logs until we see a chance to let the motor down, but not for long. The stream narrows to barely more than a trickle, and the expedition comes to its first hauling point. "There must be a beaver blockage upstream," I point out, and the boys, who started the day with no shoes, hop out and start heaving. They seem game for anything. This is only the first of five or six hauls over shallow sandbars until finally, around one bend, the culprit comes into view. It's the Hoover of all beaver dams and must've taken an industrious beaver all spring and summer to build. We joke that it has a three-car garage, satellite TV, and broadband. "Boys, we've got to dismantle enough of this thing to get by, and it's going to irk him when he discovers what we've done. Let's make fast work of it."

Ten minutes later the water is cascading where the dam had been and the three of us are easily able to sluice the canoe up through and climb aboard. Around the next turn, the lake comes into view, and a jewel of a lake it is. There isn't one other boat on it.

On route, rods are readied, hooks tied on, and sinkers attached. Bobby and Brad are going perchin', and a pretty stiff northwest wind is helping us toward the perch hole. No sooner does the anchor hit bottom than three small white perch are caught and released. The time until lunch goes by in a blur, and a good-sized pickerel happens by in time to make it onto the fish stringer. Time to find a lee shore that offers a good chance for a cook fire out of the wind. One is soon spotted—one that also boasts a silver, sandy beach and a rock jetty where the boys can cast after they build a fireplace. What a dandy it is, right between two boulders protected from wind and built up with smaller rocks so the portable grate could be laid across it level.

Brad loses a fish on his first cast off the jetty. Bobby loses a lure. I lose no time cleaning the pickerel, slicing up some "steak fries," and putting the burgers in the broiler basket. Not to mention a pot of coffee for myself. Picture us three perch bums, slumming on a secluded beach, the only humans on the whole lake, eating a surf 'n' turf lunch fit for kings topped off with dark chocolate homemade brownies. Was life ever meant to be this good? For two young, barefoot boys, it just might have been. With everybody chipping in, the site is cleaned and left better than before for the next fishermen. Now, back to perchin'!

The grown-up perch don't come to this party. They just send the kids to play and show everyone a good time. The thing is, they have about eighty kids! Talk about busy! Chub shiners and sunfish come uninvited, and by four o'clock in the afternoon, four dozen worms shrink to a few stragglers. No one wants to leave, but the boys have "promises to keep, and miles to go" before they hitch a red-eye road trip back to Vermont with Mom. As the expedition leaves the lake, a giant rainbow "blotch" forms in the sky behind us, and Bobby says it looks like a perch. The lake is saying good-bye to adventurers who treated it well, taking only one pickerel for the table, and leaving a tidy lunch ground for some lucky future perchers.

On the way out, a few casts in the stream bring an explosive strike to Brad's lure from a large freshwater "gator." It's probably that very pickerel that rose up before his mind's eye just before he dropped off to sleep in the van headed for home. My last thought before dropping off to sleep that night was that I'd just spent a day with three sports, not two: Bobby, Brad, and the twelve-year-old percher who still lives somewhere inside me.

Fall

Autumn Comes to Grand Lake Stream

A great many roads surrounding Grand Lake Stream are best negotiated in first gear. Here, devoid of urban distractions like malls or Main Streets, "riding the roads" is a legitimate pastime. Most of these rural routes were made to access timber. Contractors may only work an area for a few months, and, once finished, their roads are not maintained, the exceptions being principal woods arteries. New roads are made when needed to accommodate new timbering operations. The Stud Mill Road, a shortcut to Bangor when passable, is one example.

One never sees the same scenery twice on these deep woods excursions, especially with the change of seasons. At summer's end, there can be severe fissures caused by erosive runoffs. When hurricanes peter out in Maine, as they frequently do, their final act is to fill the streams to overflowing. Too much water is trouble for the woods roads. It is not uncommon to journey eighteen miles out only to be forced to turn around because of a washout.

If you roam well off the trails and roads in September, and the wind is right, you may pick up the scent of the bear bait sites. Guides set out these barrels and buckets of reeking treats to attract black bears at the beginning of August, and they replenish them continually until the season opens about August 30.

Horse grain soaked in Fryolater grease and vats of syrup or jellies and other sugary concoctions baked in the September sun can ferment some far-traveling, potent odors.

Along the road edges, fall die-back may already have begun, most visible in the tall grasses. The areas closest to the road are usually grown up with "whistle woods," bands of small-diameter trees running parallel to the road and choking each other for daylight and growing room. Whistle woods make excellent cover and habitat for rabbits, ruffed grouse, and woodcock, among other wildlife.

Many trees in the whistle woods are birch, and now their leaves are taking on brown spots and curling up. The same will happen to the foliage of the alders and the maples, and later, the beech. Beech trees begin to drop nuts that are a favorite and significant part of the black bear's diet. Guides often estimate the success and even the average weights of the bear harvest from this important crop. The maples that grow from the heaths, bogs, and swamps are already a brilliant red, and by month's end may be bare.

Ferns, though, are the deadest giveaway of summer's dying torch. These tall, lush bouquets come to the summer party late and leave early. Their fronds first show their inevitable demise by rusting from the tips inward. This continues toward the stem at the center until the whole plant looks toasted. When you see a large patch of these all rusted and brittle, a distinct fall feeling settles in.

Lots of the woods roads eventually steer close to West Grand Lake, and at this time of year it can be a shock to see how low the water is. The lake's September shoreline is reliable evidence of a receding season. Domtar Industries, controller of the dam, may not be the only cause. Some summers are droughty, dehydrating the lakes through evaporation, and this, combined with Domtar draw-downs, can unveil the lake's "old shoreline."

The old shoreline's distance from the modern shore varies around the lake from thirty feet to thirty yards. In some places, stumps of the trees that once stood on the old shore are still visible. West Grand's water is so clear; one can view this shelf or ridge easily and imagine what the lake looked like before any dams were built, driving its waters upland into the woods. The days of those post-dam trees were numbered, and some of the resulting driftwood (*dri-ki*) can still be found washed into piles in coves and crannies around the lake.

White men in quest of industry built dams. Seeing clearly where the water stood before they were built is to see the land and lakes the native people inhabited and fished. In a place so essentially connected to the past, the imprint of earlier times has the welcome effect of widening the view. In low water, the old Indian encampment areas can easily be picked out, as well as the narrowed waterways that must have afforded good salmon spearing. The Passamaquoddy may have built partial obstructions—mini-dams—to slow the flow and thus enhance spearing. I once saw an anthropological study in which babies were placed next to moving water. They all built dams! Today, the children's museum in Bangor features running water troughs where kids can, with blocks, make mock dams. There must be a primal urge in humans to stop water.

Thanks to fall's low water level, lakeside camp owners get a chance to improve a beach, rework a deck or dock, or maybe move a pesky boulder or two. Widening shorelines also make a favorite local pastime—arrowheading—much easier. Local collections of aboriginal artifacts would wow any archaqeologist. Collectors spend long hours at oxbows, on alluvial bars, and on cobbled beaches this time of year. It takes a skilled, or lucky, eye to see these gems dating from five hundred to five thousand years ago.

The early signs of fall are all here now, but fishing will not cease for another six weeks at least. In mid-October, the drawdowns will stop by law. Togue spawn in shallows that could expose them to danger if the lake is too low. Good, fishable stream levels will bring some of the best fishing of the year and some of the heaviest salmon, fat from a full growing season. Catching them on flies packs enough thrill to attract anglers from across the continent.

After October 1, the early archery season for deer has already begun, and the focus for many shifts to hunting. The game seasons are many and varied: upland and migratory birds, ducks, bear, moose, the regular firearms and muzzleloader seasons for deer, and finally, bobcat. While guiding for these sports is not what it once was, bear, moose, and upland bird guiding has begun to rebound.

Labor Day

Right around Labor Day, here, and all over Vacationland, someone will always say, "Love to see 'em come, love to see 'em go." They'll be referring to the guests from away who have buttered our bread all season. That old saw is without teeth or truth. When spring sprung, these visitors were responsible for bailing us out after six months of wallowing in winter. They infused us with news from the world so distant from Grand Lake Stream and melted our frozen faces into smiles. Now they have enabled us to prepay for our heating oil for the coming winter. Many of them have ensured our income next summer by booking their trips before leaving. And, some of these visitors come year after year, exceeding the category of "client" and earning that of friend.

In leaving, it should be said, they'll miss a lot, too. They'll miss those September days when the summer haze has abated, replaced by cool, clear, autumn air. Soon after that, the intensity of color becomes almost heart-rending to behold. Our lakes become bluer than blue. Cloudless days interrupted only by east-west contrails become commonplace. Our friends from away will miss the crisp, pungent smell of fall's snappy Down East mornings. It may be the first rotted leaves on the ground or the last wafts from fading flowers, but this odor is powerful indeed for what it inspires. After putting in a long season on the lakes, a rebirth of energy now catapults us into fall. And, we're going to need it. All those tasks that were too hot to handle only recently—the firewood, the chimney work, the painting, and staining—now loom large.

The fall migration of landlocked salmon into the stream is missed, too, by our short-term, summer visitors. Grand Lake Stream, almost overnight, is enlivened by a profusion of these fish on a mission. Some "drop in" from the lake above the dam, and many swim upstream from the west branch of the St. Croix drainage, including The Flowage, Lewy Lake, Long Lake, and Big Lake.

Following them will be another migration—that of the fall fly fishers, the staunchest of whom consider fishing over still water a waste of time. Many of these folks haven't set foot in a river since last June. Some are serious and stooped, stepping tenuously over the stony stream bed, wading stick in hand. Some will not only be wet from the waist down, but also behind the ears. They'll don every fly-fishing accoutrement featured in the glossy catalogs that ply this trade. They'll populate the stream until October 20, the end of the no-kill, extended season on landlocked salmon.

Following this sometimes ragtag, sometimes photo-perfect fleet of fly fishers is one more migration that everyone looks forward to—that of the eagles. By early November, an inimitable, ear-splitting screech will start just before first light, and it won't stop till the darker edge of dusk. Males and females, immature and mature, will cruise the three-mile stretch from West Grand to Big Lake doing what this most magnificent bird of prey does best. Salmon and trout caught unawares will soon find themselves air-drying on their way to a pine limb and the wrong side of dinner. The population of eagles in the St. Croix Valley has, thanks in part to the stewardship of the "Bird Group" in Maine's Inland Fisheries and Wildlife department, more than doubled in the last twelve years.

Motoring across a lake with the first color changes blazing, paddling into a stream, and then swamping through a bog to a wet meadow of ripe, wild cranberries also is something our summer visitors don't get to know. Some years these crimson heaths are bountiful beyond fantasy. Our annual October harvest means a Thanksgiving that keeps on giving until the last of the red berries run out, maybe in late winter in a good cranberry year. Cranberrying requires nothing more than a blueberry rake (a handheld, many-toothed scoop) and a reasonably good back. In good years, a Grand Laker can be half-filled in a morning. My friend, David Sockabasin, relies on an old method of culling cranberries. First, he spreads the newly harvested crop on a tarp, the corners of which have been anchored. At this time of year, one won't have long to wait for a windy day, and when it comes, it naturally blows away the light leaves and stems, leaving the heavier berries. The crop can then be frozen or put by in mason jars.

Blackberrying is another seasonal activity. We find the plump, black fruit in prime bear country at a time that coincides with the opening of the first segment of the bear hunt. Encounters with these hungry harvesters are rare, though, owed to their general repugnance for humans. The most obvious sign of the black bear's love of this wild plant is the seeded scat he leaves everywhere as proof of his presence.

Successful blackberry gatherers wear their guilt all over their hands, forearms, and clothing, because it's common to get bloodied by the barbed bushes. The reward, though, is that scrumptious blackberry pie waiting to crown a long-awaited, white perch fish fry among friends and townspeople as the season winds down.

Drummond Humchuck: Slimy Business

The end of the guided fishing season can simmer into an emotional stew for guides. So many of the sports now come and gone are friends who visit but once a year. At this moment, that year can seem an eternity. There is an unavoidable letdown when one has been in good, sociable company for months, and then, abruptly, this fellowship ends. Guided fishing income also stops, and other gainful pursuits must replace it. Guides often stitch together several employs, such as caretaking, carpentry, canoe making, and canoe repair. Those with hunting guide licenses can guide hunters of bear, moose, upland bird, deer, and bobcats in their various seasons from late August to mid-February. An unconventional livelihood, yes, but it suits the disposition of those who have chosen the guiding lifestyle. Though a master guide myself, allowed by law to guide hunters as well as an assortment of recreational trips, I have chosen to guide only fishermen. I do my audio archival work and other recording studio work through the winter months. Over the years I have bonded with many of my clients so that watching the last of them depart in autumn is a difficult period for me.

In one of these emotional stews, and with a five-gallon pail of cranberries, I set out one September morning for Township Unknown. The long haul in from the old logging yard where I parked the truck was made longer by the weight of the cranberries I carried in the pack basket on my back, even though it was snug and comfortable. Since Lola Sockabasin's passing, I prefer those made by the New England Basket Company, subsidiary of the Pine Tree Store in Grand Lake Stream. It is a taut, sturdy weave worthy of ten gallons of dunnage and can last a lifetime.

As is always the case with the guiding months, I hadn't had a free day to visit my friend, Drummond Humchuck, since spring. That worried me—someone in their mid-eighties not being checked on for five months—but then maybe Drummond's brother, Woody, had been out. In any case, Drummond has been getting on well in his hermitage for over sixty years, and yes, I had to admit the odds were good he'd eventually die there someday, my worries notwithstanding. But, all dark thoughts of this ilk were dispelled the moment I cleared the tree line bordering Drummond's haven. There he was, moving a teapot off the flames of an outdoor fire with a hookaroon. Two cups sat on a stump close by. All I could do was shake my head at a telepathy beyond my grasp.

"How'd you summer, Drum?" I hollered.

"Still here, chum," he yelled back wearing his crinkly grin.

Drummond, whose mood is generally good anyway, turns gleeful and giddy seeing the cranberries I've brought for him.

Yes, he could set out from his place and easily find cranberries, but I knew at this time of the year he'd be busy with eels.

True to form, there, off to one side of the dooryard, I saw some eel skins at the foot of Drum's "skinnin' tree." It wouldn't make polite parlor talk today, but the long and the short of it is that Drummond skins eels in the old, traditional way. After killing them, he buries them in the yard overnight. This is done because eels simply refuse to die otherwise. He then digs them up, nails the head to a tree, makes a cut completely around the serpentine fish just under the gills, muckles onto a flap of this skin with a plier, and pulls off the whole slimy hide in one yank. Drummond once made a pair of gloves for me from eel skin, a gift I'm quite proud to show off.

The American eel resides in very nearly all our local waters. It is "catadromous," meaning it spends the majority of its life in freshwater and then returns to salt water to spawn. It is also "palindromic," having the ability to swim both forward and backward.

Carter White, Bill White, Bill Sprague and his son, Sonny, and Dave Tobey were among those Grand Lakers who trapped eels for market. There are corroborated stories of one ton of eels being taken in one stormy night in the old canal along Middle Walk, which runs parallel to Grand Lake Stream in the middle of the village. A ton of eels requires some contemplation. Drummond traps them only for his own use. He eats them and sometimes uses the skin.

In Maine, the eel weir season is July 15 to November 1. Eels move best on the stormiest, most hair-raising nights with heavy rain and rising water. For the most part, those nights will be during the dark of the moon, or just eight to ten days per month. Although it's not completely understood, the most plausible theory seems to be that eels feel less vulnerable to their principal predators after man—minks and otters—during violently inclement weather, since these predators are likely to take refuge from such weather. Drummond was making ready to trap in the dark of the September moon, and he was hoping for a storm.

In the late summer, adult, sexually mature eels begin their migration out of ponds, lakes, and streams to the Atlantic Ocean. By the time they leave their acquired native habitat of freshwater, they will be nine to fifteen years old. Some have been trapped that have measured fifty inches and weighed sixteen pounds. The pilgrimage lasts three to five months and comes to fruition in the deep water on the northern edge of the Sargasso Sea in the Bermuda Triangle where every eel is born. Mating adults die after spawning.

Drummond's eel weirs have mesh, or grating configurations, each with one opening in it for a sluice. Eels go to the weir and poke around the mesh looking for a route downstream until they find the opening. Once into the sluice, they drop into a "catch box" that measures four by four by eight feet. That's a cord of eel if it's full, and they do get full. In watersheds like the St. Croix River system, the catch boxes are required to have removable panels in the deepest part of the channel, so that any errant Atlantic salmon or brook trout can freely escape during the day. At night when the trap is tended, the panels are dropped into position, and in the morning, the contents of the catch box are examined.

"Set down, chum," Drummond said, pointing to one of his homemade birch chairs. Off beside the fireplace I could see the ash kettle with floating eel steaks. I don't know where Drummond learned this method for curing fish in warm weather, but I looked it up, and it turns out it came from early

Italian missionaries. The lye in the wood ash serves as a preservative almost indefinitely. After the chunks marinate in the solution overnight, Drummond puts them out in the direct sunlight to "firm up." When he's ready to use the fish, he simply soaks them in fresh water, which removes the lye and ash.

Drummond's diet consists of indigenous foods all eaten in their season. Whether it's muskrats in the spring, eels in the fall, fish and berries in summer, or moose meat in winter, his culinary palate is varied and interesting. And, that's not to mention his mastery of wild mushroom identification. He can tell the mushrooms that make a drab meal gourmet from the ones that destroy your central nervous system. An important distinction.

As always, Drummond's premises abound with projects. His winter wood stores are well under way. Wild plants and herbs hang everywhere, especially red willow, and that's one of the reasons I suspect Drummond has some Passamaquoddy blood. Red willow, or *Nespihqamq* in Passamaquoddy, has been used in pipe mixtures for centuries for relief from headaches, eye pain, insomnia, anxiety, and even depression. Although I've never seen any medical or academic support for these claims, Drummond believes them and continues to avail himself of this remedy.

Inside the cabin are hooked rugs in progress, several whittling masterworks, and popsicle stick models of the Hoover Dam, the New York City Post Office, and one nearly finished of the *Titanic*. He has a connection, he explained, to each of these historic symbols. He'd seen the dam and the post office as a young man, and had an aunt booked on the return trip of the *Titanic* to England—the return trip that never happened.

After tea, I empty the contents of my pack basket to "ooohs and ahhhs" from my friend. In addition to the cranberries, I had brought bag balm, Cloverine, wire, duct tape, pickling salt, a pound of 16p nails, glue, a gross of popsicle sticks, wooden strike-anywhere matches, hydrogen peroxide, Band-Aids, witch hazel, Vaseline, and Vicks VapoRub. They were all guesses, but good ones judging by the reception.

Once everything is unpacked, Drummond goes into the woodshed and returns with a stringer of smoked eel. "Take these to huntin' camp, chum, and see if the boys don't love 'em."

No other person I've met lives so completely in the moment while simultaneously preparing for tomorrow as Drummond Humchuck. Every time I leave, I take a personal oath to try to do the same.

One Amazing Fish

Eels can and do travel overland, particularly in wet weather. They have been seen in great, undulating masses on beaches in search of freshwater. It is said that they are able to scale a thirty-foot dam by means of a chain/ladder method. One scurries up on the traction of its slime until it drops. Another makes it a little farther, and so on, until an eel chain can be formed along the slime trail all the way to the top. The migrating population can then scale the barrier and cross wetlands to get where they're going.

This amazing fish can breathe through its skin as well as its gills, and it has reverse gear. It can spin itself into the body cavity of a large, dead fish to eat its eggs, then unwind to get out. This same ability makes it the bane of any angler who brings up an eel on rod and reel.

For all of its unusual skills and its adaptability, it still does not even enjoy the status of "fish" among most anglers. It is nevertheless an important fish in our ecosystem, and it has been a positive development that over-harvestation of elvers, or juvenile eels just adapting to freshwater, is now being controlled. Meanwhile, the adult eel harvest is a fraction of former times, and small harvests don't make a dent.

Eels also are now farmed commercially in the Orient, a fact that negatively affects local market prices. It is claimed by some eel connoisseurs, however, that farmed eel have thinner skins and don't taste as good.

St. John's Bull

The moose hunting season in Maine is split. Each part is a week long varying from the end of September into early October, and only winners of the moose lottery are legal moose hunters. Winners may select a sub-permittee and an alternate, and they are restricted to hunt only in the zone named on their drawing. Many applicants, such as yours truly, have never hit the lottery, while others—the lucky ones—have laid claim to two or more moose hunts. Depending on where you live in Maine, a moose lottery win can cause a chain reaction of celebratory parties. I was thrilled when it happened to my good friend and guiding colleague, Master Guide John Arcaro.

Quick to deny any claim to sainthood, John owns up to the vice of loving a superior English ale like the one named after The Bull pub on St. John's Street in London—St. John's Bull. It is the need that all good stories have for good titles that summoned the beer, the bull, and the saint into service for the telling of John's first-in-a-lifetime moose saga.

John had eight years invested in the Maine moose lottery before he struck pay dirt. Compared with many, that's not bad. His sub-permittee and alternate choices came easily: eldest son John Jr. would be his right-hand man; his younger son, Mike, would be alternate. Since the sub is also allowed to shoot and since John Jr. has advanced bow-hunting skills, John Sr. would try when the time came to set up a bow shot for his son if at all possible.

When the Department of Inland Fisheries and Wildlife publishes the winners of the lottery in early June, the names of Grand Lake Stream's two or three winners are in short order known all over town. After basking briefly in his celebrity, John noticed that his permit came in for Zone 18 in the Lee and Lincoln area, about an hour and a quarter away. This would be difficult. John and his wife, Mary, own and operate Canal Side Cabins in Grand Lake Stream, and late September to early October can be very busy times with moose hunters, upland bird and waterfowl shooters, salmon fishermen, and leaf peepers all staying at Canal Side. Luckily, John, through the Sportsman's Alliance of Maine's website, found someone who was willing to swap zones. So far so good, and the stage was set for scouting work.

If you need to know what's on the move and where, who's seeing what and when, the best people to talk to are those who are constantly in the woods. Bear guides, trappers, and loggers come to know areas of the wilderness as well as a beat cop knows his city blocks. Through conversations with them, John was able to sketch out a tract where a hunt might prove fruitful. In the days that followed, consecutive sightings of a hefty bull moose in the region convinced him he had made the right choice.

When opening day of the first week of the split moose hunting season dawned, it was overcast and windy, and John with his .306 and John Jr. with his bow were on the move at four-thirty.

After a jostling half-hour woods ride, John Jr. took to a tree stand within eyeshot of his father, who was set up on the ground twenty-five to thirty feet away. Mild signs of the moose rut were around—pawings and rubs—but not at the intense level of peak mating. Those signs are unmistakable: pine trees six inches in diameter completely stripped of bark, and craters pawed out of the dirt sometimes six feet in length. John Sr. began to call. His moose call of choice: the Phantom Pro Line Series made by Extreme Dimension Wildlife Calls of Hampden, Maine. After a while, a bull responded. He seemed to be moving slowly toward the two hunters, but wind conditions and extremely jagged terrain made it difficult for them to get a good bead on direction.

Meanwhile that morning, bear guide Dale Tobey and his bear hounds had struck two bears in the same region. The sound of the baying hounds carried into the Arcaros' moose-hunting sector, and progress from the answering bull halted. The bull "hung up" or simply stopped moving except with extreme caution. In this suspenseful state, the clock played out until lunchtime, and the two hungry hunters returned to town. Had they known what lay ahead for them, they might have taken a long nap that afternoon. As it was, they were back in their shooting saddles exactly twelve hours from the time they set out that morning. Once again, John Sr. got busy on the Phantom call.

Within an hour, a bull responded, possibly the same bull from the sound of the grunt. While similar, each bull's rutting report may have subtly distinctive characteristics. Rather than risk "call shyness," John let the bull become curious by not sounding the Phantom. Slowly, the bull kept advancing. Now, from the various calls available on the Phantom Pro, John selected the "estrus cow" call. At carefully chosen intervals, he let the call bleat out again and again. At six o'clock, after what seemed like an eternity, the two men heard the bull grunt again. From then on, the moose moved steadily closer. Its responses testified to real interest, becoming deeper, more gutteral, and of longer duration. Tension in the tree stand and on the ground mounted.

"The wind was in our favor," blowing over the back of the bull and into the men's faces so it probably wouldn't "wind" them, said John Sr. of those late September evening hours. "At the same time, it also prevented us from hearing well. We were straining to hear any snap of a twig so that we could try to judge his distance from us."

At one point in the heat of anticipation, John Sr. mistakenly hit the "agitated cow" call button on the Phantom, a call that signaled to the approaching bull that another, perhaps younger bull was pestering an unwilling cow. "It may have been a happy accident," John said, "because now this bull picked up his pace."

The libidinous behemoth finally came into full view at almost six-thirty, but only for John Sr. John Jr. had no line of sight for a much more demanding bow shot. "He seemed monstrous," said John Sr., "and yet I knew my son couldn't see him. It was frustrating, but I knew it had to be now or never." John discharged his .306 and the moose made a gallop across a small clearing. Once more and the bull toppled. The Master Guide's aim had assured a quick kill.

As any moose, or bear, or deer hunter knows, after the trigger is pulled, there is always "the rest of the story." With only twenty minutes of daylight remaining, father and son's celebrations had to be brief. A four-wheeler trail had to be brushed out so that the men could drag the bull to the road for transport. They worked until almost seven o'clock, and, of course, during this period, the skies opened to release drenching downpours. No work is as heart-thumping as this. The terrain was rugged, craggy, and swailed, all culminating in an old logging yard littered with slag. At this point, the sopping hunters returned to town to drop off the guns, change into dry clothes, and pick up the dragging gear. Mike Arcaro joined them to lend a hand, and they were all back out at the site by eight o'clock. If they thought it was raining hard before, it was a sprinkle compared to now.

In the midst of the most soaking torrent, help arrived. Bear guide Dale Tobey, whose hounds had accidentally interrupted the Arcaros' hunt that morning, helped the Arcaros get the heavy bull a half a mile out to the road. Dale's truck has a forward frame on the bed so it was chosen as the vehicle to winch the moose onto and carry it back to town. Around midnight, they transferred the moose to the Arcaros' truck with the aid of the chain fall and scale tower at the Pine Tree Store. Then, it was off to Drew Plantation, north of Springfield, to D&R Custom Meat Cutters. They arrived at two-thirty in the morning.

The Arcaro bull turned in at an 830-pound dressed weight, had a forty-two-inch spread of head gear, and fourteen points. Like all successful hunters, John reflected on all the elements that led up to his trophy. Was eight years of waiting for a winning ticket the magic number? Was it the working woodsmen who put him on the right trail? Or maybe that unintended call from an "agitated cow"? Today, head, horns, and cape adorn the main lodge at Canal Side Cabins where any guest can get the whole, soggy story of St. John's Bull, and if they're a really special guest, a pint of a superior English ale.

Rags to Riches

The story of the black bear in Maine is a rags-to-riches tale. From the time of the early settlers up to the 1950s, the black bear was considered a pest and was hunted year-round, often with a bounty on its head. Widespread clearing and burgeoning farmlands drove bear populations into a downward spiral, and by the mid-twentieth century, it was estimated that there were only 5,000 bears left in the entire state. Virtually wiped out of southern coastal regions, the bears were forced to the more heavily forested regions north, east, and west.

Then, beginning in the 1960s, when the black bear was promoted from pest to big-game animal, its stock grew. What followed was the most extensive research initiative ever conducted on this Maine fur-bearer, resulting in management practices soon put in place. The growth line on the black bear population graph took a 45-degree angle upward, and it has retained that rise. At these sustained growth rates, by 2010 that population will have quintupled since the mid-1950s.

This management that produced the densest population of black bear east of the Mississippi is now the envy of wildlife agencies across the U.S. With current estimates of over 23,000 bears, an annual harvest of 1,500 to 2,500 bears—roughly 10 percent—creates a positive growth curve, satisfying nearly all objectives, including sport, public sightings, education, health, and safety.

Washington County is one of the top three counties where bear hunting and bear guiding thrive. The other two are Aroostook and Penobscot. It's the first big-game hunting season to open each fall, and, with a duration of about three months, the longest to stay open. It begins with bait season, moves into hounds season, and concludes with the regular firearms season. Washington County guides keep Plott, Walker, and Blue Tick hounds for the long-winded work of bear stalking. Here, guiding bear hunts, one of the most vigorous types of guiding, is a viable business for those who are up to it.

Family Tradition

Gary Hanlin, sixty-three, from Bloomingdale, Ohio, has personally helped grow the bear-hunting business in Grand Lake Stream. Over the many years he's been making his autumn trip, his party has grown so large that the hunters now require two rented houses. The Hanlin group helps keeps the guiding culture alive here, topping the "A-list" of loyal clients.

Gary has had his share of successes, and his son, Jason, has scored his first bear, so chances are, Jason'll be in it for the long haul, too. This father-and-son team is so enthusiastic about the annual outing that they book their following year's hunt with Master Guide Paul Laney before they leave town.

Gary Hanlin's name appeared on The Board at the Pine Tree Store in the fall of 2004. The Board lists big-game taggings, including bear, moose, and deer, and fall customers arriving at the store make a beeline for it. The list gives dates, locations, size, and weight for every big-game animal taken, as well as the successful hunters' names and home states. Even the deer that one year dented up store co-owner Kathy Cressey's Subaru made it up on The Board.

Gary's name was up there along with nineteen other successful hunters during the early bear seasons that year. What stood out to casual observers was the higher-than-average weights of the tagged bears. Several came in at 200-plus pounds. A few were over 300 pounds—one came in at 350, and one strained the scales at 375. Those, by any reckoning, are big bears, and bear guides had been expecting them since Labor Day. The reason—beechnuts.

There is probably no single influence to which the health and well-being of black bears is tied so much as to this one hardwood species. A beech blight in Maine could reverse the positive trend of the black bear population almost overnight. So could over-cutting, because it takes a beech tree forty years to become a good, annual source of beechnuts. Not every year produces a good crop, but when it's bountiful, the bear harvest jumps along with bear weights.

Gary Hanlin got his big bear that year with a Remington .35. We might all be surprised at how many hunters, upon reaching a certain age, put down a far more expensive and technologically advanced rifle, and take up a family heirloom firearm. Some think it's a harbinger of good fortune. Others that its presence confers meaning, as though a volume of family history were written on its stock. Or it may just feel right, like it did to Gary Hanlin.

"It was the first gun I ever owned," he said. "I worked at a gas station in high school making sixty-five cents an hour, saving up enough to buy it at the whopping price of fifty-two dollars. When I got older, I gave it to my brother, Ed, and when my son, Jason, became old enough, Ed gave it to him. Now Jason has his own gun, and I'm using the .35 again."

"The magic hour in bear hunting that year was six-thirty in the morning," says Gary's guide, Paul Laney. "Out in the open it was still quite bright out, but deep in the woods, the shadows were extremely long." Gary saw a shape. A small bear was visiting the area first. Later, a larger—much larger bear—crept in, nose sampling the air in every direction. At that point, the smaller bear departed.

Gary's reaction had to be instantaneous. He knew from experience that opportunities are lost in a split second when there's a slight wind shift, or "the bear looks right up and sees you sitting there." Gary saw his shot and he shouldered the rifle. The shot was quick, and clean. The family heirloom had found its mark. When he left his stand and stepped cautiously closer, his eyes widened. "The paws would make two of a man's hands," he said. "The head was broad enough of beam to set a large platter on it." Gary knew then that it was the bear of a lifetime.

This hunt went just the way everyone wanted. They don't all happen this way. Paul Laney gave an example: "Monday night of the same week we had three different hunters who saw action. One shot and killed a bear, clean. A second hunter said he missed his bear completely, and a third wounded one, which we followed until we caught up with it a mile and a quarter from where it was shot. That hunter ended up with a success and the bear was not wasted. The second hunter was a better shot than he thought. We found that animal a hundred yards from where the man had been hunting, and it was shot straight through the heart."

Hunters come to be impressed by that kind of follow-up work on the part of their hosts and guides. Many of them, like Mike Dulong, fifty, from Mason, New Hampshire, return the favor by using good judgment in the woods.

"I hunt out of Grand Lake Stream with my friend, Dave Foley. We're both guided by Paul Laney. We've been coming here for six or seven years now," Mike said. "This year, we started hunting Monday. We didn't see a thing. Tuesday there was a pretty good blow going on, but by five the wind calmed down nicely. Soon after that, I saw a cub walk into my area. Then the mother came in with two other cubs. Before long, the mother spotted me in the stand with my bow. She made noises for a bit, then walked out of the area. Two of the cubs followed her, one stayed.

"After a while, another small bear showed up. Now I was up to five bears, but I still didn't see a shot I could be confident about. I waited, and then a large male bear walked in. I estimated his weight at one hundred and eighty pounds. He also saw me in my stand, and we ended up in a staring contest. I guess I lost because he disappeared. Not long after that, I saw another male circling the area from a distance. That made seven bears in one evening, and I never fired a shot," said Mike, an experienced bow hunter who knows a good shot when he sees one.

Hunters like Gary Hanlin give others something to shoot for. That evening, his bear weighed in at the Pine Tree Store at 435 pounds! For days to come, eyes would bulge and heads would be scratched in front of the The Board at the store. Hanlin's party is now up to fourteen hunters. Next time, he'll probably have some competition to tote that .35 Remington.

Extended Season

The state hatchery in town provides three-fourths of the spring yearling salmon stocked annually in Maine lakes. These fish are raised from brood stock derived from the eggs of mature fish already in the West Grand Lake system. Egg gathering takes place in the fall after the close of the two extended seasons: October 15 on West Grand Lake, and October 20 on the stream.

It coincides with the annual fall sampling of landlocked salmon—a checkup and overview of the general health of the fishery.

Dave Marsanskis, fish culture supervisor at the hatchery, is usually accompanied by state fish pathologist Dr. Russell Danner, as they and the hatchery staff handle hundreds of spawn-ripe fish. They also will be joined for one day by Region C fish biologists who will take length and weight data on one hundred samples.

For the weeklong operation, a kind of dry dock is floated in old Hatchery Cove, the site of the original salmon hatchery just above West Grand Lake Dam on the west side. Male and female salmon, previously trapped in net cages strategically placed where the lake narrows so they interrupt the migration path toward the stream, are segregated into different pens. It's easy for a trained eye to distinguish the sex of these salmon: males stand out for their larger heads, hooked jaws, and darker hues; females are brighter, showing more silvery tones, and their heads are noticeably smaller.

About 900 salmon are viewed for the fall sampling, but only 150 pairs are spawned to meet the hatchery's annual egg quota. Before being relieved of their eggs, females are partially anesthetized with clove oil, the same natural sedative used during the spring fin-clipping process. It is applied all over their bodies and, in minutes, they are lulled into a mellow state for easy handling. When the time comes, females are held firmly in one hand and stripped with the thumb and forefinger of the other hand in a downward, milking motion. Bright orange eggs the size of lentils drop out by the dozen, and each female is good for about a thousand of them. The eggs drop into plastic bowls where they are quickly fertilized by the milt similarly stripped from males.

One year, I watched Danner take fish from the pens, sterilize them with an iodine solution, and then test them for various diseases. If these are to be the progenitors of the hatchery's brood stock—stock that will eventually travel all over Maine and out of state as well—he wants to be sure they don't carry dangerous pathogens that can be passed to thousands of hatchery-reared fish.

For decades, there's been a debate over the flow of fish into the stream and back up into Grand Lake. One school believes that after spawn-ripe salmon drop down, they're never coming back to the lake. They may hold in the stream for a time or even one of the downstream lakes, but eventually they'll pass through the St. Croix system and out to sea. In other words, they'll become, according to this school of thought, Atlantic salmon, the species from which they derive. "It's true they're in a weakened state post-spawn," said now-retired senior Region C fish biologist Ron Brokaw, "but a small percentage of them might make an effort to get back into the lake. "It's well into June when salmon would want to return to the lake, and they'd have more energy then to do so."

One of my clients, Debra Van Runkle, and I watched the hatchery crew one raw October morning as they were trying to net the contents of the cages in gusting winds. We then headed down to the Dam Pool below the gates and the fish ladder. Debra was ready to be baptized into a sport calling her back to Maine after living in California for many years. The day was miserably perfect for salmon, but Debra just donned her rain gear, tucked her blonde hair under the hood, and said with believable enthusiasm, "Let's go!" A good steady rain was falling while leaders were tied, knots were demonstrated, and reasons for fly choices were explained. Then, it was time to walk down the steep path to the stream and find our wading legs.

There is nothing so distracting or so frustrating to a fly-fishing student as a pool full of rising salmon. They had been dropping into the pool steadily since the start of October. The hatchery crew just above us on the lake was having good luck intercepting the migrating fish. They were heavy, spawn-ripe, and hungry. Debra was entranced by the spectacle of the visible salmon in the pool, including a twenty-inch fish within kicking distance. With her concentration interrupted, she bypassed the basics at first, but after a short time, she regrouped, with the assurance that everyone new to the sport faces the same challenges. Yes, the line needs time to unfurl, both backward and forward. It's a big leap of faith to believe that by working the rod a little more slowly, the line can actually stay airborne. It will, but not until all the impatient bull-whipping is out of one's system, and the beauty of the sport is allowed to make its graceful entrance. That's a special moment.

To keep things as uncomplicated as possible, I selected a black ghost streamer for Debra, one without too much hackle, which would increase wind resistance and cause "helicoptering." The rain was now in competition with the salmon for dimpling the Dam Pool's surface. I showed Debra different stripping rhythms—the action of pulling the line through the fingers—with the hope of mimicking a swimming smelt. Suddenly, in the middle of one of her practice retrieves—the rod tip was pulled down into the stream.

"Aagh! I think it's a fish!! What do I do now?"

The second most distracting thing that can happen to a fly-casting student is to hook a fish. It means fast-forwarding to chapter six before covering one through five. In spite of rain, wind, and adrenaline, Debra composed herself, even while white-knuckling the butt section of her fly rod. She heard my pleas for a tight line, but it went slack when the fish came toward her. As if part of some educational conspiracy, however, this salmon was still there when Debra took up the slack.

Debra soon realized it was possible to hold the line with her "trigger hand" and reel up slack with the other until she could play this fish from the reel. When all the slack was in, she lifted the tip and slowly worked the fish toward her as if she'd been at this longer than she had. She heard my warning that this fish would find a second wind when it saw her boots. When the eighteen-inch salmon swam in by Debra's knees, it bolted downstream with the added force of the current and its second wind. Debra's reel sang. Her mouth fell open as she felt the power being transmitted up the line and down the rod to her hands. The strong salmon did an about-face, and then swam just as fast right for her "Reel! Reel, Debra!" Inevitably, the line went slack for a moment, but the black ghost was embedded well. When her line tightened up, she shouted, "I've still got him!"

The fish was finally fatigued by its own spellbinding river dance and Debra was able to "float" it. She ran her fingers lightly over the glistening, silvery sides of the male salmon, felt the kype in its lower jaw, said her own private thank-you for the great ride, and prepared to release her prize. She put one hand under the belly and one along the tail and briefly "swam" the fish, which accepted the massage calmly, then darted away as if nothing had happened. Debra stood up straight and blew out a long sigh. "I've just caught my first salmon!! My first salmon!"

It wasn't the time to tell Debra that victory, to the beginner, bestows a premature confidence. It was, after all, her first day. Most beginners find it difficult to go back to chapters one through five when, with only a little knowledge and a lot of luck, a triumphant moment came calling. Instead, Debra seemed humbled by the experience. There are no round shoulders when we go back to hauling and line-stripping techniques. She goes on to cast all day in the rain with several more welcome interruptions from willing, sporting salmon. She made up her mind before leaving California she wasn't going to go about this in half measures. She'll see it through, learn, and tomorrow, she'll fly solo.

Escape from Beantown

A crew of television professionals from Boston's WCVB-TV 5 has graced the riffles and eddies of Grand Lake Stream through the terms of five U.S. presidents beginning with Jimmy Carter. It all started in Codyville.

Go left at the end of the ten-mile Grand Lake Stream Road, and sixteen miles north up U.S. Route 1, and you'll come to Codyville. Don't go right instead of left at this junction with Route 1, or you could wind up in Key West, Florida. Codyville boasts no post office, no police force, no Main Street with boutiques or bistros. It is something like the little brother of Topsfield, which does have a post office.

The TV crew's base of operations in Codyville was a real camp. No satellite TV, no sauna, no microwave or laundry service. There were bunks. There was a pump. There was a woodstove and a woodpile. There was an outhouse. "On the way to enlightenment, chop wood and carry water," says the eastern proverb, and in the Codyville corner of eastern Maine where it sidles up to New Brunswick, Canada, that's just what these fly fishermen from Beantown did.

The group's spring fishing jaunt to the north woods was begun by "the best TV director I ever worked with," said Bob Oliver, a WCVB cameraman. His name is Richard Puttkamer, affectionately known to his chums as "Putt."

Especially in the early years, Putt was the group's angling Pied Piper, who, instead of leading fly-fishing novitiates to their doom, led them to promising pools where their salmon skills could be honed under his watchful eye. He explained when to use certain flies, and why. He held court on lies and feeding lanes, on insect hatches and water temperatures that changed salmon behaviors. The group enthroned him as president of their "Grand Lake Stream Salmon Association."

Eventually, new anglers from in front of and behind the WCVB cameras joined the spring rite. When the Codyville camp practically fell in on itself, the then-larger group booked into Canal Side Cabins on the banks of Grand Lake Stream. Here, proprietors John and Mary Arcaro provided the freedoms that perfectly suited the free-ranging fishermen. A second annual trip was added in the fall, and GLSSA membership grew. Bob Oliver, Bob Carrol, Bob Hak, Rich Spongberg, Mike Fosco, Reggie Power, Peter Mehegan, Tony Coleman, Geoff Sullivan, and Mike Keller now comprise the core group, while guests sometimes post as honorary members.

For this group, fishing is exactly half the fun. When the final slivers of light in the western sky fade to black, it's time to troop uphill to the cabins. Wet waders and fly vests are hung on porch pegs as somebody starts rattling pots and pans in the kitchen. Later, when commotion from the cleanup quiets, a welcome sound is heard. It's the tuning of a banjo, a violin, and guitars. Then the plaintive notes of a harmonica. These sounds eventually coalesce into a first song that everyone knows and sings. The floodgates are now open. Songs move around the cabin in round-robin fashion, each musician taking his turn as maestro. All evening a crescendo builds until someone mentions "Barrett's Privateers," a boisterous, bawdy folk ballad that could bring even the lame to their feet. The last echoes of the full-voiced refrain ricochet uplake off the shores of Whitney Cove sometime around three o'clock in the morning. So go the biannual conferences of the GLSSA, reminiscent of the great fishing clubs of Teddy Roosevelt's time, only these days, this one continues without its founder.

Richard Puttkamer was a fly-fishing celebrity in Grand Lake Stream for forty years. Without intending it, his presence raised the stakes for others in a pool, as though something unassumingly authoritative and immortal attended him in all the waters he waded. Putt's body is built for rivers: not too tall, not too short, of sufficient width and breadth to stand strong current—a serendipitous composition of features given that his feet are planted there more often than on dry land. His head appears bedecked with coarse hackle rather than hair, not combed, but to all appearances, whip-finished. His refulgent, broad-cheeked smile is all bright jungle-eye and flashaboo. His jocund demeanor presents a tinseled, blood-red attractant to which no true sporting soul is immune.

Rather than take offense, Putt would agree with Steinbeck that any man who pits his intelligence against a fish and loses deserves it. Ever the student of stream life, he would earn a nugget of knowledge from each such loss, and then, the wiser, employ it against the same fish the next day. One raw October morning, my wife was crossing Grand Lake Stream on its only traffic bridge when she recognized Putt, one hundred yards upstream, a lone fisherman standing in the river. It was snowing sideways. Putt was hunched over, glaring intently at a particular spot. He was wearing fingerless gloves and had a sweatshirt hood pulled up over his head.

"How did you know it was him?" I asked.

She shrugged, "No one looks that way in the river except Putt."

She slowed, watched him for a minute longer until he lifted his rod, and in one overhead sweep, laid out practically his entire fly line. In the next instant, Putt's spine straightened, his right arm came up sharply, and the slate-gray patina of the river tableau exploded in white froth. Putt looked up and saw his witness on the bridge, and she, the teeth of his triumphant smile.

If put on a stringer, moments like these in Putt's rich fishing career would belly it in the middle. No one who has seen the hot embers in his eyes during a Hendrickson hatch could escape the contagion of Putt's fervor. After the last casts of a long day of river fishing, one might expect to find him by the fire reading Lefty Kreh or Frank Amato or William G. Tapply. Instead, he'd be holding court in the cabin among the friends of his passion. Recitations, singing, toasting, and celebrating until the wee hours never scotched Putt's posting on the river the next morning. He was always in good fetter when the salmon awoke.

His friends in the GLSSA saw the sport ennobled by Putt's presence, and now, his passion is theirs as well. Richard Puttkamer and his lengthening legend now wade the waters of the great Northwest. As the new millenium began, he moved to the state of Washington. In his absence, Bob Oliver is "acting president" of the Grand Lake Stream Salmon Association.

Fly Rods & Shotguns

The first day of October bushwhacking always evokes those earliest memories of high-stepping through thick covers with a pungent smell in the air. That J.C. Higgins, bolt-action 12-gauge from Sears—the one you deep-sixed in a stream you tried to cross—comes to mind, too, as does the face, posture, and name of each one of the springer family: Duke, Patsy, Ting, Kafka. Off to one side was Dad hounding the dog to keep to the business at hand; off to the other was a brother with a better shotgun than yours. Nothing equaled that pitch of tension when the dog began to "make game" and you knew what was coming. What you didn't know was which way the bird would break and who would get the shot. Of course, the clearest memories are of the times it broke your way and all of the day's glory belonged to you.

One early October as I was fishing the stream with the headmaster of a private school on the Maine coast, he blurted out that he looked forward to this time of year more than any other because he could pack both his fly rod and his shotgun. He's not the only one to favor the season. The census of upland bird hunters booking accommodations at local sporting lodges is up in recent years, and it appears that after a long respite, northern Washington County may again become the wingshooting destination it once was.

Estimates of ruffed grouse harvested annually in Maine are now thought to be in the range of half a million. Hard information on this Maine game bird is scant because research funding has been nearly nonexistent. Most of the "field work" is the result of polling moose permittees and their parties at check stations around the state. The last attempt at a serious survey of grouse harvested in Maine was in 1988, when around 580,000 birds were taken. Some would say it's ironic that this popular and often prolific game bird has done quite well on its own with little or no official management policy. Others would say it's remarkable that research for such an important sporting bird in Maine is so underfunded. Nevertheless, the future presents a challenge as hunter numbers and season lengths increase.

The other upland bird drawing avid wingshooters to local lodges is the American woodcock. This ground-feeder is extraordinary for more reasons than its many colloquial names—timberdoodles, mud-suckers, mud-bats, woodcock—or its classification as a shorebird when it is decidedly not one (ranging as far west as Manitoba). Hunters who are not bird-watchers miss out on "the singing grounds," the incomparable mating performance of male woodcocks in May. Males sing a trill of up to a couple dozen notes, then launch themselves, spiraling up and up, singing to the accompaniment of the wind whistling through their brindled plumage. Mate-able females are seduced by several repetitions of the singing ground spectacle.

During their life span of more or less five years, woodcocks need not one, but a variety of habitats: clearings or strips of open land; dense, soft-bottomed thickets of alders; and young forests. These account for the woodcock's three major needs of mating, feeding, and birthing.

American woodcock populations throughout their range from Canada to the eastern United States and reaching as far as east Texas have been declining at the rate of 1 percent per year for more than thirty-five years, according to the Breeding Bird Survey. That's the bad news. The good news is that Maine may be the outstanding exception. In other states, the lack of timber cutting and the absence of early development such as that resulting from abandoned farmland are chief factors in this decline. Timbering is still a viable industry in Maine, and a large share of huntable retired farmland acreage in northern Washington County has not been replaced with residential development, as is the case in points south.

The last major research effort on the federally regulated, migratory woodcock was a four-year joint study concluded in the fall of 2001. The agencies involved were U.S. Fish and Wildlife, the U.S. Geological Survey, and the Migratory Bird Project of Maine. There were three study sites in Maine, two where hunting is permitted, and one—Moosehorn National Wildlife Refuge near Calais—where it is not. Data collected from tagged and radio-fitted birds revealed that fall survival rates are very nearly the same in hunted vs. non-hunted areas. Mammals and raptors were the chief causes of death to woodcock in all areas studied. From the study, it was determined that hunting is not hampering regeneration of the species throughout its Eastern range, including Maine.

The report revealed that in 1996, 26,000 birds were taken by approximately 8,300 hunters. This increased by the year 2000 to 27,750 woodcock being harvested by 9,100 hunters. Thanks to more effective hunter surveys and the federal Woodcock Conservation Plan, these figures may continue to rise despite its "Bird of Concern" listing by the U.S. Shorebird Conservation Plan due to its thirty-five-year decline. More and more volunteer-supported efforts like the Woodcock Initiative are raising public awareness about the importance of renewed habitat for the American woodcock.

At some of the local sporting lodges, hunters use their own dogs or those provided by the lodge. Parties travel a radius, typically two or three hunters to a guide, covering some of the most productive upland bird habitat in the state.

A guide's grouse "coverts" are his lifeline in fall. They are the hard-won result of dogged, preseason driving, traipsing, and scouting. Birds tend to stay within the same ten- to thirty-acre home territory, and during the hunting season, guides will stagger visits to coverts so as not to upset or abuse one area too much. Such pay dirt only needs to be productive for about six weeks of the year, so the good guide acts as its steward and is understandably bashful about giving up its coordinates.

Newer hunters need to make the distinction between ruffed grouse and spruce grouse or risk a hunting violation. Most spruce grouse are seen roaming the woods on foot; they seldom spook and boil up in the manner of their ruffed cousin. The male wears a red eye-patch, not the female, and the overall coloration is of grayish-brown. Spruce grouse are far less numerous than ruffed grouse but can inhabit the same areas.

Ruffed grouse won't let you get too close before flushing or at least taking off at a dead run. The most obvious sign that it's a legal bird to shoot is the thick, black band running laterally across its tail feathers. Black feathers also adorn both sides of its neck. There is no open season on spruce grouse in Maine, while the ruffed grouse season runs from October 1 through the end of December.

Woodcock seasons run shorter than those for grouse, and bag limits are regulated federally. The woodcock wingshot is a favorite for hunters with dogs that point. When the release command is given and the timberdoodle takes to wing, it can fly an uncanny zigzag pattern or go straight up overhead, all the while *cheep-cheep-cheeping* with the sound of the wind in its wings.

It's now safe to say that the bird-hunting business is back in force, with lodging, guides, and dogs enough to make anyone's bushwhacking vacation a memorable one. October in Grand Lake Stream is that special month of the year when fly rods and shotguns make grand bedfellows.

The Hill Gould Horns

In October of 1910, Frank Ball, who owned the sporting camps in Grand Lake Stream now known as Weatherby's, bought a set of deer horns for ten dollars. That was a tidy sum in 1910 when frivolous purchases were necessarily few and far between. But Frank Ball had a good sense for the remarkable. Those deer horns, which he later sold after they were prepared by Bangor taxidermists S. L. Crosby Co., went on to become as renowned as the camps he sold to Beverly Weatherby in the 1920s. Both the antlers and the camps had appreciated nicely for him by then.

These weren't just any deer horns. As testimony to this, their home today is the Bass Pro Wildlife Museum in Springfield, Missouri, and alternately, other Bass Pro sites. "The most massive deer ever" was how Ron Boucher described the horns in a 1999 article he wrote for *Big Buck Magazine* based in Saskatoon, Saskatchewan.

By the time Boucher caught up with them, these antlers had had a more spangled career than some Hollywood screen actors. They had traveled all over the U.S. and Canada, had been through at least a half-dozen owners, and had left behind a trail of photographs and articles as well as a growing body of legend, mystery, and speculation.

It is the reigning Maine champion-record non-typical buck, having scored an amazing 259 Boone and Crockett points. In the B&C system, racks that score over 200 non-typical make big press. Racks in the 205 to 230 class are considered colossal. The only word for the rack that has been known for ninety years, no matter who owned it, as The Hill Gould Head, is Promethean.

Hill Mulberry Gould, Maine Guide, family man, and veteran of "the war that would make the world safe for democracy" is buried in the town of his birth, at the Grand Lake Stream cemetery. It was before he became all these things, however, that he had an encounter with the white-tailed buck of any deer hunter's dreams, never mind a young man of eighteen.

In an environment that forged "rugged individualism" long before Herbert Hoover coined the phrase, eighteen-year-olds had to be woods-savvy. Many of them were already working on the long lumbering operations by that age. They were equally handy on river drives and with explosives to free logjams. Hill Gould had more than his share of these skills, as did his twin brother, Eldon Gould, who accompanied Hill on that auspicious hunt, October 8, 1910.

Anna Cataldo, Hill Gould's daughter, was often sought out over the years to recount her father's tale. She did so for me one morning in her Grand Lake Stream home. I arrived unannounced. Anna led, and I followed her, to the smells of fresh coffee and raspberry pie in the kitchen. It is always surprising to learn how often widows bake in the morning, as though for an unexpected guest.

Anna said that around 1960, Bud Leavitt, outdoor columnist for *The Bangor Daily News*, wrote a piece on the Hill Gould Head without interviewing Hill himself. Anna was miffed. She sat her dad down at the kitchen table deciding once and for all to get straight the story of her father's famous hunt that fall day more than fifty years earlier. When she had it all down, Anna typed it up, then sent it off to Bud Leavitt. She never heard back.

Anna's retelling of Hill Gould's hunt was straight to the point, colorful, and often edged with humor. She cut me a piece of raspberry pie, poured my coffee mug full, and began.

"Dad was born with a caul over his head, and in those days, that meant good luck. If you were born with the caul, you would never want for material things, and it would seem as if good fortune always just fell in your lap."

"That day [October 8, 1910] there were four other men with Dad: his brother Eldon, Freddy Baker, Tom Shaw, and Kizzy Kennison. They hunted from a camp out where the South Branch of Little River flows into Little River proper. The camp was called The Bear's Den. On that morning, Dad walked up on the Horseback to a section that looks down on Little River. There were some shallow rips there where deer were known to have crossed since anyone could remember.

"In those days, the deer season opened October 1. With a license, you were allowed three deer and one moose, but the moose season didn't open until later in the month. Once on the Horseback, Dad decided to still-hunt from a stump that was handy to the lane used by deer crossing the stream. By and by, he heard a lot of loud crashing coming right toward him through the alders. There were several deer, mostly does. When they came into view they were still partially camouflaged by the alders. When Dad saw the horns on that buck, he thought it was a moose, and he held his fire. When he finally made it out to be a deer, he let fly with the .30-30."

Anna said her dad was a long time dressing out his prize and a long time hiking back to camp with the heart and liver. This was in pre-coyote days when successful hunters could leave a deer out overnight if need be. When Hill reached camp at dusk, the other men had the lanterns lit. He plunked the heart and liver down on the camp table and the others let out a cheer that Hill had bagged himself a moose, even if a little early in the season. When Hill told them that the parts belonged to a deer, they all decided to hike the two miles back to the site to check out Hill's claim for themselves. With lanterns shining the way, they made the trek. Arriving at the scene, the whole group marveled at the hulking deer and the unbelievable rack of horns adorning its massive head.

Next morning, the men collected a canoe from town and spent the entire day getting the Goliath out of the South Branch country and back to Grand Lake Stream. Once back, they dressed and divided up the venison. Hill Gould was able to hang a wedding ring on fifty-two points of the rack. There may have been more that were just nubbins, too small or rounded off that would not hold a ring. By 1984, Boone and Crockett had scaled the rack down by 20 points to 33 scorable points, and it still bashed all previous records. The palms of the horns mimicked those of a moose, and the biggest circumference measurement at the base of one of the horns was an awesome thirteen inches. No wonder it fetched a handsome ten dollars from Frank Ball in 1910!

There is evidence that Hill Gould's good luck was transferred with his death to the Hill Gould Head itself. One of its many purchasers had built a brand-new home and barn on Mount Desert Island. When completed, the man of the house saw the perfect place to hang the trophy—right over the fireplace mantel. The missus said, "Not on your life," and so it was relegated to the barn. In the great Mount Desert fire of 1947—which devastated huge sections of the island—the house burned, but not the barn. The Hill Gould Head survived to be purchased yet again, continuing its own career while extending the fame of Hill Mulberry Gould.

Today, a picture of the massive antlers is on display in The Pine Tree Store in Grand Lake Stream.

Old Maine Guide

Val Moore had been asked so many times by so many different people whether he was going to hunt this year that he was getting annoyed. Why was everyone pestering him? Why did they care? His guiding buddies—the ones still around—and just about anybody he ran into at the store all wanted an answer. His response was, "Don't think so," just to put them off. The seventy-one-year-old knew it was because of his age that they were asking. He knew what they were really after. If they could get a "yes," it would make them feel younger.

At what age does a man stop hunting? He guessed it varied, but he'd know when the time came for him, and he sure didn't need to advertise it. His wife, Mary, was not one of those asking about his plans. She just did the things she usually did as the season turned from fall foliage to ice in the puddles. She watched him putting wood up, doing the odd painting job here and there, scraping the leaves out of the gutters, puttying a window, and sawing out some ash.

Opening day of the regular firearms season arrived early that year—October 29. The day came and went and he didn't notice a thing. Nothing about the day, the weather, or the way he felt seemed to invoke the slightest yen. So, he just let it pass. He did muster enough interest to drive by the store a few times that day to see if there were any deer being weighed. (The scale tower stood out back of the store like a scaffold in a Western movie.) He also stopped in at closing time that day to hear the scuttlebutt and the tally of tagged deer—two.

He knew he'd put hunting on that lengthening list of things he figured himself too old to do, especially now with that one blamed, aching knee. To help himself adjust to his advancing years, he preferred to pass off these things as "nonsense." He now preferred to think of things like deer hunting as amusing, definitely not something he needed to do. He surely didn't need the meat like back in the poor times. And how ridiculous was it for a seventy-something old geezer to be chasing around in the willywacks, getting soaked, cold, played out, and skunked besides?

Yes, he used to guide hunters back when deer were plentiful and most sports left with a nice buck. He's in a lot of the old pictures with groups of guides and huge game poles with more antler points than you could shake a stick at. Every now and then some magazine writer wants to hear all about that. He does the best he can to be civil, but what he really wants to say is, "You had to be there." Nowadays, a fellow could walk all month and never see an ear or a white flag go up. "Coyotes and too much cuttin' took the best of it" was how he, and the remaining guides his age, explained what happened.

Unseasonably warm, Indian summer days the first week of November did nothing for gumption. They were the perfect excuse to continue with work that usually would've been cut short by cold weather. It also served to quiet the questioners since few folks want to hunt in the heat. He pointed up the bricks on the chimney where the masonry had cracked. He put a new downspout on the house and aimed the water away from the foundation. He even put an extra coat of varnish on the inside of his canoe. He had guided a couple dozen dates last season—mostly longtime clients who'd be back again next summer for sure. Varnishing now was one less chore he'd have in the spring.

The wind picked up to start the second week of November, and with it, he felt the air changing. The temperature dropped into the twenties Tuesday night so that by morning, there was a firm coat of frost on everything. After a second cup of coffee that morning, his wife watched him fumble around outside, come back into the house once more, then finally drive away slowly in his truck. She noticed he had changed his hat.

He had already decided he wasn't really going hunting. Yes, the .38-70 was resting, muzzle down, beside him on the bench seat of his blue, F-150 pickup, but that was no big deal. Not around here. Almost any truck this time of year had some kind of firearm in it. The fact that he slipped on a vest and stepped out of the truck at a certain spot on a certain trail that formed a "horseback" didn't mean anything, either. There had always been a well-used game crossing across this hump from swampy lowlands on one side to thick softwoods on the other, and it was fun to see if there were frosty tracks frozen into the mud. Yes, he and the sports with him had taken many deer here in the past, but today, he was just sampling the air, nosing around to see if he saw a track or two to pass the time. Anyone might do that. It doesn't mean you've gone hunting.

A little farther along that trail—past the usual deer crossing—he noticed a trampled area, and when he glanced into the softwoods to the right, he saw that an alder was rubbed bare about a foot and a half off the ground. The wind was, for a change, light. As he stepped off the horseback and into the softwoods, he felt just the slightest coolness on his face. That light breeze was coming from the west. He liked that.

He walked another twenty-five yards and there, beneath an outstretched, low hemlock limb, he saw a fresh scrape on the ground. Very fresh. In the center, he could see the cloven print. It was splayed wide at the toes, and both dew claws made their impressions behind them. "Hefty animal," he thought. He took in the sharp, almost harsh odor of the turned-up moss and humus. He let this smell linger in his nostrils. It was the smell of wonderful memories and it made him forget the pain in the knee that always bothered him.

He followed the obvious game path through the softwoods, one slow step at a time, two-handing the .38-70 at port arms. He did this from habit since it was much quicker to raise a rifle from chest to shoulder than from side or waist to shoulder. The hemlocks gave way to a thick stand of young firs, and mixed among them were a few larch trees. The terrain then lifted gently into a knoll. "Nice bedding area," he thought. On the far side of the knoll he found a stump not yet rotted through since the last cutting. It had a westerly view—into the wind—though nicely broken up by saplings. He sat down and laid the rifle across his knees. He looked up, then looked back down at the gun, and it all came back.

It was an old, family hand-me-down. He was well aware of the new, high-powered, "red dot" rifles used by younger hunters. One of the young guides showed him one he'd just bought, and Val acted impressed just to be nice. For him, this rifle stood apart from those long-range, level-shooting marvels of ballistic engineering. This rifle actually meant something. Open sighted, light as his 16-gauge, he could carry it all day and "slap shoot" when a jumped deer bounded away, making it impossible to scope with more modern rifles. "Give me open sights," he'd said a thousand times around the cribbage board in hunting camps. How many deer had fallen before this sweetheart? He couldn't even imagine. One day, it would be passed down again, and come to think of it, it was overdue for a thorough cleaning.

A loud crunch jerked his attention up off his lap and threw it to the west where the saplings ended and a stand of hardwoods began. He held his breath, then heard another crunch.

Grand Lake Stream Primers

Anna Cataldo's books, *Pod Run* and *Guides For Hire*, co-authored with her mother, Ada Chambers, were read for half a century by people hungry for the feel of life in a tiny village surrounded by wilderness. Long out of print, they can still be found on bookshelves in local homes. Sports who booked trips to Grand Lake Stream complete with accommodations and guide would sometimes ask lodge owners for reading materials to help them get the feel of their destination. Three books topped that list: Anna's *Guides For Hire*, *Up and Down the River*, by Edmund Ware Smith, and *Grand Lake Stream Plantation*, by Minnie Atkinson. These provided a crash course on Grand Lake Stream for sports from away.

He felt his heart miss a beat, and when it kicked in again, it was at twice its former rate. He opened his mouth to breathe so that the sound of air passing through his nostrils wouldn't override his ability to hear. Then something strange happened. He became aware of himself—heart pounding, short breath, and even a bead of sweat under his hat brim. He had to snicker. It was exactly this way when he was fourteen years old.

In the next moment, he felt a coolness wafting across the back of his neck. The wind had shifted! Right on cue came a loud snort and the heart-sinking, retreating sound of twigs and dead branches breaking as the buck bolted downwind. The old guide let out his breath.

Before walking into the store at four o'clock, he paused for a moment, deciding whether to change his orange hat. "Hell with it," he muttered under his breath, snickering again. As he stepped out of his truck, another truck pulled up with an eight-pointer in the bed. He joined a group of hunters milling about to hear the blow-by-blow account of the successful hunt. When Kurt Cressey came out to weigh the animal, he saw Val standing there with his orange hat on and said, "You been out, Val?" He shrugged his shoulders. "Took a walk's all."

That evening, it was *Wheel of Fortune* and *Jeopardy* on the tube as usual. He didn't let on where he'd been that day. Neither did Mary ask. She'd noticed that he'd come home wearing his orange hat, but she knew better than to bring it up. Later as she cleaned up in the kitchen, she occasionally glanced out to the living room. She saw him pull out his gun-cleaning supplies from a drawer in his rifle safe and settle in with the .38-70. He looked at it from every angle, cleaning the trigger guard, sights, stock, and forearm as carefully as he cleaned the bore and the action.

When she came out of the kitchen he looked up, then looked back at his work, blushing. He thought she might ask what he was up to, or even what his plans were for tomorrow, but she never did. She sat down across from him, turned on the floor lamp, and picked up her knitting. After a long time, he spoke.

"Might take a walk in the mornin'," he said.

Just as she knew he would.

Blind-Sided

Paul Wilbur and I had been the first ones to arrive at deer camp that year. Not a shot had been fired all week. For the most part, the rains had been steady during the days, before dropping back to a drizzle at night. The swamps had taken in more water than they could hold, and there were now new lakes that needed naming. The largest puddle in the camp road had been dubbed "The Car Wash" since everybody's truck got a thorough dousing each time through.

Most of the six men in this hunting party have known each other all of their lives, although Paul, who lives in Woodstock, Connecticut, was just approaching a decade of history with the group. All were in their mid- to late-fifties that year, but this was no couch-potato deer camp. Ours was a hunting routine that kicked in like clockwork on Day One and continued until Saturday afternoon of Day Six: Hunt all morning, break for lunch and sometimes a short nap, then hunt until dark. The entourage had hunted through the adverse conditions of the week with no shots fired, and now, all were heading out on the last morning of our annual November get-together.

Overnight Friday the rain quit, and Saturday morning was a welcome contrast. As the sun came up, steam rose from moss-coated rocks. The quiet was intense. Day Six has a way of putting the hunters in a pensive mood, but this was the first morning they could see well and hear well. Everyone's senses were enlivened. What was left of a moon that had been full as the week began still had enough candlepower to light up the pre-dawn woods. All wind had abated and the stillness that replaced it was deafening in a different way. This was a morning for checking your pulse by listening to it in your ears. This was a morning for hearing a twig snap a hundred yards away.

Since there had been no compelling signs of any real rutting activity, the hunting choices on this morning of hope were based more on previous years' experiences. Six hunters spread out on the compass—two in a southerly direction, two westerly, one went east, while I went north to the edge of a swamp only a long stone's throw from the camp.

The sun rose and the softwoods dripped loudly onto beech leaves below as one of the westerly hunters reached his destination and settled in for a long sit. Paul, who knew roughly where this chum was headed, made a mental note of that location in relation to his as he settled into his own spot—a natural ground blind, partially masked from open view by the root ball of a fallen tree.

Paul had just come through a couple of rough years and was happy to be hunting. First, there was a table saw accident that took parts of three fingers on his right hand. Of course Paul was right-handed and, of course, carpentry, cabinet-making, and skilled handyman work were his first loves next to hunting. He now had to get used to the loss of feeling, the numbness in the slightest bit of cold weather, and the thimble-like protuberances worn on the fingers to protect them following the surgery. That was enough of a life-changing experience for one year, but there was more in store the next.

A rare glaucoma-related condition had begun to cause severe, sometimes debilitating pain in Paul's right eye. Nothing brought much relief. He went through different pain prescriptions, some of them so strong that they rendered him completely immobile—definitely not Paul's thing. New doctors and new treatment plans were no more successful, and when the vision in Paul's right eye foundered and eventually failed, the excruciating pain did not. The time came when the idea of losing that eye no longer competed with the idea of losing the pain.

I was keeping in touch with my friend by e-mail and phone during this period. The surgery went successfully, and Paul was fitted for a prosthetic eye. He had months of healing and learning to see with only one eye, but the absence of pain was like a new lease on life. Paul came to hunting camp that fall compromised on his right side by the loss of fingers and sight, but not in the least bit by any loss of enthusiasm or sense of humor.

Humor in a hunting camp tends toward the thick-skinned variety. One wiseacre reminded Paul that Lord Nelson, hero of the Battle of Trafalgar, scored his greatest victories after suffering virtually the same losses as Paul's. Paul's laughs were as hearty as the rest, but then he wondered aloud how the wiseacre might like finding a glass eye at the bottom of his toddy, staring up at him like a conscience. This is never a gathering for the faint of heart.

Just before eight that morning, Alan Burnell, who had settled in east of Paul's position, caught in his peripheral vision some movement over his right shoulder. As Alan knew from a lifetime of hunting, all large bucks enter from the right if you're right-handed, and from the left if you're left-handed. In either case, your muzzle is always pointed in the wrong direction. Was this movement from a large buck or from a deer at all? At this point it could just as easily be a chickadee or a squirrel. Could he pivot his torso without drawing attention to himself? Doubtful. He was on the ground on a plane with anything else on the ground. What he needed to do was get whatever it was out of his peripheral vision and into his vision. That meant putting his neck into a slow-motion right turn.

"How did a buck that size get within twenty-five yards without me hearing it?" was all Alan could think as his heart somersaulted. As soon as Alan spotted him, the buck moved forward so that his head and shoulders were behind a big hemlock trunk. Alan had seen this happen before. It was as if the buck knew he'd been seen and was now hiding. He seized the moment to try to turn his body to the right some more. The small amount of air movement seemed to be in the hunter's favor. Holding his breath, he inched his way around. Then, something—who knows what, some sensation or presentiment on the part of the buck—caused him and his heavy headgear to bound away, keeping, of course, the hemlock tree between himself and Alan, whose rifle was now at his shoulder.

Alan reacted quickly. He came to his feet and set off high-stepping roots and rocks and runoffs to get another view of that buck. What lay ahead of the whitetail, if he kept a steady course, was a stand of blinding thick softwoods just over a ridge. The deer would surely set a course there for refuge.

It wasn't that far, but it was all uphill. There wasn't a lot of other noise in the woods competing with Alan's footfall since

Photo courtesy of Randy Spencer

Here we are at my old Grand Lake Stream camp. Left to right: Paul Wilbur, Skip Burnell, me, the late Barry Burnell, Ian Spencer, and Alan Burnell.

the ground had not frozen overnight. This was a good thing. He scaled the ridge, and for some unknown reason, the buck paused before moving into the softwoods. Had he heard something up ahead? Or was he just plain curious? All experienced hunters have seen a mature buck jeopardize himself with that kind of curiosity. Having stalled in his tracks, he finally picked up Alan's movement. He catapulted away, but not toward the softwoods. Instead, he turned—out of Alan's way—and into Paul's.

On the uphill side of Paul's root-ball ground blind, he had heard a red squirrel for the previous half hour or so. Nothing can be more nerve-wracking on a quiet morning in the woods. These busybodies have put the image of antlers into many a hunter's imagination, and an itch on the trigger finger besides. But what about that last sound the squirrel made? Something about it was different. A little too much weight maybe, or perhaps it sounded more like a step than the rodent rustle to which his ears had become accustomed. He'd better check to be sure.

Rising slowly and quietly, he was able to turn his head and look through the thick screen of roots without being seen himself. The air was in his favor. He squinted with his good (left) eye in the direction of the squirrel noise, and there it was: a twelve-point squirrel! The horizontal line of the deer's back was unmistakable. Paul's eye followed it all the way up to the glint of a bleached antler in the sun.

The buck moved forward, once again putting a mature tree between his head and the rifle. Paul brought up his .44, found the far side of the tree—awkwardly with his left eye in the scope—and waited. This time, instead of turning away and using the tree as a barrier, the buck just kept on walking. Another step put Paul's bead behind the buck's shoulder blade. Shooting left-handed was a strange sensation, but strange or not, there was now a magnificent white-tailed buck perched perfectly in his crosshairs.

Alan had frozen on the flat above the ridge, knowing the deer had chosen a perilous route. From there he heard the inimitable, thunderous *thwack!* of Paul's .44. I heard it from my position at the edge of a swamp east of Paul. *Thwack!* it went again. After a long pause, Paul fired his three consecutive shots signifying to the others that he needed some help. Alan was there before the shot's echoes played out.

The last laugh at that year's hunting camp was Paul's. For all his so-called handicaps, he had put big points on the camp scoreboard where the rest of us had none. We didn't laugh quite so loud when Paul did it again two years later.

Swamp Thing

Because of its popular association with death as well as to life forms that give us the creeps, the swamp is a paradox. It is the place that kills whole stands of trees. Then, for decades their lifeless, skeletal remains stand spookily silent over water that is ominously dark.

In Maine in November, some of the most experienced guides and hunters seek out these watery worlds. Swamps can be havens for deer, moose, bear, and many other creatures, offering a soft bed of moss, food and water, and above all, security.

Whether you float in or plod your way in on foot, you're making more noise than anything else already there. The seasoned swamp stalker knows that when he is noisy, the swamp is quiet; when he is quiet (and patient), the swamp can produce a flood of living sound.

One late deer-hunting afternoon in early November I followed a game path into a swamp I had previously scouted. It might as well have been raining. Advection fog, so common in these places when warm fronts move in over cool water, hung heavily in the air. My woolens were wet long before I reached my destination, but that's why most of us wear wool—it keeps you warm even when wet. The sound of my rubber soles snapping twigs was the only noise. No matter how far you're going into the bog, it's too far when every step is a high kick to get a leg over the cedar deadfalls, and when every few yards you put your foot into a hole that coats you to the knee with mud. Not a squirrel or a mouse was stirring as I progressed. Only later did I learn that this was a very bad time for small creatures to be on the move.

It was a full half-hour after finding a nice seat on a moss-covered stump when the ghostly silence was broken with the report of a pileated woodpecker banging the bugs out of dead trees. Hard to say how far away it was. The hollow trees and logs of a large marsh like this one create a veritable echo chamber. I marveled at what kind of shock absorber this bird must have in its neck to hammer that hard and not get whiplash. Nicknamed "Indian Hens" in the south, this variety of woodpecker was used as a model for the cartoon hero, Woody Woodpecker. Pileateds can be twenty inches tall. Their signatures on dead trees are easy to spot: large, rectangular holes where they've gone mining for carpenter ants, beetle larvae, grubs, and other insects.

Very often, if you see one pileated, you'll see two, and sure enough, a second one soon started jackhammering. Now this swamp had a rhythm section. Just as I was finding this rhythm, a chorus of crickets added their chirps in syncopation to the pileateds' log rhythms, and all this orchestra needed now was a wind instrument. At that very moment a raven flew overhead, wings whirring perfectly in concert with the swamp sonata. And to think—only minutes earlier the silence here had been deafening! After their short, impromptu performance, I finally saw the two woodpeckers that started it all, swooping through the trees in their unmistakable, peak-and-valley flight patterns.

With the subsiding din, ground noises now became audible. Of all the animals on dry and wet northern land, is any as ubiquitous as the red squirrel? As mentioned earlier, in many a deer hunter's imagination, a lot of them weigh in at two hundred pounds and have ten points. When you see them, you're a little miffed that they could make such a fool of you. Once the scurrying begins, that's all you hear. This infamous sound has masked the footfall of an approaching buck for many a hunter. For me, on this day, something did approach, but not by land.

I heard the wing-beat long before I saw the bird. When I craned my neck to see what it was, there was a four- to five-foot wingspan arching over my head. Its landing on a dead limb hanging over my seat was so unnerving, it sent a rush of blood pounding in my eardrums. The head of this bird was the size of a child's, and its swivel neck brought its dark-eyed, penetrating gaze home to me, hauntingly. Perching itself on a limb only thirty feet above, it fixed a stare on me that put a shudder in my spine. Grayish facial feathers formed a mustache, and eyebrows too. This creature loomed all too human-looking for my comfort. What's more, this bird was obviously not fazed by my presence.

The great horned owl is one of the scariest raptors to behold up close. Though its talons are hidden under ample plumage, they have a crushing power of up to five hundred pounds per square inch, while a well-conditioned man's hands might have seventy. This powerful and opportunistic predator has more than enough hair-raising physical features to suit its fearful reputation. Although this one seemed three feet tall from my position below, I guessed that its height was probably more like two and a half feet. That's awfully big for a bird. I'd already seen that its wingspan was well over four feet. Being confronted by a fierce animal in the woods, one that's not in the least bit impressed by a human presence, is a sensation wanting for good comparisons. I made "scat!" motions to which the raptor paid no attention. I knew from reading about different owls that their famous swivel necks compensated for eyeballs that cannot move in their sockets. Between their incredible eyesight in dim light and their stereo hearing, they can pinpoint prey as if with an onboard global positioning system. When it suited this giant, it gave me a good once-over, lifted its wings in horror movie fashion, and soared off. A short time after, I heard a blood-chilling scream from across the marsh, the likes of which I have never heard in a lifetime of tramping through the woods. A murder was committed that late afternoon, and its unrepentant perpetrator is still at large.

At 4:10 p.m. in mid-November, all available light is on fast fade. This is the witching hour when the heart-sinking feeling hits home that you may not encounter a whitetail on this outing. While I had seen and heard enough already to satisfy any woods traipser, I was still hoping for a crunch or a crash on the approach. Instead, a sound was delivered that made me forget all about the closest encounter I'd ever had with a killer owl. Picture Sasquatch picking up a twenty-foot hollow log and breaking it over a boulder. Imagine this being done in an echo chamber, over and over again.

I shouldered my rifle. In that instant I might've referred to it as a "weapon," so convinced was I that this sound could not be made by a game animal. Beads of sweat formed under my hat brim. I then realized that I must have stood up involuntarily. No sooner had I sat back down to ponder what in this bog could produce such a tumult, it happened again, only closer. This was not the sound of brush and branches breaking as a moose or deer advanced. It was purposeful, violent, and *loud!*

I checked my watch. It was now past the legal shooting time. I followed my feet out of that swamp much faster than they had led me in. When I reached the twitch trail from which I had taken the game path, I looked ahead and could make out a black shape several hundred yards away, crossing the same trail I was on. Was this Sasquatch leaping out of my imagination and into reality? A few more tentative steps. No—it was a black bear apparently spooked by the same racket that had prompted me to make my hasty exit.

Back in town the next day, I looked up some local bear guides. It soon came to light that the rumpus I'd heard was not Sasquatch, or even a moose. It was the sound of a bear—probably the very bear I saw—building its den. The time was right, and so, they said, was the place. Right at the edge of the swamp where the terrain rose, there were excellent opportunities for a den. Black bears, they said, will fell trees, pull apart stumps, scoop up mud and clay, and add things to a natural, cavern-like structure to make a den. The violent sounds I'd heard were now explained. The bear I'd seen wasn't fleeing those eerie sounds. He was making them.

It's a good thing to experience the swamp. Ever since the publication of Rachel Carlson's epic *Silent Spring*, which inspired a whole generation of ecological consciousness, these marshes and wetlands have slowly come to be recognized, not as wastelands, but as "cleansers" of the earth. Each one is, in its own right, a mini-ecosystem. Just as the oyster flushes and filters impurities in the sea, so does the swamp do the same work inland.

A place of teeming life, of eerie silences and blood-curdling clamor, the swamp is full of mystery. As havens for a broad array of wildlife, and sometimes for wintering deer herds, it is an important habitat that deserves both respect and protection.

Winded

The very sight of the bouldery road leading into camp produces an emotional pang, bringing back memories of seasons long gone, of deer lost and won, of many years of heart-warming fellowship. By early November, the way in is littered with gold—fallen maple leaves paving the path to the camp door. It's worth stopping for a moment just to take it all in.

The camp itself is standing there like a diary of the card games, cribbage, laughter, roasting and toasting, and practical pranks. Nothing here changes much. Everything is as it should be, right down to the old fifteen-gallon galvanized tub hanging on the outside wall of the woodshed. And there's the outhouse, or "backhouse" as folks used to say. The very sight of it is, according to one of the hunters on his way here, "enough to keep you reglah."

The arrival of each hunter to this annual summit is a jubilant, raucous affair. When all of us do finally arrive—some fatter, some thinner, some balder, some grayer, all older—we're each a sight for sore eyes, and say so. Convening here marks the passage of another year, and very few stones in that year will be left unturned during the full-voiced, nightly banters to come.

These sessions invariably bring back everyone's earliest hunting experiences, usually having to do with Dad or Gramp, or maybe an uncle. They always have to do with a Winchester Model 94 .30-30. What young hunter didn't start with this rifle? One of the guys reminds us of how, as a young boy, he once emptied his over the back of a ten-pointer because he was looking at the deer instead of the sights. As we got older, most of us followed a progression of calibers, say to a .35, then a .270, and finally a .306 or a .308. One of us still lugs his grandfather's .32 Special into camp every year, saying, "It just needs to be here."

And so, First Night reminiscences have begun. All the favorites are going to be retold. It's unclear now, after so many years, whether these things really happened or if the stories merely took on lives of their own. Or, is it that just enough of these old yarns are true to make the rest seem plausible? Who hasn't, for example, seen a crown of horns that turned him into a sculpture of a hunter, frozen in his tracks with an acute attack of buck fever? It happened to the hunter in one of the stories always told on First Night.

He was walking with his buddy to their respective deer stands. Tracks in the mud testified to the near presence of a heavy deer. Split toe, dew claws touching down with every step—an inspiring sight to behold first thing in the morning. The trail they were on soon opened to view for almost seventy-five yards, and at the end of this run they saw rotating antlers. The buck never suspected anything. It stepped into the trail side-to, head turned away, clearly showing twelve points. The deer was browsing on some head-high sapling shoots. Our hero shouldered his Browning .308. Trouble was, his mind-body coordination was compromised. His extremities were not following orders from his brain. All he could do was shake. As if to help out, the buck held its pose, sniffing and rubbernecking every which way, but not making the two hunters downwind in the trail. Finally, the shooter got his fingers to move, and the .308 announced itself, once, then again, then again. *Pow! Pow! Pow!* went shots reverberating through the hardwoods. The buck never flinched. It did, however, take another step giving the two hunters an even better view. The clip held a total of five rounds, and the hunter emptied it before the buck, looking rather bored, took another couple of steps. In utter exasperation, the foiled hunter slung the rifle and a handful of cartridges over to his chum and said, "Here, you shoot for a while."

It's a late night, this first one in camp. When the tales wind down, someone has to brave the first bedward move before anyone will follow suit. As a true, old woods camp, this one was originally built for crews who slept two to a bunk in double bunk beds, accommodating eight. Those have been torn out and an extra bunkroom built on for more space. The table and benches are in the middle of the floor just as they traditionally were, with the woodstove off to one side, kitchen along the opposite wall. The smaller "guest cabin" is where the cookee and his wife stayed when this was a working camp. Now, two of the guys bunk out there.

Each of us has staked out his usual bunk. As the bottom bunker is just crawling in, his chum on the top bunk launches into a snoring racket that threatens to loosen roofing nails. Figuring he'd better nip this in the bud, he yells up, "Hey! Pipe down up there!" This interrupts the din for a good five minutes, by which time the bottom guy has time to fall asleep and start snoring himself. A third party to this pas de deux who also has been accused of loud snoring, decides to make a little extra racket loading the woodstove for the night and getting the coffeepot ready. It does the trick, and buys him enough time to fall into la-la land before the racket resumes. The snoring symphony then comes to full pitch to keep the mice awake all night.

At about four-thirty, a flashlight beam points this way, then that, inside the two-bed guest cabin. A blast of smoke and sparks bursts out of the stovepipe. After a few minutes and a little more rummaging around, the cabin door opens and the flashlight beam is leading a man toward the main camp. There's no guesswork as to who it might be. In most hunting camps the same person gets up first every day, and the same person gets up last. Once in the door he makes a beeline for the gas range. He trusts that someone did their duty and filled the coffee pot before going to bed.

Each hunter is responsible for a full day of meals, and today is his day. Putting down the flashlight, he fumbles for a match and lights the gaslight over the stove. Ah, good! Someone did load the coffee pot. He opens the gas spigot and touches off the burner under it. He does all this, gloating to himself that he is the only one up, and that when the stragglers do finally emerge, they will see that he's got the jump on them as usual.

In truth, all the wood-sawing and gurgling, all the sweet dreams of being the sole judge for the next recruitment of Dallas Cowboy cheerleaders, ceased the moment the main camp door opened. All are listening to his every move, content to allow him these few moments of exultation.

"Got my tea water on?" a voice grunts from the bottom bunk in the back room.

"Yep." It's a fixed tradition that the cook-of-the-day lights a burner under the small white enamel saucepan for the one tea-drinker in camp. Soon after that, it's the sound and smell of bacon in a skillet that inspires the entire camp to take to its feet.

"What's for breakfast?" someone pipes.

"Just give me some elbow room here and you'll find out soon enough." A drum solo of pots and pans provides the last blast of reveille and now the camp is a rumble of hunters pulling on polypro long johns, wool pants, and boots. Someone turns on the radio for a weather report. "Winds southwest five to ten, highs in the mid-thirties."

The five-minute warning has been given for the breakfast table to be set and someone rises to the occasion. We don't eat like this every morning the rest of the year, but we permit ourselves an extra measure of self-indulgence during deer camp. Hash, eggs cooked short-order the way you want them, sausage, ham, or bacon, toasted homemade bread. Formidable fuel is required for the kind of walking that will take place today.

When the dishes are cleared and stacked in the sink for some generous volunteer later in the day, and when the table is wiped down, a topo map is spread out and oriented with a compass. A huddle forms around the table and slowly, a plan develops.

Everyone finishes dressing for the day: wool coat, wool pants, and wool socks, but some draw the line when it comes to wool long johns. It's cold out. All envision the rut beginning with this first good cold snap, and even if this isn't completely accurate, it sure quickens the step. To these guys, cold can be a profound stimulus, something akin to an endorphin / adrenaline cocktail.

I barely slept all night. It seems dumb to admit it, but it was just plain excitement that kept me awake. I tossed and turned and waited, and finally, Mr. First-One-Up mercifully broke the silence. Now, after breakfast with all plans and best intentions laid, I'm out the door and hiking. I go slowly so as not to perspire and clear the country of downwind deer and so as not to crunch too many twigs underfoot. Soon enough, perspiration forms under the bill of my hat, so I stop for a breather and listen. "What's your rush?" I ask myself.

After a few moments, my progress resumes and it can't be helped—that last fifty yards to my stand is always much too noisy. I selected it because of the nearby stand of hardwoods. On cold mornings like this, though, those frozen leaves and the twigs under them announce my arrival to any living thing within a broad radius. Every twenty yards or so in a semicircle around my stand, I set out scent wicks, old film canisters filled with cotton swabs. Before setting each one down, I pull out some buck lure, unscrew the dropper and soak each wick. I set them on a stump or rock about fifteen inches off the ground. Now, if I'm lucky, I'll make it up into my stand quietly just in case there's already an old moss-horns in the vicinity sampling these wafting scents.

This is where I always sweat the most. Getting up the tree with all those clothes on as well as other assorted gear causes me to pull the bandana out of my back pocket. I wipe my brow with it and put it back into my pocket fast. Right about now I start to think about what I could trim off the equipment list that would lighten up this load. Buck knife? Nope, need that. Deer call? Nope, you never know. Survival kit? No way! Map and compass? What, are you nuts? Wicks? Hey, a guy's got to give himself a fighting chance, doesn't he? And so it goes until I'm right back where I started—I need all this stuff! Including the extra cartridges in case I need to signal for help. Including the blaze-orange poncho in case it pours. Including the stocking hat in case my ears get cold. Including everything!

Now comes my favorite part—watching dawn break. I consider it prime time. When I look back on my hunting career, it's true I've taken as many deer at dusk as at dawn, but somehow I prefer this time of day. There's something invigorating about watching and listening to a new day coming alive. The first sound I hear is the pulse in my own ears from having climbed the tree. When that quiets, I quietly clear my throat in case there are any coughs lurking there to spoil the day. I remember that one time when I sneezed and a buck "blew" no more than thirty feet away. It was flag up and sayonara. Funny how an incident like that stays with you forever.

All right now, what was that? I ratchet my neck around slowly and strain my eyes even further until I make out a mouse scurrying from cover to cover under a blowdown. Well, I really didn't think it was much of anything anyway. Now, as the eastern sky lights up with orange, something makes a noise from way out on the edge of my hearing. I try to turn it into the sound I want to hear: that steady, rhythmic, deliberate shuffle, a crunching cadence that can only mean one thing: Here he comes. For a while I swear this sound is coming closer, then it returns to the periphery of my hearing where it's a toss-up whether it's real or imagined. But now—son-of-a-gun!—here it is again, and this time I'm able to rule out imagination.

I do the neck-ratcheting maneuver again. I learned in my twenties that fast turns of the head, even in a tree stand, can be the equivalent of flashing a pie plate at an oncoming buck. I can hear the nitrogen popping out of the vertebrae in my neck as it creaks around. Can the deer hear this too, I wonder? Simultaneously I begin working my gluteal muscles to allow me to turn to the right very slowly. I swear, out of all the ways for a deer to walk into an area, he comes in over your right shoulder nine times out of ten. Now I at least have most of my torso facing the noise, even if my neck is still craned.

It was 20 degrees when I had left the camp, and those frozen leaves made the sound I'm hearing now seem closer than it really is. With my neck pressed against the collar of my coat, the blood flow to that one carotid artery is compromised. I get a slight rush of lightheadedness. "C'mon, c'mon . . . don't stop," I implore the imagined big buck as I strain to see movement. It stops, but only briefly. If my life had depended on a guess as to how far away the noise was now, I couldn't have made that guess. Fifty yards? Seventy-five? Just then a flicker of something light-colored captures my eye. Is that where the sound was coming from? Yes! In a few seconds it begins again, and I decide there is enough light to shoot if it comes to that.

As I've been monitoring this one sound in the woods, a new day has dawned. Chickadees chirp a chorus interrupted by an occasional screech from a jay, but I am too one-track-minded and tunnel-visioned to take it all in. Now, when I'm about to black out and fall out of the tree stand unless I relieve the pressure on my jugular, I see another flash. Hey—it's a tail! It's swishing up and down. My eyes follow it up, then along a horizontal line forward. The head is of course hidden behind a tree. Another step and I'll know what I need to know. The Maine buck law is clear: Make sure the head gear is at least three inches tall or don't shoot.

How long can a deer possibly stand frozen in one place? All sense of time evaporates. Even the pulse in my ears eases. Well, almost. I take advantage of the tree between the deer and me to raise my rifle enough to see through the scope. Suddenly—what was that? A loud crashing comes from behind my right shoulder. I can't turn or my movement will be made. The noise keeps coming. *Crash! Crash!* Now the deer I've been looking at through my scope picks up her head. Yes—her head. That must mean—yes—oh no!—there she goes and there he goes, right under my stand at a gallop, pushing the doe in front of him.

No shot. It would have been sloppy at best. I want no deer with a bullet in its hindquarter wandering around suffering for days to come. Obviously, this buck had either winded me or saw the movement when I shouldered my rifle to look at the doe through the scope. From the brief glimpse I'd gotten of its size, this buck has been at this a long time. I blow out a long sigh, reflect on whether or not I'm angry, and then laugh to myself.

All is not lost. To my own surprise, as my blood and pulse quicken, as my respirations shorten and my throat closes up, I feel like the kid in one of those camp stories toting the Model 94. This morning, I'd seen a trophy, and it felt like a gift. The older I get, having that happen seems to be trophy enough. That, and the new edition I was adding to the camp's repertoire of stories was enough to tide me over.

Drummond Humchuck: Blood Trail

"You see any rabbits on the way in?

"Yeah, as a matter of fact, I did. Nice to see you, too, Drum."

"What color?"

"About half white."

"Yup. I see a ermine yesdee almost all turned."

Drummond Humchuck doesn't go in for big salutations. When I get to his place in Township Unknown, it's as though the last sentence spoken on my last visit was merely interrupted by the distractions of a few months. He's somehow able to make me feel, from the first moment I arrive, as if we're together all the time.

His questions as I was walking into his dooryard referred to the only two Maine fur bearers that exchange their summer and fall coats for white ones at the start of winter. Drummond gauges the progress of the seasons by such things.

I had hiked in on a Saturday in early December, the last day of the muzzleloader season. Muskets tend to be a little heavier than most deer rifles. I was glad to set mine down. I had carried it much of the way in at port arms in hopes of seeing something, but this hike had gone the way of all my other hikes this deer season: lovely walks in the woods. No thundering hooves, no flagging tails, no snorts or blows. I'd hunted hard, though, because it seems a shame to let the season go by and not be there in case something spectacular happens. Those things, when they do occur, have a way of becoming folklore around here. They can take on a life all their own beginning at the Liar's Bench in the Pine Tree Store. It's these epic tales, told and retold and sometimes sung that paint a local history colorfully, brimming with distinctive characters and deeds.

The man presently serving me tea doesn't, in my view, have to wait to enter that Hall of Characters posthumously. Drummond Humchuck is as one-of-a-kind as they come, living a life that most in modern times would call a catastrophe. He has no access to any goods and services in the conventional sense, but in the unconventional sense, he has everything. By any ruler I can conjure, the man is unique.

I suppose I was looking a little round-shouldered to Drummond after showing up skunked on the last day of the deer season. My friend took a long sip of his tea and looked up at the rafters in his cabin. "Seein' that musket a yers reminds me of the year I hunted five weeks and never missed a day and never see a deer."

"Yup," I said. "Sounds like the season I just had."

"I s'pose I was close to givin' up. Then she snowed and snowed good one afternoon. I see that and was cured. No more down around the gills. I headed out just like it was openin' day. Chum, I hadn't gone four hundred yards inta them woods when I see him. Tall 'n' handsome and two trees growin' outa his head. I shoulder'd the musket, let fly with a ball, and that buck looked at me through the fallin' snow as if to say, 'Who invited you to this party?' He jumped straight up in the air and took off runnin' while I reloaded the musket. I could barely pour powder I was so shook. When I see him again it was only his head, the rest of him bein' hidden in the whistle woods. I passed up that shot and lived to regret it. He was off and me after him, followin' tracks and red dots on the snow 'til after dark. I walked two miles back here.

"If I slept that night someone forgot to tell me. I was dressed and out the door 'fore first light next mornin'. I worked the woods where I left off 'til I cut the track, and once I did I jumped him right quick. The blood had slowed to a trickle, but he hadn't slowed a little bit. When I had to go through young hemlock and jack pines, I pushed up my sleeves, slung the rifle over my shoulder by the strap, and walked with my bare arms held out. Blood showed up on them where that buck had walked.

"That deer took such a curly-cue route, I got all confused. I didn't have no compass, but I had my old pocket watch."

I interrupted Drummond. "Your watch? What good did that do?"

"Just point the hour hand at the sun. Halfway between that and the 12 on the watch dial is south.

"So anyway, that buck stayed out ahead of me, always runnin' at the right time so's I could never see him very good. After 'bout an hour of this I realize he's headed right for the river. Now I really didn't want to wade that, 'specially in December, but a'course he crossed it and wade it I did. Once I got to the other side, I found a log to set on and I was wringin' out my socks when a mink come right up that log and run up my back! I had to jump up and dance a jig to get him off'n me. Wasn't that critta' dumbstruck to see that log come alive! By the time I cut the trail again, that buck had had a chance to get pretty well ahead a me. After a hour or so I realize my feet felt like blocks I was liftin' with my knees. They was froze. So, I stopped and built a fire. Hated to but had to.

"Them woods was wet's a snout, but they was plenty a birch 'round to get a good fire goin'. I hung my woolens includin' my socks up on sticks and set there in the altogether eatin' a piece a jerky from last year's deer. I was warmed up and on my way with dry socks in half an hour. I see from the tracks that that deer never slowed at all. He crossed another brook, kept a goin', and finally went into a cedar swamp where a man couldn't crawl, never mind walk. I see the last little red drop just 'fore dark, then walked four miles home. You know, chum, a man's never so one-track-minded as when he's on a blood trail. If they told him right then Judgment Day is nigh and it's high time to get ready, a real hunter'd stay right on that trail and cast his fate to the wind.

"Next day, I combed and zigzagged that country enough to scare all the moles outa their holes. I never cut a track. Then, it come to me. Bein' hurt, that deer would stay to water. Wounded, they'll lay in it, drink, but just want to stay close. The best water I knew was behind me. So I doubled back 'til I come to that brook. I followed it, one slow step at a time, downstream cause I knew in a roundabout way it eventually emptied into that same swamp. I guess I'd walked a half-hour when I see three fresh red spots on a rock in that stream. I froze 'cause I knew I wasn't alone there. Without pickin' up my head, I rolled up my eyes and between me and a deadwater forty yards downstream, I see horns rotatin' back and forth. That buck was bedded in moss. Hadn't winded me far as I could tell. Hadn't heard me neither 'cause a that babblin' brook. I waited 'til that head rotated away from me, and I raised the musket.

"Look here, my tea's all gone. Yers?" Drummond asked, standing up slowly.

"Sit back down here!" I piped to let him know I knew exactly what he was doing.

"Back in a flash, Chum."

To my exasperation, he took the teapot off the stove, poured slowly until both our cups were full, then sat back down and reached for his pouch of red willow. He loaded his pipe carefully, savoring the moment. Touching off the tiny shavings with a wooden match and drawing deeply, he blew out a fog of red willow smoke and said,

"Got yer wood up, Chum?"

"Very funny, Drum. What happened?"

"Oh, oh yeah," he sputtered. "Had to quarter it and bring it in by pack basket."

"So you got him!"

" 'Course I got him."

Drummond puffed again on his pipe and blew a ring that looked to me like a smile above his head. I had to laugh. Any self-pity I'd felt over being skunked that season was disappearing as fast as that willow smoke into the rafters. We would interrupt our conversation now. When we resumed it, the hares and ermines would be white as the driven snow.

Fall Foods

Words like "killing frost," smells like wood smoke, and sounds like honking Canada geese heading south on the Atlantic Flyway prompt us to take an extra comforter out of the cedar chest. These changes are soon reflected at the dinner table. The work, and even the fun activities of fall, produce appetites that tower over those of summer. Fall dishes must serve up enough fuel for long hikes in the woods, afternoons of cordwood splitting, Sundays of cranberrying, and nippy days of "tipping" (gathering spruce and fir boughs for wreaths). When the shift of the seasonal axis is felt in the stomach, some dishes seem to answer the challenge better than others.

Stout Stew *(with thanks to Melissa Duffy)*

It was a succession of bitter May days fishing for salmon that called this recipe to Melissa's mind, but here, we apply it after ample testing, to the appetites of autumn.

Ingredients:

¼ C vegetable oil

2 ½ lbs beef stew meat

1 ½ lbs yellow onions, diced

1 Tbsp unsalted butter

2 tsp sugar
2 Tbsp flour
1 ½ tsp dried thyme
3 carrots, sliced ½-inch wide
1 bottle Guinness, Murphy's, or any good stout beer
1 C beef broth
1 Tbsp tomato paste
1 clove garlic

Instructions:
Preheat oven to 350°. Brown meat over medium heat until crusty, a few pieces at a time. Put meat aside on a plate. In the same pot, add butter and diced onions, cook for about 5 minutes, add sugar, and cook until golden brown. Add flour, thyme, carrots. Raise heat to high, add the beer, stirring constantly until boiling. Add broth and tomato paste and bring back to a boil. Reduce heat, and add the meat to the mixture. Put this in the oven for 2–3 hours. Remove and refrigerate overnight. Ladle the fat off the top, and 1 hour before serving time, place in the oven at 225°.

Tips: Use a large stew pot that is oven-safe. When serving, use bread bowls (round bread with centers cut out) or mashed potatoes with a bowl-shaped area to contain the stew.

Note: Since acquiring this recipe from Melissa, we've tried Stout Stew out on hunters and fishermen at the end of chilly days on the trails and in the stream. It never fails to restart the inner furnace in record time.

Stuffed Pumpkin *(with thanks to Shelley Spencer)*

Shelley first guinea-pigged this recipe on the Grand Lake Stream Salmon Association, a group seriously game for adventure. It went over so well, it is now deemed safe to serve to other very special fall guests. I still remember the way the table looked that first time with a gold tablecloth and linen napkins to match the fall motif of plump pumpkins ready for scooping.

Ingredients:

1 pumpkin, 5–6 lbs
1 lb ground beef
3 lbs potatoes
1 large onion, chopped
½ tsp ground clove
½ tsp nutmeg
1 tsp ground sage
1 tsp allspice
1 tsp pepper
1 large cube of salt pork

Instructions:

Brown hamburger in a pan with the onions. When cooked, add all spices to meat mixture and set aside. Boil potatoes and mash. Add mashed potatoes to meat mixture. Cut off top of pumpkin big enough to fit your hands inside to clean out. Stuff pumpkin with mixture and replace top. Cut the large cube of salt pork into small, ½-inch cubes and poke toothpicks through them and into the sides of the pumpkin all around it (to moisten during baking). Cover pumpkin with foil and place in square pan. Bake at 350° for 4 hours. When you can easily poke a fork through the pumpkin, it's done. Allow to sit for 20 minutes after removing from oven. Cut into slices just as you would a cake or pie. Scrape off pumpkin skin and discard, mix everything together, and add salt and pepper and butter to taste. Serves 6–8 people.

Hint: A pumpkin with rich, orange color will be sweeter to the taste.

Venison Stroganoff *(with thanks to Nancy Norris)*

There are vacationers who have been coming to The Pines Lodge on Sysladobsis Lake for many years who have not the least bit of interest in fishing. They come for Nancy's cooking! There's virtually nothing she serves up that doesn't live after itself in the memories of her clientele. If you're lucky enough to stumble onto some venison in the fall, see if this dish doesn't find a prominent place in your memory.

Ingredients:

2 lbs venison round steak, cut ¾-inch thick
2 Tbsp shortening
1 large onion, peeled and chopped
¼ lbs fresh mushrooms
2 Tbsp butter or margarine
2 Tbsp flour
½ tsp salt
⅛ tsp pepper
1 tsp prepared mustard
1 can (10 ½ oz) beef bouillon
1 C dairy sour cream

Instructions:

Remove bone and fat from meat and cut into strips about ¼ inch wide and 1 ½ inches long. Brown meat in shortening in a heavy skillet. Transfer meat to a 2-quart casserole and add onion, salt, and pepper. Heat bouillon in skillet, scraping bottom of pan to loosen all particles. Pour over meat and bake, covered, in pre-heated moderate oven (350°) for 1 ½ hours, stirring occasionally if meat on top becomes dry. Wash and slice mushrooms and sauté in butter until golden. Stir in flour. Drain the liquid from the meat and add gradually while stirring. Cook over low heat, stirring constantly until smooth and thickened. Add mustard and sour cream and blend well. Pour over meat. Serve over cooked noodles or rice. Makes 4–6 servings.

Aunt Lizzy Smith's Baked Mackerel

(with thanks to Lucille Harrington)

Lucille, of Milbridge, Maine, says that this old favorite comes from the family archives. Trouble is, of all the Smiths in the family tree, no one seems to know which branch was Lizzy's. Passamaquoddy Bay yields plenty of mackerel in September and October, but so does Harrington Bay, handy to where Lucille and Rodney Harrington live. Mackerel is an easily taken fish which we now know to be the quintessential health food thanks to omega-3 fatty acids. In Lizzy's day, people commonly put up mackerel in mason jars, then opened them to use in this recipe. The cider vinegar was key, Lucille says, as it is in so many other dishes. So simple a meal to make and yet so good, especially when served with a platter of fall vegetables like rutabaga, brussels sprouts, and red potatoes.

Ingredients:

1 tinker mackerel per person, *or* ½ medium mackerel per person
apple cider vinegar
several whole cloves
lemon (optional)

Instructions:

Place fish on baker's sheet and pour on cider vinegar to a depth of ¼ inch. Sprinkle with a few whole cloves to taste, and bake at 350°–375° for ½ hour, or until browned on top. Don't let them go until completely dry. Many of our guests have found the addition of a pinch of lemon an enhancement to this dish. Don't forget: With all those natural fish oils, you're doing your heart a big favor.

Portuguese Stew *(with thanks to Martha Spencer)*

Some Portuguese culinary influences came to Down East when it was still part of Massachusetts Bay Colony, and we should all be thankful for that. My sister-in-law says everyone she serves this to asks for the recipe. When the weather turns cold, turn to this stew to warm up.

Ingredients:

1 ½–2 lbs haddock, cod, or pollock
1 C chopped onion
½ C chopped red pepper
2 cloves chopped garlic
4–5 hot Italian sausages
1 large can peeled tomatoes (crush by hand)
1 C water
1 C red wine

2 C diced potatoes
½ tsp each oregano, basil, and thyme
salt and pepper to taste

Instructions:
Sauté in a little olive oil the chopped onion, red pepper, garlic, and sausage. Then add and bring to a boil the peeled tomatoes, water, red wine, potatoes, and spices. Turn back to a simmer for 30 minutes, then add the fish, bring to a simmer again, then turn off heat. Martha says this stew is best when made a day ahead and served with Parmesan cheese.

Mincemeat *(with thanks to Edith Sprague)*

This solution to dinner got more than a few Maine families through the lean times and the cold, but there's no reason to consign it to those occasions exclusively. If this wasn't your year for a deer, you can still make it with top round. Talk about a dish that sticks to your ribs!

Ingredients:
venison or top round enough to make 2 lbs ground meat
6 lbs apples, cut up finely
2 ½ one-pound pkgs. ground raisins
2 C molasses
½ C vinegar
salt to taste
5 tsp each of ground cinnamon and cloves
3 lbs margarine
2 lemons, 4 oranges, 1 one-pound box whole white raisins (all ground including peels)

Instructions:

Combine the ground meat with the other ingredients and cook very slowly (approximately 2 hours) at 350°. When ready, seal into quart canning jars while very hot. Anytime you're pressed for a quick meal during the cold months, take out a quart, heat, and serve with a good root crop vegetable for a truly hearty Maine dinner.

Shelley's Fabulous Fish Cakes

(with thanks to Shelley Spencer)

This is the house dish that reminds us that Shelley is from Annapolis, Maryland, where they can make good fish cakes out of anything that swims. A good, fresh tartar sauce is the frosting on these cakes, so we've included a recipe for that, too.

Ingredients:

3–4 lbs of fish, chopped or pulsed in food processor (may be white perch, togue, pollock, haddock, or cod)
½ C each of minced celery and onion
2 minced garlic cloves
1 large egg
½ C mayonnaise
1 tsp Worcestershire sauce
1 Tbsp Old Bay Seasoning
⅓ tsp red pepper flakes

Instructions:

Mix all ingredients in a large bowl and blend well. Mixture will be moist. Mold into small cakes/patties and place on a cookie sheet covered with waxed paper. Allow to sit for 30-60 minutes.

Heat oil for frying, and make sure it is hot before cooking fish cakes. Pat each cake lightly with bread or cracker crumbs just before frying. Brown each side, turning only once. Drain, and serve with tartar sauce.

Tartar Sauce

1 small onion, minced
2–3 pickles minced
1 C mayonnaise

Mix all ingredients and chill.

Lean Times Kale Soup *(with thanks to Shelley Spencer)*

You can make a lot of this hearty fall soup cheaply. Each time it's reheated, it seems to taste better than the time before. We have substituted both Swiss chard and Georgia collards for kale with no discernible difference in the outcome.

Ingredients:

1 lb kielbasa, sliced in ¼-inch chunks
vegetable oil
1 C chopped onion
4 cloves minced garlic
5–6 C chicken broth
1 large can of diced tomatoes
1 small can of kidney or cannelli beans
¼–½ lbs chopped kale
4 peeled and sliced carrots
2 C of sliced and chopped potatoes

Instructions:

Sauté onions, garlic, and kielbasa in vegetable oil. Add all ingredients to soup pot and simmer on low heat until vegetables are tender. Best after sitting for 24 hours.

Logging Camp Cornmeal Pancakes

(with thanks to Bonnie Gagner)

The men who worked the woods camps ate five times a day. The first breakfast came well before daylight and it had to be hearty for the work in front of them. Bonnie Gagner's father was Sonny Sprague, who worked in the camps and appreciated a morning start-up like this one.

Ingredients:

1 ½ C cornmeal
2 ½ C white flour
4 level tsp K C Baking Powder
1 tsp salt
¼ C sugar
¼ C shortening
2 eggs or 2 additional tsp of K C Baking Powder
½ C condensed milk
1 C cold water
8 or 10 thin slices of bacon, cut in bits

Instructions:

Sift together three times—the meal, the flour, the baking powder, salt, and sugar. Chop in the shortening, beat the eggs, add the milk mixed with the water, and stir into the dry ingredients. Have ready iron frying pans, preheated and rubbed with a slice of bacon. Turn in the mixture to the depth of a scant three-fourths of an inch, sprinkle with the bits of bacon, cover, and let cook about 4 minutes, or until well filled with bubbles. Turn to cook the other side. Serve cut in triangles. Or, put into the pan in large spoonfuls, sprinkle with bits of bacon, and cook more slowly and covered. Good hot or cold. Can (and used to) be made over open fire outside.

Florence's Hot Dog Relish *(with thanks to Florence Wilbur)*

When I've had this relish at Florence's house, I've thought it deserved a much higher classification than "condiment." It is worthy of being served as a side dish. Of course, it goes well on hot dogs and hamburgers, and sometimes Florence uses it with roasts. Most of the ingredients for this recipe are typically harvested from the vegetable garden in the fall.

Ingredients:
4 C finely chopped onions
1 medium-sized head of cabbage
10 large green tomatoes
12 green peppers
6 red sweet peppers
½ C salt
6 C sugar
1 Tbsp celery seed
2 Tbsp mustard seed
1 ½ tsp turmeric
4 C vinegar

Instructions:
Grind together the onions, cabbage, tomatoes, and peppers and cover with the salt. Let this stand for 1 hour, then drain. Add the sugar and spices and vinegar. Boil mixture slowly until it thickens. Seal in jars and boil them for 15 minutes. Enjoy!

Fall Desserts

Some of the desserts that follow are the ones we use in September and October in picnic baskets for traditional shore lunches.

Apple Upside-down Cake *(with thanks to Kathy Cressey)*

This recipe came from the maternal grandmother of Kathy Cressey, proprietress of the Pine Tree Store in Grand Lake Stream. She says, "I don't know if it was a recipe she created or not; however, she passed it to my mother, and she passed it on to me. I can only assume its origin came from using common ingredients that were staples in many kitchens in my grandmother's day. The iron frying pan, as used in this recipe, was a versatile kitchen item—used on top of the stove, as a baking dish, and as a serving dish! This dessert always seemed to appear in our household in the fall when the temperatures started to dip and the apples were plentiful."

Ingredients:
4 Tbsp butter
1 C sugar
1 Tbsp molasses

4 medium-sized apples, peeled and sliced
1 egg
¼ C milk
1 C flour
1 tsp baking powder
½ tsp salt
1 tsp vanilla

Instructions:
Melt 3 Tbsp butter in a large iron frying pan (my mother always called it a "spider"). Add ½ C sugar, 1 Tbsp molasses, and stir until all is melted. Remove from heat. Peel and slice the 4 medium apples (my mother always used Macs) and arrange on the sugar mixture.

In a separate bowl, beat 1 egg, ½ C sugar, ¼ C milk, 1 C flour, 1 tsp baking powder, ½ tsp salt, and 1 tsp vanilla. Beat well and then add 1 Tbsp melted butter. Pour batter onto apple mixture. Bake at 350° for 30 minutes. Serve warm with whipped cream or vanilla ice cream.

Fresh Blueberry Cake

Cooking Down East by Marjorie Standish, *Maine Sunday Telegram*, Guy Gannett Publishing Co., 1969 offers a blueberry cake recipe that's hard to beat for guides' baskets.

Ingredients:
4 eggs (separated)
2 C sugar
½ tsp salt

1 C shortening
2 tsp vanilla
3 C sifted flour
2 tsp baking powder
⅔ C milk
3 C blueberries

Instructions:
Marjorie says to beat the egg whites until stiff. Add about ¼ C of the sugar to keep them stiff. Cream shortening, add salt and vanilla to this. Add remaining sugar gradually. Add unbeaten egg yolks and beat until light and creamy. Add sifted dry ingredients alternately with the milk. Fold in beaten whites. Fold in the fresh blueberries. (Take a bit of the flour called for in recipe and gently shake berries in it so they won't settle.) Turn into a greased 9 x 13 pan. Sprinkle top of batter lightly with granulated sugar. Bake at 350° for 50 to 60 minutes. Serves eight.

Fresh Apple Cake

Apple trees all over Grand Lake Stream are bowed low with fruit by September. Many are no longer tended, but the apple truck from Aroostook County comes conveniently to Princeton just in time for this seasonal delight. This cake packs powerful appeal for sports who love a treat after a shore lunch. It comes from Marce Mitchell and Joan Sedgwick's *Bakery Lane Cookbook* (Random House, 1976).

Ingredients:
2 ⅓ C flour
2 C sugar

2 tsp baking soda

¾ tsp salt

1 tsp cinnamon

¼ tsp each, nutmeg and clove

4 C chopped, peeled apples

½ C shortening

2 eggs

½ C chopped walnuts

Instructions:

Combine flour, soda, salt, and spices in a bowl and mix well. Add apples, shortening, nuts, and eggs. Beat at medium speed until well blended. Pour into a greased and floured 9 x 13 pan. Bake at 325° for 45 minutes. Frost with caramel frosting when cake is cool.

Caramel Frosting

Ingredients:

⅓ C butter

12 C brown sugar

3 Tbsp milk

1 ½ C confectioners' sugar

¼ tsp vanilla

Instructions:

Melt butter in saucepan. Add brown sugar. Stir over medium heat until sugar melts. Add milk and bring to a boil. Pour into mixing bowl and cool for 10 minutes. Add confectioners' sugar and vanilla and beat to spreading consistency, adding additional confectioners' sugar if necessary.

Suet Pudding *(with thanks to Harriet Standish Spencer)*

Today, it may sound like something you're supposed to tie in a cheesecloth and hang off the bird feeder. Then, it was a strong finish to a Thanksgiving Day feast. This recipe was passed from my great-grandmother, Harriet Lake Wilmarth, to my grandmother, Nellie Wilmarth Standish, and finally to my mother, Harriet Standish Spencer. It goes back even further, since Harriet Lake actually got it from her mother who made it during the Civil War. This delicious topped dessert may not sound like health food today, so let's check the health record: Harriet Lake was the youngest of eleven siblings, nearly all of whom lived well into their nineties. My grandmother, Nellie Standish lived to be ninety-nine and a half years old. My mother, ninety, and a big fan of this recipe, attests that no one, at a single memorial service, ever said, "It was the suet pudding that got her!"

Ingredients:
1 C molasses
1 C milk
¾ C chopped suet
1 C raisins
2 tsp baking soda
1 tsp cinnamon
½ tsp salt
½ tsp clove
½ tsp allspice
½ tsp nutmeg
1 tsp vanilla
3 C flour

Instructions:

Thoroughly grease the insides of a few 1-pound coffee cans. Mix all ingredients together. Bring a large kettle of water to a full boil. Fill the cans with ingredients, cover them, and place them three-quarters deep in kettle water. Boil 2 ½ hours, adding water as needed to maintain depth. Serve with hard sauce.

Hard Sauce

Ingredients:

1 C confectioners' sugar
5 Tbsp butter
⅛ tsp salt
2 tsp rum, whiskey, or brandy
¼ C cream

Instructions:

Beat the butter until soft. Gradually add sugar. Add salt and spirits; beat until smooth. Beat in the cream. When sauce is very smooth, chill thoroughly. Sauce may be spread in a dish to the thickness of ¾ inch. When firm, cut into small shapes suitable to individual servings.

Winter

Snow in the Air

To listen to weather forecasters today, it seems that most people now either fear winter, or at least take a dim view of it. Approaching snowstorms receive news coverage once reserved for catastrophes. This is surprising to us in a corner of the world where snow and ice mean more activity, not less.

The official start of winter comes after the close of muzzle-loader season, the year's last chance to stalk a deer. Partridge season lasts another ten days, but by this time, deep snows can make bird hunting all but impossible. Bobcat season, already open for three weeks, has five to go.

After the holidays, even though the arc of the sun is rising and the days are getting longer, the coldest days are yet to come. As the old saying goes, "When the days lengthen, the cold strengthens."

Sandwiched between 17,000 acres of water, winter is unique here for its brooding silences and its roaring, wailing upheavals. It is both downy-soft and rock-hard. It is sometimes translucent with whiteouts, sometimes transparent with stark clarity. On some cloudless February days it is hard to believe the world could be so harsh and so beautiful at the same time.

When the snows arrive they erase everything. In some sense, life starts anew after each storm. Winter shows us the tracks of forest inhabitants, hidden from us in other seasons. It allows us

Photo courtesy of Randy Spencer

Grand Lake Stream's winter transportation—Skip by a snowmobile.

to walk on water as each lake becomes a Big Sky country unto itself. Winter opens the way to remote places via skis, sleds, or snowshoes, places otherwise barred to snooping humans. In secluded, crude camps, snow is the ultimate insulator, allowing for cozy nights beside warm woodstoves. Sometimes in these outlying places in the depths of the season, one might find the reward of a fully embraced winter—the tracks, that if followed faithfully, lead back to one's self.

A Cass Family Christmas

The Cass family was the region's first family of white settlers. Many clues to their life and times appear in Minnie

Atkinson's *Hinckley Township or Grand Lake Stream Plantation*. This Christmas legend is well-known, often retold, and treasured in the area.

It was eleven-year-old Edward Cass, wrapped in three blankets and huddled as close to the fire as his mother dared let him, who was telling his own story. Every few minutes Nellie Cass adjusted the blankets, pulling them up around his neck, but he was plenty warm. It was really just an excuse to touch him. The shock of the previous night—when she feared her firstborn was dead—had still not completely left her.

As young a mother as she was, Nellie wore the face of a middle-aged woman. As the first white settlers of Range 3, Township 1, the fact that David and Nellie Cass were alive at all was a tale of triumph over steep adversity. They had, in the year 1820, literally hacked their home out of the wilderness on a bluff overlooking the north end of Big Lake. After settling, hardship stayed on as a perpetual houseguest, the sort of guest that ages you. When David was gone days at a time tending traplines, she had beaten bears back from the cabin door while holding an infant on one hip. She seemed always to have an infant clinging to some body part, for she had arrived there with two, then birthed six more in that house. In the ten years since they'd moved from Saint Stephen, New Brunswick, she had seen the face of another white woman exactly twice.

Christmases were scant of gifts, but generally not of food. Since building a more formidable framed house, David consigned the original cabin to a pigpen. David managed to exceed 380 pounds, an impressive weight even for his tall stature. Part amateur doctor, part pig farmer, trapper, and lumberjack, he was probably the perfect pioneer. Gruff by nature, he made whiskey friends of gangs of lumbermen who happened through the area and stayed over with the Casses, to Nellie's lament. They called him "The General." In contrast to this expansive, "liquid personality," his sober demeanor was cross-grained, winning few admirers among his native, tribal neighbors for whom he seemed to bear some umbrage of unknown origin.

It had been a good fall for furs. Using his father's hand-me-downs, young Edward had his own trapline on the mile and a half or so between home and "the marker," about halfway to Governor's Point and the tribal settlement. Both the Casses and the Passamaquoddy let the marker be their silently agreed-upon boundary. Along his trail, Edward had made hash marks in trees facing in both directions just in case.

"In case" happened on Christmas Eve day, 1832, when Edward was eleven. David was due back from a three-day run up Big Musquash, then up the East Branch to what is now called East Musquash Lake. It was an exceptional year for otter. Their pelts were fetching seventy cents apiece at the Milltown market (thirty-five miles east) at a time when the going rate for a whole pig was twenty-five cents. Nellie wanted her eldest son to wait until his father returned, but he made a strong case that these were the shortest days of the year, and if he got a move on he could tend his whole line and make it home before dark. The younger children were competing for Nellie's attention, and she was in the middle of making a batch of soap. In short, she was in a bad position to argue. Edward already had the will of his father, and she capitulated. In gratitude, a jubilant Edward promised her two rabbits for a Christmas stew. Watching him snowshoe effortlessly across the clearing, rifle over one shoulder, and over the other his pack into which she had slipped some jerky and a wedge of cornbread, she wagged her head in disbelief at how quickly he'd grown.

Father David, on his way home in the open Big Musquash heath, had seen the weather coming on the southeastern horizon. Snow to be sure, and serious. There was already a foot and a half over a solid base which made for good shoeing, but the prospect of a big snow now made the sight of his homestead that much more welcome. By the time he hung his snowshoes on a buckhorn under the porch roof, it was coming down heavily.

"You what?" The news that his wife had let Edward start out that morning brought The General instantly to a full lather. Spit flew everywhere as he bounded back and forth in front of the kitchen cookstove shouting epithets to which her ears were well-accustomed. The floorboards sagged under his tromping weight. For her own part, Nellie felt a tightening in the pit of her stomach. She had not seen the weather coming and now feared for Edward just as her husband did. It was only their manners of expressing it that differed.

Young Edward had made good progress that day, but no money. Three traps were tripped and five were baitless as well as furless. He stuck several of them into his pack, having determined they were once again in need of repairs.

It was on his way back that the snow came. Good enough—he'd follow his hash marks. Then he remembered his promise of two rabbits for Christmas stew and recalled approximately where he'd seen tracks on his way in. When he reached the spot, they were visible only as impressions under the snow. Having more confidence than years, Edward followed them to a softwood knoll. Despite the pine and hemlock canopy, the snow was blanketing everything at an alarming rate and he promised himself if he didn't see a tail soon, he'd turn back. His snowshoes were loading up and his legs tiring.

No rabbits. Time to turn back. Back? No sooner had he turned around than everything looked completely different than it had a moment ago. Then he realized it was because he was now traveling in the opposite direction. Or was he? He turned around again. And again. His own tracks were gone. His usual good sense of direction abandoned him, and in a moment of horror that took away his breath, he didn't know which way home was. Crying in the Cass household was never tolerated by The General, so Edward had not really learned how. His reaction to outright fear was to run until all his wind was gone. He then fell in a heap, breathless, and saw that it was now becoming dark. He pulled himself up, then trod on just as aimlessly as before. "Help! Help! Hello! Anyone?" He embarrassed himself to think there would be a living soul within earshot of his screams. After his desperate callings, the softwood forest sounded even quieter.

Now, the weight of Edward's fear was crushing him. He couldn't think straight, couldn't walk or breathe well. All he could think to do was burrow against the cold. He started digging under a blowdown, first with his hands, then with a snowshoe. It was now very dark. The last thing he remembered after crawling into the hutch he'd carved out was that being asleep—or even dead—would be better than being this afraid.

He left that part of his story out while swathed in blankets in front of the fireplace. He might as well have told them, for it was tame compared to what he did tell them. He said that during the night he thought he awoke, or maybe he was dreaming, he wasn't sure which. When this happened, he saw that there was a fire going beside him and he realized he was not freezing cold. Through the smoke he saw a man squatting, a Passamaquoddy with a rifle across his knees, traps over one shoulder, warming his hands and squinting at the boy as if smiling. The company of another living soul and the warm fire completely overtook his terror. He confessed everything to the stranger—the empty traps, the return trip, the remembered promise to his mother, the rabbit tracks, leaving his trail, and finally, becoming hopelessly, helplessly lost. He confessed his bottomless fear, too. He had never known how bad a person's fear could be. The Passamaquoddy man stoked the fire and his smile deepened. He never spoke a word.

For his part, The General had been out all night looking for his eldest son. Unknowingly, he had walked right past the spot where Edward had left the trail. The snow had covered all clues. He even walked out onto Big Lake until he felt the snow slushing underfoot, and he had to abandon the idea. "Edward wouldn't try to shoe the lake this time of year," he tried to reassure himself. But there was simply no sign of his son.

Nellie had never seen a more desolate man than the one standing on the porch at daybreak. All he did was shake his head, and that's when the real shock hit her. She crumbled, crying in the snow on the porch until David Cass gathered her in his hulking arms and carried her inside. He motioned for the other children to leave the room, and they scattered, only to peek out from behind doors.

Edward said that when he awoke in the woods in his snow cave, it was daylight, it had stopped snowing, and he could see that a fire had been burning beside him. It wasn't just a dream! He saw tracks leading away from the fire. He gathered up his pack and rifle, put on his snowshoes, and followed them. Having huddled in the hutch all night made everything he was carrying seem heavier, but his heart felt light. The tracks led to Edward's own trail, not 100 yards from where he'd spent the night. They then took a left turn heading toward Governor's Point. Edward took a right, and in three-quarters of an hour stood before his home, much older than when he'd set out from it.

Not a word had been spoken for a very long time inside the cabin when a sound from outside broke the silence. "Hello? Hello?" Nellie broke a hinge on the door bursting through to the outside. She ran at her son who dropped his pack and caught her in his arms. He wanted to cry with her but he saw The General standing on the porch, hands on his belt.

Everything seemed explained to everyone's satisfaction. Everyone agreed on the mistakes made, and on how lucky Edward was to be alive, but there was no scolding. Not this time. For the parents, their son seemed resurrected. They knew who to thank in heaven, but not on earth. In the days and months that followed, Nellie found her husband's disposition toward their Passamaquoddy neighbors softening.

That Christmas, a holiday that had gone undercelebrated in the Cass household before this time, was their most memorable of all. The General sawed down a fair-looking fir tree and the Cass kids attached everything they could think of to it: cranberry and popcorn chains, feathers, even two rabbit tails.

"Where'd those come from?" Edward asked when he saw them dangling from the tree.

"From those two rabbits I pulled out of your pack," Nellie Cass said. "I meant to thank you for keeping your promise, dear. Just like you said—it's rabbit stew for Christmas dinner this year!"

Baying Hounds

Suzie holds her head up high, and well she should. Her breed was officially adopted as the State Dog of North Carolina in 1989. She's royalty and knows it. None of the other dogs passing by, craning their necks out of truck windows, can claim this distinction. Maine doesn't have a State Dog. The Maine Coon Cat is the mammal of note in this state, not an animal that would like to see a Plott hound like Suzie on its trail.

Jonathan Plott and his brother brought a German cur breed of canine to their farm in Plott Creek, Haywood County, North Carolina, around 1750. They bred the animals with bloodhounds, and once the new breed was established, the results were impressive. The Plotts had very possibly created the world's most perfect tracking, treeing, coon, boar, and bear dog. It is the only American breed of hound in this country with no British ancestry.

Ferocious to a game adversary, friendly to the family, the Plott is intelligent, lean, fast, has a glossy, usually brindle coat, and yelps a high-pitched note unmistakable to its handler. It can run all day on a little fuel. Its feet are what set it apart from the other most popular tracking and treeing hounds in Maine, the Walker and the Blue Tick. The pads of Plotts, while webbed, are tougher and less susceptible to cuts and tears when running on ice and snow, which they're called upon to do in Maine during the bobcat season.

Suzie's owner, Master Guide Paul Laney, learned cat-tracking skills from his father, Dick Laney. Dick is also a Registered Maine Guide, and he helps Laney's Guide Service, based in Grand Lake Stream, on guided bobcat hunts. Paul and his new bride, Marie, who helps run the guide service with her husband, keep ten other dogs, too, but Paul doesn't use the same hounds for hunting cats that he uses during the dog season for bears. Paul's dogs are specialists. Their ancestors may not have been expressly bred for the bobcat chase, but they have proven their worth again and again to Paul, who has not guided an unsuccessful cat hunt in eight years.

Lynx rufus is the slightly misleading Latin name of one of the most sporting species in all of Maine hunting. This animal is neither a lynx (except in its genus classification), nor is it red (rufus in Latin), though its coat does take on a russet hue during spring and summer. It is coy and antisocial in the extreme.

Bobcats were once a bounty animal in Maine. This was true in many northern states before the spread of coyotes from the western prairies all the way to the eastern seaboard and as far as Newfoundland. Previously, bobcats were the principal threat to deer, followed by harsh winters and starvation. Though whitetails are still prey, the chief staple of the bobcat's diet tends to be the varying hare (snowshoe rabbit), cottontails, partridge, and squirrels. Even so, if their numbers were to sharply increase in Maine, they would presumably kill more deer to sustain those numbers. A 10 percent annual harvest, including trapping and hunting, has been instrumental in helping to sustain the bobcat balance.

Their range is wide—up to twenty-five square miles for toms, and in winter, they'll move two and a half miles per day. Toms rut in late winter, and females deliver in early June, usually two or three kittens. If given the chance, the tom will eat its own offspring.

Where do bobcats hole up? Cover—the thicker the better. Plenty of alders, pucker brush, cedar, spruce, and tangled webs of understory are the likely homes of this extremely retiring animal. As with so many other game animals, early successional growth is the friend and benefactor of the bobcat. Paul Laney, to his own surprise, has found evidence that bobcats love coastal regions for the shellfish and other sea life they can scavenge on the beaches to supplement their rabbit regimen. Even there, it will be the thickest brambles, barred to human traffic, where they will seek refuge. Outdoorsmen, unless they are specifically hunting the cats, will probably not encounter even a half-dozen of them in a lifetime of hunting.

The average weight of an adult male is twenty pounds. His paw print in new snow is not much bigger than a house cat's, but his identifying markers are truly eye-catching: protruding tufts of sideburn whiskers, pointy ears, and a tail that looks like it was docked at the vet's office. The overall color impression is a dark gray or light brown, dappled with black streaks and blotches. It's the "killing claw" on the inside of the front paws, several inches up the leg, that makes the bobcat such a formidable foe. Their deer kills, often found by bobcat hunters, show no evidence of the languishing deaths suffered from coyotes—marked by hindquarters torn and slow evisceration. The bobcat's killing claw, like that of the mountain lion, swipes the windpipe or jugular for a quick kill. Bobcats will feed on this carrion episodically, burying it between times by pawing snow over it.

Best-case bobcat hunting scenarios begin in December, though there have been years when Paul has had to wait until January for good conditions. The hardest part is bringing this disappointing news to hunters who are on call and willing to travel far for this adrenaline-charged hunt. Snow is the critical mass, and early snow means the bobcat is on the move when the season opens—December 1.

The first order of any bobcat hunt is to find a track. Guides on trucks, snowmobiles, and snowshoes start searching well before daylight. It can happen in the first ten minutes, or when the sun is on the down side of the low arc it scribes during those shortest days of the year. Having cut a track, the guide may not settle on it as a starting point. Knowing the country, he may calculate its direction and intercept a fresher track from the same cat crossing another road or trail. The freshest track means less work for dogs, guide, and hunter. An experienced guide can size the animal from its track. Paul had two opportunities during the 2008 season to guess bobcat weights for another guide just by seeing the track. Both animals were eventually harvested, both weighing in within a pound of Paul's prediction.

Both hunter and guide are equipped with two-way radios. When a track is chosen and the dogs are released, they can coordinate a plan on the fly. As the bobcat runs, it gives off more and more musk, which in turns keeps the hounds true to its trail. It's the baying that gives the guide the progress report he needs. Once the cat is "bayed up," it has turned and faced the dogs, teeth showing, killing claw at the ready.

Paul's policy is to take two Plotts along for the hunt—one mature and experienced hound like Suzie, and one younger dog in need of some on-the-job training. The dogs don't eat much before going out because of the breed's tendency toward looped bowel syndrome. They will, if allowed, eat large quantities very quickly. This can put them at risk of intestinal strangulation when they lay down. They are fed a more generous, but controlled portion after the hunt. For the rigorous work of tracking and baying, the guide wants his dogs in top condition. Only after the bobcat season do Plotts thicken a bit. When the months play out and fall rolls around again, the hound hunter begins "roading" his dogs. They run alongside or in front of the truck for miles on dirt roads, conditioning themselves for the work they love.

Dream Trophy

Starting at about the time he turned eleven, Charlie Ben of Indian Township began saving money for something that didn't yet exist. In his mind's eye, and sometimes in his dreams, he saw the taxidermied mount of a trophy bobcat that he himself would harvest. The time was fast approaching when he'd turn twelve and be allowed the thrill of the hunt itself. So far, he'd only gone as a spectator. He was saving money on the faith that in his near future, there would be good reason for it. The kind of mount he envisioned would cost between five hundred and six hundred dollars. To everyone's amazement, he had already saved four hundred and forty dollars.

One morning in the December after he'd obtained his junior hunting license, Charlie and his nine-year-old brother, Toby, were rousted out of their slumber at five. By six, the hunting party was on the road, and Charlie, the "designated shooter," had the rare advantage of having four experienced guides along on the trip: his grandfather, Dave Tobey, Dale Tobey (Dave's brother), Lee Whitely, and Paul Laney. If that wasn't enough for favorable odds, Suzie, the proud Plott hound, and Lily, a juvenile still in training, were along, too. Charlie's hopes were high as he gripped his 16-gauge and headed out in the dark to find telltale imprints in the snow.

About seven miles out of town, they cut an unmistakable cat track. The party walked for about ten minutes, dogs out ahead, hot on the musky scent. In less than fifteen minutes, the bobcat was "jumped" where it had apparently paused for a breather.

The best outcome is for the hounds to push the cat in a circle back to the hunter. Before this happens, the dogs may go by the hunters several times at full speed, pushing the cat ahead of them. Hunters are instructed at this point to stand as still as a statue. Bobcats have an uncanny knack for distinguishing outlines and seeing "what's wrong with this picture." Suzie was showing Lily all the ropes as they raced past the hunters in a blur. Charlie, Toby, and their guides were in cover so thick it was difficult to see the progress of the circular chase, although they had no problem hearing the barking, baying pandemonium going on around them.

Photo courtesy of Randy Spencer

Charlie Ben's bobcat.

Finally, the cat "bayed up." As Charlie was about to raise his 16-gauge, Paul Laney stepped forward and handed him his .22 Colt Woodsman, the sidearm of choice for the experienced guide. If that wasn't a memorable enough moment for the junior hunter, finding out that this cat weighed in at thirty-five pounds brought him back to his dream and the realization that it was coming true.

Today, Charlie Ben's prize stands majestically on a piece of driftwood perched high in his grandfather's cathedral-ceilinged camp. At sixteen, he's still "wicked proud" of the trophy.

First Skim

I knew a man who lived for ice fishing. His name was Whitey Weimann.

Well into his eighties, Whitey would show up in his restored Model A Ford at eighty-acre Roseland Lake in early winter. He'd take an ice chisel down to the lake and walk out, one slow step at a time, pecking away with the chisel. When he wasn't satisfied, he'd look out longingly, pause awhile, then, dejectedly, get back in the Ford and go home. Finally, the day would come when his proddings with the chisel gave him enough confidence to go. Sometimes there were no more than three or four inches of ice for his first foray. And, weather, no matter what the severity, was of no consequence to Whitey. He was going, and that was that.

I had a caretaking job at the time on the shore of this same lake. Very early on winter mornings from December to March, I could almost set my watch by Whitey's arrival. It was barely light out and I would just be stirring. From the comfort of my overstuffed platform rocker next to the woodstove, cup of coffee in one hand, binoculars in the other, I'd watch as Whitey sauntered out to one of his favorite two or three spots for yellow perch, jig stick in one hand, a five-gallon pail in the other. In the days before global positioning systems, he knew how to use shore coordinates to go directly to his honey holes. Sometimes he'd have to wade through fifteen inches of slush or drifted moguls of new-fallen snow without snowshoes, but he'd do it and eventually get where he wanted to be. He'd then flip the five-gallon bucket upside down for his seat.

Whitey caught one hundred yellow perch on a good day. This pond was a veritable perch production factory, and it did no harm to relieve the gamefish (bass and brown trout) of some of the pressure brought to bear by these swarms of pan fish. Whitey subscribed to the axiom that yellow perch taste muddy in the summer, but sweet as haddock in the winter. Even so, he didn't keep all he caught, and when he did keep a mess, he was generous. Sometimes he'd stop by the house before leaving and drop off a sapling tree limb stringer loaded with yellow perch, all for me.

Sometimes I'd see Whitey out there on the ice in the pouring rain when it looked as if a canoe would be the best means of propulsion. Meanwhile, a lot of guys Whitey's age were sitting in the donut shop, wagging their heads over the baleful state to which the world had sunk. On the days when "Arthur" (his arthritis) was visiting, Whitey could just as easily have joined the bellyachers at the donut shop, or simply stayed home and felt sorry for himself. These were days when no automatic momentum was there to greet him when he awoke, but he'd make himself go out to the lake, anyway. For Whitey, there was a payoff.

For one thing, Whitey liked to be among other fishermen and outdoor-types whose conversation he enjoyed. Somehow, the outlook didn't seem as bleak out there among sporting types as they did around the indoor, coffee-and-donuts crowd. There was always a remembered fish story or the discovery of a new jigging lure that was working magic. There was the excitement when a flag went up for somebody else, or when Whitey got another perch on his jig stick. He swore by his large Swedish Pimple lures with a yellow perch eyeball impaled on one hook. That setup never stopped working so far as I knew, and it probably still would if somebody put the time in that Whitey did.

He and his wife, Ev, traveled in their younger years to different sporting destinations, and they had wonderful stories and memories to share. Whitey believed there was such a thing as too much introspection. The dividend, he said, for getting out of the house and onto the lake was that it got him out of himself as well. It was Whitey's way of preventing himself from getting "too down around the chops," and Ev fully supported this philosophy.

Whitey learned an important lesson earlier in life, one he still practiced in his eighties. He summed it up for me one day: "Ev and I know a lot of folks our age who talk about all the regrets they have over things they didn't do. We don't have those regrets because we did them. Do them while you can. There'll be too much time to regret it later if you don't."

Before long, I stopped seeing Whitey's car pull up in the morning. A cancer, never mentioned, one he had beaten ten years earlier, had returned. I visited him at his house. He asked me to follow him into the basement. There, spread out on a pool table, were several fly rods, reels, spare fly lines wound onto an old L.L. Bean fly-line spooling rack, and some thick, fleecy fly books stuffed with streamers. He told me that he and Ev had discussed it and had decided to leave these things to my son, who was then ten years old. A lump in my throat prevented me from responding.

These days, when I see the first skim of ice on the local lakes and ponds, I can only think of Whitey Weimann. Then I start to think about where I stored my traps and jig sticks the previous March. I get them all out and assess the condition of my tackle. Then, my son and I walk very slowly out on some clear-water pond with good weed beds, testing thicknesses. What we're after, on these first-of-the-season trips, are a mess of yellow perch. We're always pretty confident when we do this, that a special supper is in the bag for that evening.

Whitey passed on about a year after the visit when he took me down to his basement. Ev died after falling down a flight of stairs several years later. Today, my son is still using the tackle bequeathed to him by Whitey Weimann. What my fishing friend bequeathed to me, through his example, was a philosophy on aging that is standing the test of time.

Yellow Perch

Perca flavescens, or yellow perch, share no lineage with white perch. It is, however, a cousin to the walleye. Its six to eight wide, vertical bars reaching all the way to the belly set it apart from other perch, as do its orange fins. Speaking of fins, the yellow perch has spiny fins enough to unmake your day, and handling them on the ice can be bloody work. They do extremely well in ponds that aren't too deep, but offer fairly clean water with weed beds. Traveling in schools, the larger fish tend toward the deeper water, while the juveniles stay to the shallows and to the weeds.

The run of fish that winter anglers encounter is usually in the six- to ten-inch range. They can live to be twelve years old. If the habitat is stressed for forage, the average size will run less. If it's bountiful and doesn't suffer too much from pickerel predation, their size can surprise you. The largest yellow perch on record was twenty-one inches and more than four pounds! The ten- to twelve-inch variety make an elegant winter feast, sometimes served with roe. Since this species spawns in April, the females are fat with egg sacs during prime winter fishing. These are prized by some fishermen, placed on a par with shad roe for their unique taste and texture.

A schooling fish, the yellow perch, especially the young, are such voracious feeders of zooplankton that they have a reputation, when they're introduced to a body of water, for crashing native trout populations. The older fish feed on almost any aquatic offering: insects, snails, crayfish, worms, grubs, eggs, and other small fish, including their own.

The flag that goes up when a yellow perch has taken the bait is sometimes vibrating violently when the angler arrives. The reel, sitting below the ice, will likely be unspooling so fast that the fishermen will need to get hold of the line before it spools out. This is a running fish, and a feisty fight is in store for the fisherman who ties into one. Catch one, and you'll almost always catch more since you have interrupted a school of perch in session.

Because of their firm flesh, they are easily cleaned and skinned. Pierce the skin just below the back of the head and run a sharp knife tip down along the ridge of its back. Cut to one side and then the other of the dorsal fin so it can be easily removed. Make a similar cut along the underside from tail to gills. Connect these cuts under the gills, and then grab a corner of skin between thumb and knife blade. Pull back and simply "undress" the perch, revealing its delectable, white meat. Clean out the body cavity, remove head and tail, and the whole process has probably not consumed two minutes. Bake, or batter-fry with breadcrumbs, and the taste will compete with any winter meal on the menu.

First-Timer

The day dawns clear and cold. Four snowmobiles, two of them pulling tote sleds, set out from Grand Lake Stream at just past seven. Both totes are top-heavy with bait, firewood, ice augers, food, cookware, axes, chain saws, and other wangan. The two toteless sleds each have cargo cages holding jumbo-sized pack baskets filled with still more dunnage. Today will be a day of firsts for one of our guests, including every single aspect of the adventure about to begin.

David Farmer is new to snowmobiles, having hailed from Abingdon, Virginia. I point and say, "There's the throttle and there's the brake," knowing already that my son-in-law is a quick study. His maiden voyage is to be a fifty-mile round-trip to a distant body of hardwater holding salmon, togue, smallmouth bass, whitefish, white perch, pickerel, yellow perch, and brook trout—practically the entire eastern Maine freshwater spectrum.

People make steep sacrifices to come to this region in the winter to catch landlocked salmon. The lake we will fish is connected to one of only four bodies of water where landlocked salmon are native in Maine. Fish can move into and out of this lake via two thoroughfares, and there is even a possibility of catching a wild, as opposed to a stocked, salmon here. And finally, I tell David, the landlocked salmon we're after were actually Atlantic, sea-run salmon to begin with, until they were walled inland by a mile-thick sheet of glacial ice over 10,000 years ago.

There is one long-track sled in the group with enough "footprint" to take the lead and break trail in virgin snow. The others fall in behind, traveling about one hundred feet apart. Thin shards of icy crust formed by a brief bout of freezing rain at the end of a recent snowstorm fly up behind each sled's track. The dry, white powder under the crust billows over the cowlings. Fortunately, everyone is in snowmobiling uniform, including goggles. After the first three sleds precede him, the Virginian glides over a freshly groomed trail as though on a magic carpet. Keeping the sled in the new trail seems effortless to him, and he settles into a comfortable cruising speed, especially on the long straightaways.

Periodic pit stops confirm that the whole caravan is still intact, with all thumbs up down the line. At about the six-mile mark—the first mishap. A pickle pail full of sucker bait flies out of one of the totes on a bump and upsets in the trail. The lid flies off, leaving that section of the trail looking like a deep-woods fish market with all the suckers you could eat displayed helter-skelter on snow ice. Nice thing about suckers—they're tough. Every one of them rebounds with a little water poured into the bucket, enough to hold them for seventeen more miles until they can be freshened with lake water. These are not for landlocked salmon, but for togue.

Cold, single-digit temperatures had settled in for the previous several days, along with a foot of new snow, but the brooks still run across the trails. This creates a deep crevice, which cannot be seen from a distance. The best defense, as usual, is being familiar with the country and knowing where to expect them. Otherwise, it's going slow. If a sled hits these fissures going too fast, it stops dead, probably breaks one or both skis, and throws the operator over the handlebars and through the windshield.

The January snow is as yet unpacked. Absent are the factors that pack trails: traffic, groomers with drags, rain, wet snow, and time. Even with two feet of snow under the tracks, it's all relatively recent and mostly powder, so each sledder can feel the occasional rock as a ski catches it just right. In the thicker woods where the trail narrows to moose-horn width, there are blowdowns and snow-weighted boughs to negotiate, but a chain saw comes out only once. A thick spruce has fallen directly across the trail. While everyone stretches their legs, one of the guys not pulling a tote notices his pack basket in the cargo cage has been impaled by a birch sapling. If anyone had been riding "two up" on that sled with him, they would've been speared clean through. That earns a moment's thought. The trail is once again open and the convoy is back up to speed.

The route being traveled is none other than the infamous "Black and Blue Trail" hacked out in the 1980s by the late Sonny Sprague. An overland shortcut between woods roads, no rougher terrain exists in all that country. It was blazed with brute force, some of the time during black-fly season, which explains the name. It's a wonder it wasn't called the "Black, Blue, and Blood Trail."

Moose conventions had recently convened along this route. Given a chance, the ungainly animals will use man-made trails since they're so much easier to navigate than the thick woods. Not an ear or a tail is seen that morning, but they were there—somewhere close—the sign was fresh. After an hour and a half on the go, all four sleds turn down a trackless trail and all thumbs come up. Nobody has been here! Ours will be the first lines wetted in this lake this season. On his first twenty-five miles ever on a snowmobile, the gentleman from Virginia has acquitted himself impressively.

We select a campsite with consideration for wind, sun, and proximity to good fishing grounds. I immediately build a fire, and put a pot of water on a makeshift grill. Meanwhile, augers are unlashed from the totes, engines started, and the others set traps randomly over a few acres of good, fourteen-inch-thick black ice. Then, the next mishap: One of the augers had iced up around the carburetor during transit. It will not come up to speed. This might not have been a minor mishap except that someone had anticipated the company of an uninvited guest named Murphy, and brought two of everything critical.

Coy fish, bait thieves that get away with murder but leave the anglers perplexed as to the culprit, trip the first flags. One in the group has his own idea. Picking a spot over the deepest water in the lake, he drills a jigging hole, then hunkers down to work it. It's not long before the others hear his yelp. Looking his way, squinting, they see him doing the American crawl with his arms; he's yarding line out of the hole. Then, a fat, green fish flies into the air and flops down onto the ice, probably stunned by the bends. "A bass!" he yells, and we all chime in unison, "A bass?"

Smallmouth bass are supposed to be in a kind of underwater hibernation in winter; a lulled state of dormancy, not feeding, not traveling, metabolism slowed, just biding time until lake temperatures rise in May. This fish hadn't gotten the memo. It was thinking outside the bass box, feeding on fresh shiners in early January with good girth to show for it.

No sooner does the basser regroup and settle in to some more jigging, than one of his deepwater flags goes up. More American crawl strokes and, "Look!" he yells. "A white perch." Not just any white perch, but a "humpback," meaning a fourteen-inch adult that would taste as good as filet mignon on any January night.

Other flags keep the group busy until lunchtime: a pickerel, a couple of yellow perch, a small togue. Home base is the fire I'm tending on shore. With the sunlight bathing this lee side of the lake, the day feels much warmer than it actually is. Hot ham and bean soup, guide's coffee, and homemade brownies demonstrate to the first-timer that not every winter outing is a Jack London experience. He's warm, well-fed, and happy. At one point, he pulls out a cell phone, calls Virginia, and tells a friend he's "standing out in the middle of a frozen lake!" No one in the group could relate to how this sounded to his friend.

The interruptions of running for flags make the day fly by in a blur. These are the shortest days of the year. The sun never gets what anyone would call "high." There are scarcely two and a half hours to fish after lunch if the plan to reach town before dark is to be realized.

Without fanfare, "The Moment" arrives, the one all these fishermen have been privately hoping for. Bells and whistles should have gone off, maybe a cannon shot, but instead, it's merely a flag up, and it's noticed by the neophyte. Then he notices it's his! He runs for the snowmobile, pull-starts it, and before climbing on, thumbs the throttle of the now-moving machine. It's a Pony Express mount—running, jumping, leg slung over until he's bestride the seat, and off he goes. He squeezes the brake and almost slides into the tip-up, dismounting in time to see the reel unspooling at the speed of panic. The other sleds have now pulled up, too.

Amid too much advice, he calmly kneels beside the hole. He then gently lifts the trap so that the reel continues to unspool freely. He sets it down with one hand, clasps the nylon ice-fishing line in the other, and gives one sharp yank. "It's there!" He begins yarding line with long pulls. It's looping over his boots and every which way, but the fish is obviously heavy, and still on. All the experts caution him to slow down when he sees the leader, but he's doing fine without counsel. What everyone fears is that the fish will lever itself loose on the bottom edge of the ice hole.

With four faces glued to the ten-inch-diameter hole, the late afternoon sun still bright enough to see down it, a landlocked salmon does a swim-by, silvery sides flashing in the sun.

"Whoa!" The first-timer holds on, not forcing, not hurrying, somehow just doing everything right. The rest of the group falls silent, perhaps in fear, perhaps in admiration. Finally, the fish's head is vertical in the hole. In the next instant, the most beautiful thing under the day's sinking sun is lying on the ice. A quick length and girth measurement is taken and the fish is calculated to weigh three pounds. A male fish, bottom jaw nicely kyped, hefty and healthy, and what's this—no fin clips! It's a wild salmon, directly descended from those swimming these waters when the weight of the glacier was lifting from the land. The first-timer gets out his cell phone and calls his Virginia friend back.

The temperature drops like a stone in the waning daylight. Everything is lashed down. Bare hands are warmed by the fire before it's doused, and then, all engines are thrumming away. Reaching a knoll at the top of the trail that had led us onto the lake, a red sun is sitting on the dark green horizon. On the opposite horizon, a full moon has just risen. The lead sled stops, gazing in one direction, then the other, and everyone follows suit as though there's a tennis match in the trail. A celestial postcard has arrived to help everyone remember the day. Once sufficiently admired, it helps light the way back through the old Black and Blue. The moose convention has reconvened and now, here are four moose galloping in the trail ahead of the lead sled. The sledder points and makes antler gestures so the others will see. The behemoths take a hard right and pull a disappearing act that should be impossible for something so big.

The speed picks up out on the open trail that in the warm months is a fair woods road. Skidder trails lead off this main route, and on one of them, two more moose—a bull not yet rid of his heavy horns, and a cow, standing statuesque and staring as the four gawkers pass.

Slowing down for one of the watery crevices, a couple of sleds tilt a little too much and roll gently on their side. The first-timer's sled is one of them. They're easily righted, but in the process, some water comes in over the top of his boot. If we have to build a fire we can, but he waves the group forward. Stars and moonlight could have precluded the need for snowmobile headlights as the caravan hits the borders of town. Mist rising off the stream is already coating the tree limbs on its banks with glistening frost.

Fifty miles by snowmobile. Not a hard day, but a big day. A day of firsts for my son-in-law. It's all distilled near the fire, where four faces glow crimson from a winter's day out in the elements. The sucker spill, the impaled pack basket, the unexpected bass, the humpback perch, the shore dinner, the moose—they all ended up as stage props for one wild salmon. That's what will get top billing when the story's told and retold. That, more than anything else, made the trip memorable for our first-timer.

Grateful Deadline

Maybe it starts from a conviction that you've put in your time, paid your dues, come in from the cold one too many times when it took most of the next day to thaw out. You've ice-fished for years and years in the sometimes brutally chilly open, often with nothing more than an up-ended tote sled or a tarp on two poles to break the bitter wind. Or maybe it's because you've reached a "certain age." Now, you're going to fish from the cushy comfort of a heated shanty, watching with gloating satisfaction while the "have-nots" shiver just like you did for so long. So, in the winter of 1999, I decided to build myself an ice-fishing shack.

What an interesting study ice-fishing shacks make—the almost limitless variations of styles and features you come across once you start to really notice them. Some have a sloped "hen shed" roofline formed by one wall being higher than the other; some are peaked, some flat. Some sit on wide skis, some closer to the center so they run in the snowmobile track, some out on the edges for more stability. One finds skis covered with steel, tin, and Teflon. Some shacks sit simply on two-by-fours. Some have one or two windows, some have five or six, and even skylights! There are ice palaces appointed with furniture, appliances, and other amenities fit to host the governor if he chanced to stop by. Nevertheless, everyone who undertakes to build one must entertain the pivotal consideration—weight! What will be done to minimize the chances of bogging down and needing all kinds of humbling help and heroics to bail you out?

The range of materials to help with light construction is boundless. Three-eighths ply, luan, corrugated fiberglass, aluminum, canvas, plastic—if you can name it you can find it on some ice shack somewhere. There's even a website that features several different plans for building your own shack. One plan has plywood gabled ends with poly-plastic walls and roof. It's quite ingenious, but in a stiff Washington County wind, I wonder if it could stand the flapping.

Hand in hand with the weight consideration goes size.

"Four-by-eight is all anyone needs to get in out of the cold and jig up a togue," says the light traveler.

Then someone chimes in who's built a four-by-eight and later enlarged it. "Do yourself a favor and make it bigger in the first place. You'll end up doing it eventually, anyway."

I think I'm already convinced, but he does some more selling.

"There's always somebody else who'd like to go along, and you won't have room for them. And even for two people—by the time the place heats up and you start shedding coats, there's barely enough room to turn around!"

All of this must be decided before building. And, there's another hill to climb—height.

"Most people add unnecessary weight by making them too tall," says one builder of several shacks. "The only time you stand up is when you leave!"

It seems true enough. Rarely do you find fishermen standing around inside a fishing shack. Some sit on old summer chairs, some on five-gallon buckets, some on benches hinged from the wall. A six-foot-eight ceiling is good if the University of Maine basketball team is visiting for the weekend, but be sure to invite them back when it's time to tow the thing home.

Sheathing choices can undo everything gained by the other choices, since most things with an obvious upside also have a less obvious downside. If it's wood, it's going to need paint and plenty of it, or you'll be building another shack too soon. The wood and the coats of paint add weight. Some plastic or rubber fibers are definitely light enough, but may too quickly break down under UV rays.

Well, I guess that's the fun of it for the shack builder who sets out to build his home away from home for the coldest part of winter—choosing materials and deciding on design.

"The whole thing's only as good as the floor," says a friend who has thirty years on me. With that in mind, I opt in favor of pressure-treated plywood for a fish-shack floor, since it will receive more than its share of ice, snow, and water over time. But what about the size? In my personal survey of shacks, I've seen eight-by-eights, seven-by-tens, and eight-by-tens. I even saw one eight-by-sixteen! (I wonder if it was really his camp, and he just put skis on it in the winter.) In all of these, the space is certainly nice, but they have to be heavy. Searching for a middle ground, I settle on six-by-eight. Big enough to fish four if necessary, but plenty spacious for two or three.

My research and thinking take the first two weeks of January. Now I have pressure bearing down on me, since winter fishing on West Grand Lake opens February 1.

Joisting the floor with two-by-fours is easy enough, but it requires another decision: Where will the fishing holes be? It's nice to set out tip-ups and view them from the comfort of your warm winter paddock, but everyone wants to jig up a fish from inside. There is room enough for four, so I go with two right-handed holes, and two left-handed. Two will be close enough to the front wall to rig "fixed" lines from the ceiling for whitefishing, and the other two can be jigged in the traditional manner. I frame out the holes, saw out the pressure-treated plywood, and screw it down with galvanized, inch-and-a-quarter screws. Then, I flip the newly constructed floor, trace out the ten-inch circles using the bottom of a sheetrock compound pail, and with a small bit, drill through to give the jigsaw a starting point. Soon enough, the floor looks like a symmetrical piece of swiss cheese. I am ready to build walls.

I'd seen that two-by-threes and two-by-twos were common choices for studding walls. But most people who use them are still looking for ways to lighten their shack. It usually takes either a wide-track snowmobile or a truck to tow them. Somewhere along the line, someone had mentioned to me the idea of taking a one-by-four pine board, ripping it down the middle, and then "marrying" the two halves with nails or screws. The resulting stud is considerably lighter than a spruce stud of the same dimension. I go for it.

I like windows, and the more heavenly light the better. If I could think of a way to have four bay windows I'd do it. I decide to put one on either side of the door on the front wall, and a larger one on each of the remaining three walls. I know, that's a lot for an ice shack, but that's my wrinkle—light! We all know that single-paned windows with heat on one side and freezing cold on the other will frost up. So, I let Johnson's True Value in Calais saw out my five double-paned quarter-inch plexiglass windows, thinking that at least broken glass wouldn't be one of my headaches if an errant partridge flies into it onshore. I frame and head my walls accordingly, screw the plexi into place (making the screw holes larger for contraction and expansion), and add a double bead of silicone all around.

Time for a research trip to Bangor. I heard from a Pennsylvania friend, the late Bill Hartman, about Chemlite, a material used for many years to line the inside walls of long-hauling trailers. Made of fiberglass, it's extremely durable and light. Bangor has a good supply of trucking depots, so I start where anyone on such a mission would—Dysart's. I strike out there, but go right down the line to Pottle's. They have it! Odd pieces, ends of rolls and the like, so I load it up as fast as I can before they change their minds.

Chemlite is great stuff, but it's murder to work with and can make hash of your hands. This is what I learned working with it: wear work gloves, eye protection, and a mask. A Skilsaw, Sawzall, or jigsaw will cut Chemlite well enough, but airborne fiberglass particles traveling at high velocity are lethal mini-missiles.

With a week to go, I am sitting pretty—or so I thought. I have a floor, walls, light sheathing, a great set of skis under construction thanks to the skilled welding of friend and fellow guide Jack Perkins. Now, I only need a roof and something to line the inside walls.

Then someone dropped by—as many do when you have something under construction.

"Gonna have 'er ready for Wednesday?" he asks.

"What do you mean Wednesday? The season opens Saturday," I bark back.

Then he corrects me. It is a week until opening day all right, but the law says you can install a shack on the ice three days before opening day. And everyone does. That way, you can "hosie" your spot and be where you want. Just that fast, I am a short-timer with a deadlier deadline. I pour the coffee and pick up the pace.

Luan wins out as the lightest walling material that is also relatively easy to work with. I figure I am still ahead in the weight game so I can afford the luxury of walls. Now here's some time-consuming, labor-intensive work—measuring and cutting out walls to go around a door and five windows. After which comes the fun part—affixing them to my narrow studs. I never lift a hammer. Of all the great inventions of western civilization, the screw gun must be on the short list. Saves your wrist, saves your arm, saves yourself! Missing the nail you're hammering and hitting your thumb or finger full-stroke so that it sounds like you hit a pumpkin—who doesn't remember each of those moments with a painful pang? Enough epithets are spewed to embarrass a merchant marine, then the fingernail blackens, dies, and falls off. Many have chosen instead to worship the goddess Makita.

"Make it a flat roof and save some time. There's never any snow on it anyway with all the wind out there." Most of my nosy visitors have at least two cents to share, but I like this one. It will save more lumber, and therefore weight. I decide on spruce two-by-threes for added rafter strength. Wait—if there's no pitch in the roof, are they rafters or are they simply wall ties? I don't know, but I put luan on top of the spruce, then some rolled roofing. I stand back, do several laps around the rectangular shack, and pronounce it ready for skis.

It is Monday. I'm not going to push Jack Perkins, who, in addition to my less-important job order of fabricating skis for my project, is building a new Grand Laker from scratch with the help of his admiring grandson, Brett. I don't want to get in the way of that, so I use the time to make my door, a corner shelf to hold a small propane heater, and a pine chest that will serve the dual purpose of seat and storage bin. By Monday evening, it is down to the finishing touches: screwing red reflectors into the corner trim boards for the wayward snowmobiler riding too fast at night, doorstops, and finally, hanging a yard-sale bookcase on the back wall for everything from coffee cans to spare radio batteries.

Tuesday morning, to my surprise, Jack shows up in time for coffee. He never says a word about the skis, and I never bring it up because that might seem like pressure. We speak of the coming season and of the progress he and Brett are making on the new canoe. When Jack gets up to go, I see him out to his truck, and instead of opening the driver's side door, he leads me around to the bed. Laying there side by side, are a perfectly matched set of the most beautiful ice-shack skis I've seen. Not only that, but there's also a towing bar that will slide through rings on the front of the skis. Jack wears a mischievous grin. He helps me unload them, then stays to help me jack up the shack one side at a time, slide the skis under, and carriage bolt them to the floor. The ski bottoms are Teflon-coated, and when we let the shack down after the second ski is attached, you can push it on the snow with one hand. "That Teflon won't take up the frost either," Jack says, meaning these skis won't freeze to the lake even with fluctuating temperatures. I know from experience there is no thanking Jack enough. He waves it off saying, "Day comes I can't help out a neighbor, I just soon not be around."

It's late afternoon. I winch the shack into the shop and start the woodstove. The one thing I've completely forgotten is paint. The Chemlite is white—not a good option for an ice shack on a snow-covered lake. I'm not willing to lose an hour by going to

Princeton and back, so I resolve that whatever paint I have in the shop from former odd jobs is what I'll use. Turns out I have spray cans of green and brown and they surely won't give me total coverage. Solution: I'll take more than a fair share of creative license and approach this thing "freestyle."

I put on a mask, shake up my cans and set to work, moving quickly with gyrating passes circling back onto themselves, then spiraling into other patterns on all four walls. I do this with both green and brown until the last breaths of paint mist come out of the nozzles. I stand back. The room is a fog. I throw open the doors for ventilation, then walk around my ice-fishing Taj Mahal several times. I close the doors. I take more laps, but I can't quite form an opinion.

Shelley had come home while I was in the thick of it. She said she peeked in but didn't want to disturb the artist at work. Now, she follows me out to the shop, arms folded in front of her against the biting cold.

"Now be honest with me," I beseech her. "Tell me what you think." To any married person, this is a question that means different things at different times. When I throw open the doors, her eyes widen. She looks from the shack, back to me, then to the shack again. Then she bends forward at the waist, grabs her middle, and bellows into hysterics. Out comes her honesty in paroxysms of laughter that end with me patting her on the back so she won't choke.

"No, no," I say, "let it all out."

Her laughter is of course infectious, and soon both of us are coughing and gasping and wiping tears away. Only then do I see what she, from her objective vantage, sees: It is either the most godawful attempt at a camouflaged ground blind, or it is the Jerry Garcia Memorial Ice Shack. We decide on the latter.

Next morning, Wednesday, I trailer it to the lakeshore, hook up the tow bar to my snowmobile, and off we go, truckin' up the lake. I'd made the deadline.

King in a Commoner's Suit

Coregonus clupeaformis, our own lake whitefish, is more famous and praised elsewhere than here. In Canada, for example, it's an important commercial freshwater fish, especially prized for the caviar made from its roe. It has long been coveted in the Great Lakes, perhaps too much so, because in addition to environmental catalysts, overfishing has led to a population decline there. Our local whitefish are but one variety of a whole range of similar species, all part of the *Salmonidae* family. The laker class goes by many names in other parts of the world—high back, bow back, buffalo back, humpback, common whitefish, eastern whitefish, inland whitefish, among others—but in our region, this low-profile haunter of the dark depths enjoys the respect of only a certain sect of patient, persistent fishermen.

At first glance, you might say it's an overgrown mud chub: heavily scaled, small head, dark back. Closer inspection reveals that an adipose fin is present just as it is on all salmonids. This might be the whitefish's sole claim to a higher lineage, since the adipose is usually associated with more sought-after gamefish. A side view shows a small head, a double lip flap, and a somewhat unattractive overbite, called a subterminal mouth. Yes, subterminal. It reminds you of a sucker, and it also is primarily a bottom-feeder. It may be these humble outward traits that have kept the whitefish's public image down, and to that certain sect of fishermen, that's just perfect. To them, this is freshwater haddock in generous supply. To other winter fishermen, it is a nuisance fish that puts flags up, steals bait, and is grudgingly tolerated during the more-important pursuit of landlocked salmon and togue.

The most common length of whitefish derived from local waters is eighteen inches; the most common weight, two pounds. A considerable number are caught in the twenty- to twenty-two-inch range, and up to four pounds. The world, any-tackle record is fourteen pounds, six ounces, caught in Ontario in 1984. A six-pound taxidermied whitefish hung on the wall of Leen's Lodge in Grand Lake Stream for many years.

This breed can live for up to eighteen years, and in the West Grand Lake system they exist in abundance. There seem to be no clear and present dangers to threaten this prolific, deepwater fish, which, if possible, opts for water temperatures in the 50- to 55-degree range.

Cut open the stomach and more often than not you will find freshwater snails—mollusks found only on the bottom of our lakes. This is the preferred feed, followed by insect larvae, followed by small baitfish, including smelts. They are therefore a contender in the competition for smelts, but perhaps not on a par with salmon and togue. An interesting characteristic of whitefish is that they can swim out of local waters and survive perfectly well in the brackish waters of, say, the tidal portions of the St. Croix River.

One good reason we don't make caviar from whitefish roe in this region is timing. Our lake whitefish spawn in late fall after open-water fishing is closed. Few are seen in the warmer months of the year, although they can be caught on deep-trolling spoons. Only occasionally does a summer salmon fisherman accidentally hook a whitefish. The lion's share of them is taken through the ice—on jigs, on tip-ups, and on hand lines fished from the relative warmth of ice shacks. The methods employed can be as comical as they are colorful.

Whitefishing techniques are always being invented and polished with the principal objective of outwitting this very adept bait thief. Often, shacks are set up over depths of thirty to forty feet, where the lake bottom is muddy. A sounder is used to locate bottom and a loop in the line marks the desired depth. Some anglers hold the line between thumb and forefinger all day long, much as they do in the saltwater smelt shacks in the Dresden and Brunswick areas. This way they can detect the sometimes very subtle strike of the whitefish. Others attach the line to something flexible that will "give" when the strike comes, anything from a piece of sheet metal cut out of a stovepipe, an old hacksaw blade, or a slice of plastic cut out of a five-gallon pail. Sometimes a bell or other noisemaker is attached to this flexible material, providing an automatic alarm system that sounds at even the slightest meddling with the bait. Bait varies from grubs to small shiners to small jigs to cut bait. Shrimp, slices of liver, and even hot dogs have all been tried, sometimes with success.

On a good, snowy winter day with a falling barometer, a whitefishing shack can appear tranquil to the point of lifeless from the outside. Inside, though, bells are ringing while line is being hand-over-fisted until portly, humpbacked whitefish are flopping on the floor. When you're hot you're hot, so there's no time to waste in getting those hooks rebaited and down there ASAP. On days like this, the eight-fish limit can be realized in half an hour, but days like these don't come routinely.

Whitefish Cuisine

From the kitchen of one great Pennsylvanian cook, Pat Hartman, comes two ways of preparing the delectable meat of the whitefish: Make a fish batter using one cup flour, one cup water, one tablespoon sugar, one teaspoon salt, and one and a half teaspoons of baking powder. Dip the fish in the batter, roll them in crushed cracker crumbs (Pat prefers Waverly crackers), and fry in oil.

Whitefish is also perfect for pickling because its meat is firm and "hangs together" so well. To do so, freeze three to four fillets for forty-eight hours. Cut into chunks and soak for two days in a brine of eight cups vinegar and one-quarter cup pickling salt. Remove and rinse fish well, but save three cups of brine. Add one and one-third cups of sugar, three tablespoons pickling spice, and one chopped red sweet pepper. Heat to a boil and until sugar is dissolved, then cool. Layer the fish in wide-mouth jars along with one large onion, sliced. Pour the brine in and refrigerate for one week. Cuisine like this, once you taste it, is liable to raise the stock of this common lake fish from commoner to king.

Ice Palace

The propane heater, which doubles as a mini-cookstove, set on "low," makes the sound of a tiny afterburner. In the late afternoon when shadows are long and darkness has already found a home under the table, the heater's orange glow provides a faint light, making it easier to tidy up before heading home. The coffeepot and cups have been rinsed out in the nearest auger hole.

Only two guests stopped by today so it was an easy cleanup compared to some days.

A quick look around the inside of my shack shows everything more or less in its place. One corner looks like a mini-hardware/tackle/convenience store. Here's a small box of finishing and roofing nails, wood screws, and brads. I've called them all into service at one time or another. Two years ago when a fifty-mile-an-hour blow kicked up overnight, the windward strip of rolled roofing peeled back like the outer skin on a Spanish onion. The next afternoon a fool could be seen standing atop his shack hammering away. Another time, the ice auger blade caught a piece of door trim on the way out, but it was an easy fix with extra finishing nails on hand. I survey my store of backup supplies with a sense of satisfaction. They are the result of hard-earned foresight and a healthy respect for redundancy.

Not everyone keeps a running log of fish caught, but I do, and then my son, Ian, turns the data into a colored chart showing comparisons between years. There it is on the wall, a whole litany of opening days and the days that followed, the year, the fish lengths, weights, and numbers, all tacked up in a row as an easy, available reference. The opening day three years ago is still the one to beat.

Days like that one begin before they begin. The angler who is truly connected to the weather knows before opening his eyes in the morning that something changed overnight. True, it could be the smell of the pulp mill, around here a sure presager of incoming weather. When you're located northwest of a pulp mill and you can smell it, a low is arriving from the southeast. Beyond this, there's a certain feel to the air when the barometer is falling fast. Suddenly, birds and squirrels are on the move for food, and so are deer and other game animals—and fish.

That opening day clouds were layered in folds that looked like grayish-white pillowcases. The forecast said the storm wouldn't begin in earnest until mid-afternoon, but it was spitting snow just the same. It was a good morning to get the holes augered, get four lines in, and then retire to the shack, the coffeepot, the radio, and the jig stick.

That was the plan, but immediately it was thwarted. The flag on the first trap was up while the second hole was being drilled. A twenty-two-inch togue started the day right despite frozen fingers to show for it. As hole number four was dug, flag number three went up. The twin of the first togue had come calling. Well, if the fish were going to bite like this, better let this one go and hold out for that fish known by the handle, "Bubba."

Back in the shack after all tip-ups are set and baited, a white strip of belly flesh is incised from the togue in the creel. The meat is separated from the leathery skin with a sharp Leatherman Tool, and the skin itself is carved into a "Y" shape. The narrow end is hooked onto one of the treble hooks on a Leadfish jigging lure, and let down to the loop previously made in the line, indicating bottom. In this case, it was about twenty-five feet. When jigged, the belly mimicks a struggling baitfish or some other unidentifiable tasty morsel. Before it ever makes bottom, something has it. Being caught off guard causes an overreaction. Arms flying akimbo, the freshly poured coffee is knocked onto the floor and the cup almost down the hole. A fast kick saves the day, since, as the old-timers say, drop any hardware down the hole and you might as well move the shack, because you'll never catch anything in that spot.

Up comes a whitefish, and a big one. Why aren't more fishermen out here? Didn't they get the same message? A biplane may as well have smoked the letters FISH NOW! across the sky, the conditions seemed so obvious.

The Leadfish can't be rebaited fast enough. A lot of good it did, because no sooner was it fathoming the depths again than flag number four went up. This one wasn't retrieving like a whitefish. Every inch had to be earned, and then the reason became clear. Sixteen inches of writhing, liquid silver flopped down next to the hole, fat as a football—a salmon. I sent the beauty back to grow an inch and a pound by September.

The trap was reset just in time to run for trap number one. A whitefish. Good—there's dinner. Another try at a cup of coffee tempts the fates every time on a day like this. While running for that salmon flag, the Leadfish on the jig stick in the shack had found its own way to bottom. Now, when it's lifted, it catches. Is it a stump? Maybe, but this stump is swimming away. Now, things turn serious. Repositioning for a fish fight knocks over the coffee again, only this time the cup makes the side pocket. *Ploosh!* It's deep-sixing itself alongside a line being stretched to the breaking point.

The whole morning has a "pass-the-ammunition" feel to it, and, as if to confuse things, two flags are waving in the breeze during the fish fight going on inside the shack. Sometimes, it's too bad not to have a witness. Days like this always pale in the telling. The twenty-seven-inch togue fought like it got the last sip of coffee out of the blue enamel coffee cup that went by as it was being pulled up. Several missed attempts at getting the head started up the hole gave this fish new energy, which it used to yank the line hard enough to break the skin on two fingers. I lay the togue out on the ice in hopes that some social caller would be suitably impressed by this eight-pounder. Never happened. Neither did the old-timer theory about hardware down the hole. In fact, that blue enamel may have served as an attractant. And there it is on the shack log, the whole account tacked up with all the other years' catches.

Today is a very different day than that one. Today, there are fishermen everywhere because it's a beautiful day to be out. There's no smell of pulp, no pillowcase clouds, no spitting snow, and no fish. A good day for taking inventory inside the well-outfitted shanty before leaving.

Barrel swivels, spare treble hooks, leader material, and different sizes of split shot are items that need replenishing each year. On nails along one shelf are leadered, snelled hooks from size six to size two, some short-shanked, some long. And then, the colorful array of jigging spoons. It depends on the day, the mood, and other factors, but in the end, some lures seem to emanate confidence while some haven't yet. Those retain their sheen unlike the veterans.

Duct tape, blaze orange tape for the tie-down lines that anchor the building to the lake, peanuts, chocolate, hard candy, Tums, Band-Aids, and other sundries fill up the shelves in one corner. Another shelf is built just big enough to hold the radio. Some shacks have TVs with roof antennas, and we're all still waiting for the first guy to show up with his portable satellite dish. In the meantime, a radio is an absolute necessity, especially for those times when conditions on the lake are whiteout, or fogged in, and you feel like the Ancient Mariner marooned in a winter purgatory. That's why there's also a compass on the shelf—to get you home when all your shore coordinates have disappeared.

There's the mechanical jack, the chisel, the shovel, and the broom. Each year, usually more than once, conditions produce water on top of the ice. Even though you set the shack on blocks, this water can get deep, and then you've got skis socked into new ice. Chisel it out, shovel it away, jack up the shack, and get some new blocks out of the combination bench / chest. It's just a fact of life during a typical ice-fishing season—where you set it on day one is not exactly where it will be when you take it off the lake.

The chest also has spare fuel for the propane heater and the ice auger. Screwdrivers, hammer, ax, saw, rope, rags, garbage bags, and even a blanket! It also holds some old tip-ups to be recruited into service if some of the newfangled ones fail. If they'll only admit it, all ice fishermen are sitting ducks for any and all new incarnations of the the basic tip-up design. We will try virtually any prototype no matter how far-fetched it may first seem. From cat bells to spring-loaded flags that launch like missiles, to tripod traps, to anything you can name, we'll try it. And, if anyone knows of a rig that sets off a firecracker when a fish is on, we'd like to see that, too.

Before locking up, one final glance shows all the traps dripping from where they hang on nails along the tops of the walls. They're always iced up at the end of the day when they're extracted from the lake. Most of the heat in a shack is close to the ceiling, and even after the heater is turned off, enough warmth will be retained to melt and dry them for the next outing.

That last glance also revealed something else: That what this really is, is a little home. A fellow could spend the night here if he felt so inclined, and many do. An unexpected sense of security comes with this knowledge. When things get too out-of-control, too mixed-up and confused in that other world, he is reassured to know that he can always retreat to this one. That's why there's a blanket in that chest. And some frozen hot dogs. Find me alone in my ice palace, and I'm probably at peace.

Photo courtesy of Randy Spencer

My son, Ian, and my brother, Jon, outside my ice-fishing shack.

Drummond Humchuck: Togue Chowder

"Jeez, my feet ache. I think these new boots are too tight," I whined.

"What time a day'd you buy 'em, chum?"

"Huh? Uh . . . well, first thing in the morning, I guess, right after the store opened."

"There's yer trouble."

"What?"

"Figured you knew better. Always want to buy shoe leather noon to three o'clock."

"C'mon."

"A fella's feet swell some every day. By that time a day, they've swelled up all they're gonna, so if you buy yer boots then, they'll never be too tight."

I blow out a long sigh and look at the treetops bordering Drummond Humchuck's dooryard. White, puffy clouds are sailing by under a blue sky that looks even bluer framed by those hemlocks.

"Okay, so when do you buy snowshoes?"

"Don't. Make 'em myself."

I guess the best policy is to just be quiet and listen when you're in the company of a woods wizard. I don't think five minutes goes by in the presence of Drummond without my learning something. For his part, he assumes no teaching posture, nor does he consider himself wiser than anyone else, much less a wizard. His cabin is a classroom only because the life lived there is out of our time.

It is the third week of March, and, observing a tradition I'd established of bringing the last togue of the season to Drummond, I plunked it down, wrapped in newspaper. Drummond's face opened like a sun through clouds of gray-white whiskers.

"Don't get any fresher'n that!" he pipes.

"Let's make a chowder, Drum," I offer, knowing that a togue chowder to him is like a four-star repast to someone in the world I'd just come from.

Not that Drummond's incapable of catching a togue on his own. He ice-fishes, even if his methods are unrecognizable to any modern hardwater angler. For example, he sprinkles the "fluff" from cattails that grow along shorelines into the ice holes he has chiseled, and this, amazingly, keeps them from freezing over. Moreover, Drummond never uses tip-ups. Instead, he uses bobbers! I would have thought, the first time I saw this, that it was a joke, had I not known Drummond better. There had to be something to it (there always is), and I had to ask.

"There's weights just above the hook down near bottom," he said. "See how that bobber only half floats? Don't take much to sink it the rest of the way." He explained that in winter, many fish tend to take bait lightly—especially the kind he uses, grubs. If you let the bobber have its full flotation, you can't tell when you're getting one of these subtle strikes.

That didn't take the cake, though. I once watched Drummond take an old soup can and drop two pieces of cold charcoal from his woodstove into it. He had first dripped candle wax onto these hunks of half-burned hardwood. We were fishing on a pond with no cattails on shore. Once out on the ice, he lit the charcoal with the help of the candle wax and set the can in the newly dug ice hole. The smoldering charcoal inside the can heated the water in that hole all day, enough so that it never froze. He also taught me that when an iced-over body of water has only patches of snow on it, I should fish under the patches. They serve as cover, just as logs, boulders, and other structures do in the summertime. I have successfully tested this nugget several times since.

Lola Sockabasin, the legendary Passamaquoddy guide, is the author of the togue chowder recipe I was about to share with Drummond. When Lola gave me the recipe, he told me that he expected me to pass it along, because that's what you're supposed to do with recipes, jokes, stories, songs, and just about everything else but the flu and the measles. Pass them along. To do this, I had picked the most gracious, chowder-loving soul I knew.

A kitchen like Drummond's is perfectly equipped to make Lola's togue chowder. He got the wood cookstove up to temperature nicely, then took a spider off a spike in the log wall and began rendering the chopped salt pork I'd brought along with the togue. I cut up some onions and potatoes and threw them in, too. After it cooked for a few minutes, we transferred it to a chowder pot and covered it with water. We let it simmer while we had our tea and I unpacked the other stores I'd brought Drummond: epoxy glue, more strike-anywhere matches, duct tape, several balls of wool, and of course, another gross of popsicle sticks. Also, evaporated milk and butter for the chowder.

When it had simmered long enough (about fifteen minutes), I got out the togue and dressed it out, then dropped it into the pot. In no time at all it turned white and I netted it once again with one of Drummond's whittled spruce spatulas. With the other hand, I grasped the tail end of the backbone and peeled it out of the flesh, then released the boneless togue back into the chowder. I broke the meat into chunks, put the pot onto Drummond's cookstove warmer, and added the evaporated milk and a wad of butter. Drummond had saved some pork rinds from his rendering which he sprinkled over the surface.

"What a dandy!" he exclaimed, taking two gray enamel bowls off a shelf.

As we finished up the last of the chowder—the whole chowder—I nodded toward the section of the cabin where Drummond's models are on display, along with hooked rugs in progress, and several whittling masterworks.

"Why do you work so much, Drum? Do you really have to?"

"Bein' busy's a good thing, chum. We all got to work."

He stood up, walked over to the models, took a cloth off one, and held it up for me to see. His finished, popsicle-stick representation of the *Titanic* took my breath away. If there are any deities in the details of this work, it couldn't be the devil unless he's reformed. I marveled at what Drummond does with those little sticks of wood and some glue. He then showed me an elongated, hollowed-out piece of wood he'd been whittling. "See that?" he says. "That's one of the lifeboats off'n this here ship."

Drummond asked me his usual spate of questions about life back in town. As his sole messenger from civilization, I take the liberty of filtering the news. I don't, for example, go into the garden-variety squabbles that happened at Town Meeting. I also withhold information on how A is not talking to B since A heard from C that B said so-and-so about A.

Instead, I told him that the ice was breaking up and pulling away from the shoreline. The stream was running high, but everyone expects the gates will be dropped in time for opening day the first of April. A very scruffy fox has been seen repeatedly on lower Church Street, and a moose made a cameo appearance up on the Tough End. It appeared to be a young adult male that was unimpressed with the humans who came out to gape and gawk, then went back inside to call and alert people farther down the road.

"Don't you live on the Tough End?" Drummond asks.

"Yup."

"And that's where that moose walked?"

"Yup."

"I'd get my name in the moose lottery, and soon, if I were you."

I'd been saving a story for Drummond. Stories, for him, rate on a par with togue chowder. It had happened earlier in the winter, not long after I'd seen Drummond the last time. Beaver-trapping season had just begun. We'd had a cold start to winter so that there was already ice on the streams, deadwaters, and flowages where trappers go to trap near promising beaver lodges. Word was, the pelts would be fetching around thity-five dollars this year. As usual, they'd all go to Canada, then be sold on the world market from there.

I told him that two guiding colleagues of mine went out together the first week. One of them was a Passamaquoddy with whom I frequently guide fishermen. It was a morning so cold, whenever either of them picked up an ice chisel, it instantly froze to his glove. It is wise to work in pairs beaver trapping. Anything can happen, and when it does, you're likely to be a long way from home or a hospital. I noticed Drummond arching his eyebrows and sitting up in his chair.

The big snows had not come yet, so it was still possible to use the pickup instead of snowmobiles. My friends had scouted a deadwater in Township 41, and now they were back to lay some traps. They used the Conibear-type, laid strategically on the crossover of a dam. Beavers tend to build their dams where the water is slow-moving. Once built, they actually add, as a finishing touch, a kind of walkway for them to cross easily over the top of it. The trapper sometimes sets a trap in this walkway, attached by wire to the very sticks the beaver used in construction. When he puts his head in the trap or swims into it from underwater, it springs and he pulls the trap loose from the sticks and out into deeper water where the weight of the trap takes him down. Some trappers observe an ethic of taking only two beavers per lodge. This leaves more coming each season, amounting to money in the bank for the serious fur trader.

I told Drummond how my friend, the Passamaquoddy guide, walked out on the ice first. He immediately realized that because of all the rain we'd had in late fall, the current under the clear ice was much stronger than when he had scouted the place in November. He could actually feel it under the soles of his boots. His next thought was about to be unsafe ice, but that half-thought went down with him. Throwing his arms out, the chisel he was holding in his right hand went one way, and the Conibear in his left went the other. Before he could yell or even reach up to grab anything, the current swept his legs downstream, and his forehead banged the edge of the hole.

His friend, having taken a Thermos of coffee from the pickup, had just paused on shore to pour himself a cup when he looked up and saw . . . nothing! Nothing but a hole and a dark, undulating shape moving downstream like a shadow beneath the snowless ice. He dropped the Thermos and cup, picked up his chisel, and ran. He bounded down the shore—leaping over logs and rocks—on the kind of strength that only comes from panic. He saw, up ahead, where he would try to run out to a spot on the ice before his buddy reached it.

For the Passamaquoddy guide, the fall through the ice had happened too fast to feel cold or much of anything else. Wide-eyed, he watched everything as if from outside his body, he later told me. He was amazed at how fast he was moving. Amazed that he could not plant his feet anywhere and stop. He watched himself beating, with the palms of his hands, against the underside of the ice. It was solid enough to prevent him from breaking it, but obviously not enough to keep him from falling through it. He marveled that there were still grasses reaching up like long fingers from the bottom in winter. They seemed to be gracefully waving him downstream, but to what? His poundings were useless. Looking up, he could see the blue sky through the ice, and then . . . what was this? A shape. Was it coming for him? It could have been the shock of the cold or banging his head on the edge of the ice before he went under, but the idea came to him that this shape above him might be the soul of one of his ancestors come to carry him over to the spirit world.

The blows of the chisel were so powerful, they skewered the ice with ease. The first stab made a hole, and the next two widened it. The rescuing guide, adrenaline still coursing through his veins, threw the chisel aside, dropped to his knees, and thrust his arm under water up to his shoulder.

I leaned back in my chair just then and said, "You got any more tea, Drum?" He slapped his knee like only the proud master can, broke into a chest-heaving chuckle, and we both had a good laugh. He poured some more tea, sat down, and said, "Okay, okay."

I continued, telling how my Passamaquoddy friend was completely entranced as he approached the apparition of his ancestor hovering over the ice. The die was cast, and, after all, if this was how it was to be, it wasn't so bad. He exhaled the breath he'd been holding up to now, said good-bye to his life, and reached up to be received by his ancestor.

The same panic that had put fire in his legs and brimstone in his chisel blows now helped the rescuer hoist his friend up through the hole and flop him onto the ice like a stunned seal. But there was no time to rest. He gathered him to his feet and force-walked him to shore, toward the truck. He threw him onto the cab seat, started the engine, put on the heater blower full blast, and ran back for the Thermos.

As usual, Drummond took everything in, put his head back, and gazed up at the rafters, examining every detail of the story in his mind as if he were watching a movie. Stories are his movies. Satisfied at having seen it all, he looked back at me and nodded approvingly.

I went on with news from town, telling him that shop stoves were now belching smoke as canoe makers wrapped steamed, ash ribs around a mold, and guides armed with orbital sanders filled the air with cedar and varnish dust. The shelves of the Pine Tree Store were piling up with hats, T-shirts, sweatshirts, gifts, and sundries as well as a new line of rods, reels, hundreds of flies, and a whole wall devoted to eye-catching lures designed to catch fishermen first. I told him the Pine Tree Store folks had woven enough pack baskets this winter to outfit the Swiss Army and were happy to give their hands a rest until October.

I also told him that I'd begun to hear from my sports, who, as spring approached, were beginning to think more and more about fishing and Grand Lakers and cooking outdoors. Along about March, they begin to write and call, wanting to know when the ice will go out.

"What about yer canoe, chum? You got it done?"

"Nope. But it's up on sawhorses."

"The book?"

"Yup." I wasn't completely sure how Drummond felt about my writing this book, so I took the opportunity to explain the care I'd taken to ensure his privacy. I didn't want him thinking he'd become fodder for gapers and gawkers just like that moose up on the Tough End back in town. I swore another oath that Township Unknown—that forgotten plot, or surveyor's mistake, or whatever it is—would remain Township Unknown, and besides, it's next to impossible to find, anyway. I reminded him that the only way I'd found it was as a result of being lost.

Drummond gave me the same crinkly grin I get every time I clear the tree line bordering his cabin and find him making tea for both of us. He stroked his beard and looked back up at the ceiling.

"Writin' a book—that's hard work, ain't it?" he said, arching one eyebrow. I said I'd rather portage a canoe on each shoulder from here to Haynesville and back, and I watched a broad smile steal over his face. "Well, good," he said. "We all got to work, chum. Bein' busy's a good thing."

Epilogue

If phones are ringing off hooks in the homes of guides, in sporting lodge offices, and in the Pine Tree Store, it must be spring in Grand Lake Stream. These are mostly long-distance calls from Texas, Pennsylvania, Massachusetts, British Columbia, Ohio, Connecticut. The calls are from sports. They ask whether their favorite cabin will be available at the lodge. Can they book the same guide as last year? What are the salmon hitting on? Any dry-fly action in the stream yet? Think there'll be an early bass spawn?

Just making telephone contact will satisfy the other question—the real reason for calling—that is never asked: Will Grand Lake Stream still be there when they return? Just as generations of Grand Lake guides before me have done, I have listened for hours, in the privacy of a canoe, to people trying to put into words what this special place means to them. Apart from the fun they have when they come, they describe it as something that serves them, in an important way, when they're not here. They use it as a kind of virtual retreat. They come to it in their imaginations to relive moments, hear the lap of waves against the side of the canoe, see those impossibly blue skies and those clear, star-bejeweled nights. They depend on Grand Lake Stream as a kind of mental Xanadu, which, whenever they need or want to, they're able to conjure up.

I've also heard it described as the psychological equivalent of a private cache—that cabinet in the den or basement that holds the oldest scotch, Dad's chipping iron, the gifted Cuban cigars, the 1956 Hardy fly reel in the original green cloth bag, the Ansley Fox 12-gauge, the picture of the service pal from forty years ago, the Carrie Stevens flies framed under glass, and the Model 94 Winchester. They say that among those possessions, they are transported to this place. I don't doubt it, for I have learned, as most guides do, that what is uttered between guide and sport within that crucible—the canoe—is usually the truth.

It would seem like a lot to live up to on this end. Here's this isolated hamlet, hacked like a garden plot out of a wilderness that would otherwise swallow it whole. You have to come here on purpose, since it's not on the way to anyplace else. At a glance, you wouldn't guess that Grand Lake Stream props up the lives and mental health of people all over the country. It may seem like a lot to live up to, but it's not.

As a guide in a place like this, you have everything going for you. The stage is set: the comfortable, rustic-but-civilized lodge; the quaint general store brimming with personality; the sleek, graceful Grand Laker set to take sports to fish, fully outfitted with a three-course shore lunch; the seemingly endless lakescapes serving up scenery typical of our better dreams. The client is mesmerized. You stay alert and watchful, offer counsel when you can, cook, talk a little, and listen. That's the experience and the picture they'll take with them. Throughout the year, they'll visit it, nourish it, and relive it until they return the following year. As a guide, you've hit a home run.

And yet, all that never quells clients' small, abiding anxiety that it may not last—that they might call one spring and learn that Grand Lake Stream simply went out of business. The sporting lodges were unable to make a go of it and closed up. The Pine Tree Store was converted into condos. The guides moved away to look for other work that allowed them to earn a living. And it's easy for sports to fuel their worst fears. Certain signs have not escaped their notice, especially those who were brought here by parents, and now bring children and grandchildren of their own. The demography has changed. In the span of only ten years, the number of local kids boarding the bus for schools in Princeton and Baileyville (Grand Lake Stream no longer has a school of its own) shrank from thirty-five to five. Young families find it harder to earn a living and raise children in a seasonal economy where the scope of opportunity narrows the remaining seven or eight months of the year. With no industry or commerce within commutable distances, few new families are attracted here. It has been said that a town without children is a dying town, and the one consequence of this not missed by the sporting clientele is the steadily rising median age of guides.

From there, they wonder, isn't it a small leap to Grand Lake Stream's final chapter? Aren't the foundations of the local culture shifting like tectonic plates to obliterate the old order? And once it's gone, what then? Surely the remaining population could only be a blend of those able to afford second homes here and those who couldn't afford to leave.

And what about all the lands and lakeshores that have been preserved against development? By cordoning off vast tracts from which no commercial enterprise could throw a lifeline, won't those efforts have the result of keeping the scope of opportunity narrow?

Something, the worriers say, is needed to sustain local families, not just visitors. Otherwise, years from now, a photograph of a Grand Laker flotilla leaving a lunch ground, paddles agleam in the sun, will be the postcard and postscript of the guiding era in Grand Lake Stream.

In those private canoe conversations, I have found it difficult to simply brush this view aside. The doomsayer's prognosis is founded on having seen beautiful, wild places lost precisely this way back where they came from—parks and developments that sprung up like garden rows with names memorializing the life and times they replaced. They've tracked the trend northward, and now, they fear, it could threaten the necklace of sparkling lakes encircling Grand Lake Stream, the place they love, the place they depend on, the place that once boasted a Registered Maine Guide in every family.

I, however, don't quite hear the trumpets of doom. Something—difficult to pinpoint—prevents me from seeing what a few say they see through a dark lens. I attribute this less to starry-eyed optimism than to the appreciation I've gained over the years of Grand Lake Stream's own story. From Minnie Atkinson's chronicle of the town's beginnings right up to the present, this story has mostly been about adversity. Grand Lake Stream was sawed, felled, and hewed into existence despite its isolation, climate, and proximity to the open maw of a wilderness. Its population soared to five hundred at the peak of tannery times, but was then halved by an exodus of the unemployed following its demise. It was those who stayed on who built a guiding business based on the abundant natural resources, but not much else. They did receive timely boosts from the railroad, the newly invented outboard motor, and the sporting lodges that sprang up to answer the call of the new clientele. They also had the native guides to learn from since they had already been guiding sports for many years. The rest—learning how to create special, memorable days with complete strangers—was up to them.

Even the Great Depression could not achieve full amplification in a hardscrabble town already used to making do in hard times. It surely took a toll, as did the wars, but soon after, pavement and electricity removed some of the rough edges from life and spiked business besides. Then, it wasn't long before men working on farms or in the woods succumbed to the prospect of steady income offered by a pulp and paper mill, leaving the seasonal guiding trade to older men and young upstarts who kept it afloat.

The gloom that some can see today seems, if anything, less onerous than many of the challenging chapters in Grand Lake Stream's past—chapters that did not manage to spell its doom. That perseverance in the face of adversity—a theme throughout its story—must be owed to the brand of individual who has been drawn to this place.

Had it ever been a town for seeking fortunes, it might never have survived. The life sought here was a different life, a unique, rugged subsistence that paid a greater share of freedom and independence than currency. There was something called "room to move" that always agreed with a certain type of personality or constitution. Success rested on the ingenuity that could be consigned to one's own hands. Sonny Sprague loved to say you had to be a "jack of all trades and master of none." That could be as apt a description of today's guide as of those who started it all.

Glimmers of Grand Lake Stream's next chapter are already in the works if one cares to look. Young men like Paul Laney live and work as year-round guides, building up their business with each new season. The ground broken by Cornelia Thurza Crosby as Maine's first female guide is finally bearing fruit as talented professionals such as Susan Hurd capably ply the trade today. More guides have extended their spring and summer seasons to become bird-hunting guides in the growing fall business. Several of the sporting lodges have new, forward-thinking owners full of youthful, entrepreneurial spirit. The Pine Tree Store now has a subsidiary: the New England Basket Company, weaving pack baskets for L.L. Bean and other markets in Maine and beyond. Brett Vose, grandson of Grand Lake Stream's most senior guide, Jack Perkins, recently passed his written and oral exams with the state and, at eighteen, became the town's youngest licensed guide. He's now guiding sports in the town that still boasts the highest concentration of working guides in Maine.

It seems not at all unlikely that the same thing that pointed the way forward in 1900 is doing so again. Dare we imagine that it ought to be less treacherous this time since the trail has been blazed before? It seems to await a certain kind of person with the right blend of abilities to be able to discern it. It is a gregarious soul and a keen observer who can't help being attuned (probably since birth) to a thousand subtle vibrations in the worlds of fish and wildlife, and to the rhythms of the outdoors. It is someone called to the guiding profession, and through time, that person keeps appearing as though some unseen rhizome sprouts exactly what Grand Lake Stream needs, and right on time.

That's why it's easy for me to envision, years from now, an emblematic scene replaying itself: A Grand Laker is pulled up at a lunch ground next to where cool waters flow. A guide kneels beside a fire pit to touch off some birch bark, then breaks an egg into some coffee grinds. At the shutter speed of lightning, an adult and a child are taking mind's-eye snapshots of every move—mental pictures to be savored later. After lunch, the guide leads the youngster down the shoreline, finds the perfect sapling, and whittles a hookaroon for the admiring child to take home. The guide's red bandana is dipped in the lake for a cooling swipe across the brow. Without being able to put a name to the face, I know roughly who it is. It is someone for whom the lure of this life was simply too strong.

Glossary

Blowdown—Whole or part of a tree that has fallen in the woods or into the water, often due to high winds.

Bow bag—The usually canvas, rubber, or otherwise rain-resistant bag used for storing cookware for traditional shore lunches, often kept in the bow of the guide's Grand Laker.

Deadfall—Same as a blowdown, only caused by age and rot.

Deadwater—Part of a stream that is flattened out for lack of current, sometimes caused by beaver dams, sometimes by streambed terrain. Can be productive for trout fishing in early spring.

Dooryard—The area, whether paved, dirt, gravel, or grass, in the immediate vicinity of the entranceway to a home or camp.

Dry bag—Waterproof bag used by guides and sports for cameras, matches, spare gloves, etc.

Dunnage—Similar to wangan, most often used pertaining to anyone's personal baggage.

Grand Laker—The indigenous guided fishing craft in the Grand Lake Stream region. Invented by Herbert "Beaver" Bacon, early 1900s. Usually measures nineteen feet six inches.

Guide's coffee—Coffee made by guides as part of traditional shore lunch, made with whole eggs including shells. Coffee grinds adhere to egg yolks forming a floating raft in the coffee pot. When removed from heat, the raft sinks to the bottom, and the coffee poured out is clear.

Hash marks—Bare marks on a tree where bark has been cut away with knife or hatchet. Used to mark trails.

Head of the Lake—That portion of West Grand Lake that begins at The Narrows and includes Junior Bay, Bear Island and Mink Carry, The Pug, and Junior Stream.

Hookaroon—One of many names applied to the hooked stick whittled from a sapling or tree limb branches, for picking up coffee, potato, and chowder pots by bails, sparing hands from flames.

Horseback—A long ridge, often glacially formed, that provides a good opportunity for a trail or road through otherwise "unnavigable" country.

Ice-out—As per the traditional definition on West Grand Lake, when a boat can pass freely through The Narrows at the Head of the Lake.

Jig stick—Short, usually rigid ice-fishing implement with a whittled or fastened "reel" for winding up the line.

Kype—The upward (and sometimes downward), hooked configuration of the jaw(s) of mature male salmon.

Ouananiche—Passamaquoddy word for salmon.

Racer—Skinny salmon, resulting from poor health, stress, or adverse conditions. Sometimes caught in the stream during the early season.

Spider—Heavy, black, cast-iron frying pan.

Timberdoodle—Woodcock. Sometimes called mud-bats, or mud-suckers.

Tip-up—Vertical piece of wood with a reel at the bottom submerged in a hole in the ice, with a flag on top which trips when the reel turns. A horizontal piece of wood attached to the vertical piece stabilizes the trap over the hole.

Togue—Wabanaki name for lake trout.

Tote sled—Homemade or store-bought wangan carrier on skis, usually towed behind a snowmobile.

Twitch trail—The rough trail made by a skidder for hauling tree-length logs out of the woods to a yard.

Wangan—Gear, equipment, a load of baggage, food, tools, loaded into a pack basket or canoe for woods or water travel, hunting, trapping, fishing, or just going to camp. Known historically to Maine lumbermen as a boat conveying these provisions.

Weir—Used to raise the level of a body of water, sometimes includes a sluice gate to control a flow of water and/or fish (eels).

Yard—The clearing, usually off to the side of a woods road, where tree-length or pulp-length logs are piled up, awaiting transport to mill.

About the Author

Randy Spencer is a Master Maine Guide, which means he is qualified and certified by the State of Maine to guide clients on fishing, hunting, or recreational adventures, although Randy's specialty is fishing. Randy's guiding business is based in the remote eastern Maine town of Grand Lake Stream, home

Photo courtesy of Dean L. Lunt

Randy Spencer

to some of the most beautiful scenery and some of the best fishing in the nation. Randy also maintains a home in Holden, Maine. In addition to guiding, Randy is a talented singer/songwriter who has released five CDs, including his latest, *Footprints in the Sand*. In fact, he regularly writes a column for the *Northwoods Sporting Journal* that is titled "The Singing Maine Guide." He is also a freelance writer for other outdoor publications. In 2008, *Yankee* magazine named Randy one of the "25 People You Need to Meet Most This Summer," and *Portland* magazine named him one of the "10 Most Intriguing People in Maine."

Where Cool Waters Flow is Randy's first book.

☒ → 10:30